State of India's Livelihoods Report 2013

Contributors

Savitha Suresh Babu
Resmi P. Bhaskaran
Adarsh Kumar
Tara Nair
Suryamani Roul
Orlanda Ruthven
Ashok Kumar Sircar
Kirti Vardhana
Gayathri Vasudevan

State of India's Livelihoods Report 2013

An ACCESS Publication

⑤SAGE www.sagepublications.com
Los Angeles • London • New Delhi • Singapore • Washington DC

Jointly published in 2014 by

 SAGE Publications India Pvt Ltd
B1/I-1 Mohan Cooperative Industrial Area
Mathura Road, New Delhi 110 044, India
www.sagepub.in

ACCESS Development Services
28, Hauz Khas Village
New Delhi 110 016
www.accessdev.org

SAGE Publications Inc
2455 Teller Road
Thousand Oaks, California 91320, USA

SAGE Publications Ltd
1 Oliver's Yard, 55 City Road
London EC1Y 1SP, United Kingdom

SAGE Publications Asia-Pacific Pte Ltd
3 Church Street
#10-04 Samsung Hub
Singapore 049483

Published by Vivek Mehra for SAGE Publications India Pvt Ltd, Phototypeset in 10/13 pt Minion by Diligent Typesetter, Delhi, and printed at Saurabh Printers Pvt Ltd, New Delhi.

Library of Congress Cataloging-in-Publication Data

State of India's livelihoods report 2013 : an Access publication.
    pages cm
    Includes bibliographical references.
    1. Sustainable development—India. 2. Sustainable development reporting—India.
    HC440.E5S795   338.954'07—dc23   2013   2013047086

ISBN: 978-81-321-1662-2 (PB)

The SAGE Team: Rudra Narayan, Archita Mandal, Rajib Chatterjee, Anju Saxena, Umesh Kashyap and Rajinder Kaur

Cover photograph courtesy: ACCESS.

Contents

Thank you for choosing a SAGE product! If you have any comment,
observation or feedback, I would like to personally hear from you.
Please write to me at <u>contactceo@sagepub.in</u>

—Vivek Mehra, Managing Director and CEO,
SAGE Publications India Pvt Ltd, New Delhi

Bulk Sales

SAGE India offers special discounts for purchase of books in bulk.
We also make available special imprints and excerpts from our
books on demand.

For orders and enquiries, write to us at

Marketing Department
SAGE Publications India Pvt Ltd
B1/I-1, Mohan Cooperative Industrial Area
Mathura Road, Post Bag 7
New Delhi 110044, India
E-mail us at <u>marketing@sagepub.in</u>

Get to know more about SAGE, be invited to SAGE events, get on
our mailing list. Write today to <u>marketing@sagepub.in</u>

This book is also available as an e-book.

List of Tables

List of Figures

List of Boxes

List of Boxes

List of Abbreviations

ABCTCL	Amalgamated Bean Coffee Trading Company Limited
AIACA	All India Artisans and Craftworkers Welfare Association
AICTE	All India Council for Technical Education
AIDS	Acquired Immunodeficiency Syndrome
AKRSP	Aga Khan Rural Support Programme
ANM	Auxiliary Nurse Midwife
AOSAR	Agricultural Outlook and Situation Analysis Reports
APEDA	Agricultural and Processed Food Products Export Development Authority
APL	Above Poverty Line
APMCs	Agricultural Produce Marketing Centres
ASA	Action for Social Advancement
ASDC	Automotive Skills Development Council
ASER	Annual Status of Education Report
ASHA	Alliance for Sustainable & Holistic Agriculture/Accredited Social Health Activist
ATDCs	Apparel Training & Design Centres
ATM	Automated Teller Machine
ATMA	Agricultural Technology Management Agency
BCWCA	Building and Construction Workers Cess Act
BGREI	Bringing Green Revolution to Eastern India
BIPCL	Banana India Producer Company Limited
BOCWA	Building and Other Construction Workers Act
BP	Branch Penetration
BPL	Below Poverty Line
CAD	Current Account Deficit
CAG	Comptroller and Auditor General
CBGA	Centre of Budget Governance and Accountability
CEOs	Chief Executive Officers
CPI	Consumer Price Index
CPIS	Coconut Palm Insurance Scheme
CSC	Common Service Centre
CSO	Civil Society Organization
CSR	Corporate Social Responsibility
CUTM	Centurion University of Technology & Management
CWB	Construction Welfare Board
DBT	Direct Benefit Transfer
DFID	Department for International Development
DGET	Directorate General of Employment and Training
DP	Deposit Penetration
DWCD	Department of Women and Child Development
ESI	Employees' State Insurance
FDCs	Forest Development Corporations

FDI	Foreign Direct Investment
FII	Foreign Institutional Investment
FIR	First Information Report
FRA	Forest Rights Act
GCC	General Credit Card
GCF	Gross Capital Formation
GCSE	General Certificate of Secondary Education
GDP	Gross Domestic Product
GER	Gross Enrolment Rate
GoI	Government of India
GoM	Group of Ministers
GSDP	Gross State Domestic Product
HDI	Human Development Index
HIV	Human Immunodeficiency Virus
HLEG	High Level Expert Group
IAP	Integrated Action Plan
ICDS	Integrated Child Development Services
IDE	International Development Enterprises
IFPRI	International Food Policy Research Institute
IGIDR	Indira Gandhi Institute of Development Research
IHDS	India Human Development Survey
IIP	Index of Industrial Production
IMC	Institutional Management Committee
ITC	Industrial Training Centre
ITIs	Industrial Training Institutes
IWMI	International Water Management Institute
JNNURM	Jawaharlal Nehru National Urban Renewal Mission
JSS	Jan Shikshan Sansthan
KCCs	Kisan Credit Cards
KYC	Know Your Customer
LARR	Land Acquisition and Resettlement and Rehabilitation
LEC	Livelihoods Equity Connect
LWE	Left-Wing Extremism
MDG	Millennium Development Goal
MES	Modular Employability Scheme/Modular Employability Skills
MFIs	Microfinance Institutions
MFP	Minor Forest Produce
MGNREGA	Mahatma Gandhi National Rural Employment Guarantee Act
MIS	Management Information System
MKSP	Mahila Kisan Shashaktikaran Pariyojana
MNAIS	Modified National Agricultural Insurance Scheme
MoHRD	Ministry of Human Resource Development
MoLE	Ministry of Labour and Employment
MoRD	Ministry of Rural Development
MoU	Memorandum of Understanding
MPCE	Monthly Per Capita Expenditure
MPDPIP	Madhya Pradesh District Poverty Initiatives Project
MRP	Maximum Retail Price
MSME	Micro, Small, and Medium Enterprise

MSP	Minimum Support Price
NABARD	National Bank for Agriculture and Rural Development
NAC	National Advisory Council
NAIS	National Agricultural Insurance Scheme
NASVI	National Association of Street Vendors of India
NBFC	Non-Banking Financial Company
NBS	Nutrient-Based Subsidy
NCAER	National Council for Applied Economic Research
NCEUS	National Commission for Enterprises in the Unorganized Sector
NCR	National Capital Region
NCVT	National Council for Vocational Training
NDC	National Development Council
NDDB	National Dairy Development Board
NFHS	National Family Health Survey
NFS	National Food Security
NFSA	National Food Security Act
NFSO	National Food Security Ordinance
NGO	Non-Governmental Organization
NIAM	National Institute of Agricultural Marketing
NIMZ	National Investment Manufacturing Zone
NIOS	National Institute of Open Schooling
NLRP	National Land Reform Policy
NPMSHF	National Project on Management of Soil Health and Fertility
NREGA	National Rural Employment Guarantee Act
NREGS	National Rural Employment Guarantee Scheme
NRHB	National Rural Homestead Bill
NRHM	National Rural Health Mission
NRLM	National Rural Livelihoods Mission
NRLP	National Rural Livelihoods Project
NRLPS	National Rural Livelihoods Promotion Society
NSAP	National Social Assistance Programme
NSDC	National Skill Development Corporation
NSQF	National Skills Qualification Framework
NSSO	National Sample Survey Organization
NTTF	Nettur Technical Training Foundation
NULM	National Urban Livelihoods Mission
NVQF	National Vocational Qualifications Framework
OBCs	Other Backward Classes
OECD	Organization for Economic Cooperation and Development
OPD	Outpatient Department
OTP	One Time Password
PDS	Public Distribution System
PIP	Participatory Identification of the Poor
PMEAC	Prime Ministers Economic Advisory Council
PPP	Public–Private Partnerships/Purchasing Power Parity
PSL	Priority Sector Lending
RBI	Reserve Bank of India
RKVY	Rastriya Krishi Vikas Yojana
RPL	Recognition of Prior Learning

RRA	Revitalizing Rain-fed Agriculture
RRBs	Regional Rural Banks
RSBY	*Rashtriya Swasthya Bhima Yojana*
RTE	Right to Education
RTI	Right to Information
SAP	State Advised Price
SBLP	SHG Bank Linkage Programme
SCBs	Scheduled Commercial Banks
SCs	Scheduled Castes
SCVT	State Council for Vocational Training
SERP	Society for Eradication of Rural Poverty
SEWA	Self-Employed Women's Association
SGSY	Swarnajayanti Gram Swarojgar Yojana
SHG	Self-Help Group
SIA	Social Impact Assessment
SJSRY	Swarna Jayanti Shahari Rozgar Yojana
SME	Small and Medium Enterprises
SMO	Sewing Machine Operator
SOIL	State of India's Livelihoods
SRI	System of Rice Intensification
SRLMs	State Rural Livelihoods Missions
SSA	Sarva Shiksha Abhyan
SSCs	Sector Skills Councils
STAR	Skill Certification and Monetary Reward Scheme
STLs	Soil Testing Laboratories
STs	Scheduled Tribes
TPDS	Targeted Public Distribution System
TVET	Technical Vocational Education and Training
UID	Unique Identification Number
UNDP	United Nations Development Programme
UNFCC	United Nations Framework Convention on Climate Change
UNICEF	United Nations Children's Fund
VAPCOL	Vasundhara Agri-Horti Producer Company Limited
VE	Vocational Education
VET	Vocational Education and Training
VLE	Village-Level Entrepreneurs
WBCIS	Weather Based Crop Insurance Scheme
WDRA	Warehousing Development and Regulation Authority
WPR	Worker Population Ratio/Workforce Participation Rate
WRF	Warehouse Receipt Financing
WRMS	Weather Risk Management Services
WTO	World Trade Organization

Preface

Given the diverse complexity within the livelihoods promotion landscape, to bring out an annual publication that would track trends and progress would always be difficult. After several rounds of brainstorming and consultation, we narrowed down on a simple 4-P framework to design the structure of this annual report. Five years down the line, I feel the structure, though not strictly adhered to, has helped in bringing together the publication, fifth year in a row. The *State of India's Livelihoods* (SOIL) *Report* assimilates current debates and developments around the poor and their plight, the potential livelihood opportunities, the role of promoters, and the private sector and policies that impede and advance the possibilities for strengthening the livelihoods of the poor. I am happy that a clutch of sector experts are coming together as a core group to bring together the SOIL Report.

The 2013 SOIL Report has six chapters authored by some well-known sector experts: Resmi P. Bhaskaran, Tara Nair, Ashok Kumar Sircar, Suryamani Roul, Adarsh Kumar, Kirti Vardhana, Savitha Suresh Babu, Gayathri Vasudevan, and Orlanda Ruthven. While a few of them have come on board the first time, Professor Sircar, Suryamani, and Orlanda have played a crucial role in bringing out the past reports.

The opening chapter 'Overview: Economic Crisis and Livelihoods' contributed by Resmi P. Bhaskaran attempts to explore whether the current economic woes are a result of lack of reforms and policy paralysis. To do so, she revisits some of the tenets of economic nationalism, reviews the macroeconomic situation, the status of investment and the 'policy paralysis' that has surrounded it, and some of the critical political challenges faced by the Indian state in overcoming crisis before going on to discuss education, health, infrastructure, and finance, which underlie industrial and private sector growth.

Tara Nair, in her chapter 'A Statistical Atlas of Livelihoods', illustrates some of the major indictors of the status of livelihoods, especially rural livelihoods, with the help of disaggregated data at the state level. Based on the conceptual understanding of livelihood security as a multifaceted phenomenon that combines elements of means of earning a living, ownership of and control over assets, capabilities, and the ability to stake claims, the chapter analyses the changes in a range of indicators relating to employment, assets, capabilities, and poverty over the last two decades.

Continuing from where he left off in 2012, Ashok Sircar, in Chapter 3 'Policy Initiatives and Policy Paralysis', provides an annual policy update centring his discussion on the current union budget; analysis of the Twelfth Five-Year Plan; ongoing policy initiatives; and new policy initiatives such as the land reform policy, Foreign Direct Investment (FDI) in retail, direct benefit transfers, Corporate Social Responsibility (CSR) for corporate, and reform of the sugar sector.

The Government in 2013 commemorated completion of two years of its flagship poverty reduction programme National Rural Livelihoods Mission (NRLM). In the section on NRLM, Suryamani Roul this year takes a look at the several key shifts from the earlier programme that Aajeevika has incorporated changes in its guidelines during the year and the progress made so far at the end of two years.

Chapter 4 on 'Agriculture and Livelihoods' by Adarsh Kumar aims at providing livelihood practitioners a summary of the current state of the sector last time covered comprehensively through the Report in 2010. The chapter brings together a wide range of evidence with the objective of identifying key trends in the agricultural sector, highlighting vulnerable populations that need livelihoods support, and identifying key gaps and bottlenecks that need to be addressed to provide such livelihoods support.

In the chapter 'Social Protection and Livelihoods', contributed by LabourNet, the links between livelihood outcomes and behaviour and social protection is explored with a focus specifically on informal or unorganized workers. The chapter looks at the role of the Government with respect to provision of social protection through an analysis of specific schemes and entitlements, and their links to livelihood behaviour and outcomes, both for rural population and urban (migrant) population.

The final chapter, 'Skilling India', by Orlanda Ruthven explores the current state of skills policy in India and the evidence that we have so far, of its impact and effectiveness for poor people's livelihoods.

I take this opportunity to thank all stakeholders who have continued to support this initiative. I would like to thank Prema Gera of UNDP and Maneesha Chadha from Citi Foundation who have continued to commit support to the SOIL Report. In response to our request, the Ford Foundation also stepped in with critical support that helped us meet the resource gap for coming out with the Report. I appreciate their faith in ACCESS's abilities to deliver on this critical sectoral report and hope we have been able to meet their expectations with this output.

Centurion University has joined the effort as technical partner this year. Orlanda Ruthven who anchored the Report at Centurion University, has done a tremendous job, from helping in indentifying the authors and themes for the year, to looking at the author–theme fit, giving qualitative inputs to the authors at different stages to help them improve their final output to finally editing, and tightening the whole document and bringing it together as a cogent, composite report. The Report has hugely benefited from her strong support to the entire process.

I would like to thank all those who have helped in enriching the content of the Report through their inputs. I deeply appreciate the efforts of Dr Shambu Prasad and D.N. Rao for their inputs at all stages, when the themes for this Report were being decided and also later, when the contributors were ready with their draft chapters. Their inputs have definitely helped shape the Report.

From within ACCESS, I would like to thank Puja and Natasha ably supervised by Suryamani for support and coordination with the authors and managing the process for coming out with the Report smoothly. As a team they played a super anchor role to the whole process.

SAGE continues to be the publishing partner for ACCESS for this sectoral initiative. I hope that with our combined efforts this year the SOIL Report reaches a larger readership base, is referred to widely, and is able to contribute to knowledge and sharing within the sector.

Vipin Sharma
CEO
ACCESS Development Services
New Delhi

Overview: Economic Crisis and Livelihoods

Resmi P. Bhaskaran

1. Introduction

The Indian economy is going through one of its toughest periods since the implementation of neo-liberal economic policies in 1991. Down from a routine high of 8 to 9 per cent growth a year for a decade, we are now at 5 per cent. At the same time, Pranab Mukherjee in his first speech as the President of India admitted that 'trickle-down theories do not address the legitimate aspirations of the poor and cannot eliminate poverty'.[1] While the Indian economy has grown to 10th largest in the world,[2] it also accounts for one-third of the world's poor people (around 230 million), a sharp increase from one-fifth in 1981.[3]

As per the current population growth, the economy must produce 20 million new jobs every year,[4] a rate which was not achieved even when the economy was growing at 8 per cent. Slipping growth affects the overall living conditions of the majority of the population, especially those close to or below the poverty line (BPL), about 841 million people or nearly 70 per cent of Indian population.[5] Growth is now the key challenge for the present and the subsequent government following next year's elections. Any delays now contribute further to the plummeting confidence of industrialists, traders, farmers, and the 'aam aadmi' and, thus, risk deepening the impact of the economic downturn.

At present, India is facing unhistorical levels of depreciation in the value of the rupee, a sharply fluctuating Sensex, declining foreign exchange reserves, and uncontrolled inflation. Industrial stagnation follows. By contrast, the agricultural sector, still the mainstay of well over half of India's workforce, has shown good growth, while the sustainability of this continues to be in question, as farm sizes decline, farming practices tax the environment, and low investment keeps infrastructure and supply chains starved of development funds. Besides, the country has had to bear a fair quota of droughts in some parts and floods and landslides in other parts, with agricultural production and procurement taking the hit and throwing a challenge to the ambitious food security agenda.

The macroeconomic drama and contraction of growth have heightened the call for

---

[1] http://www.dnaindia.com/india/1719749/report-trickle-effect-wont-work-in-india-feels-president-pranabda (5 August 2013).

[2] This figure is by nominal gross domestic product (GDP) (nearly US$2 trillion). In purchasing power parity (PPP) terms, it is the third largest. During 1981–85 the GDP was US$179 billion and it was ranked 17th in 1981–85 (Narendra Jadhav, India and the Global Economy. Available at: http://drnarendrajadhav.info/drnjadhav_web_files/speeches/EXIM%20Bank%20Speech%20-%20India%20Global%20Economy.pdf) (22 August 2013).

[3] http://www.worldbank.org/content/dam/Worldbank/document/State_of_the_poor_paper_April17.pdf (6 August 2013).

[4] Choudhury, Gaurav and Zia Haq. 2013. 'Spinning New Jobs, Critical for India's Long-Term Economic Equilibrium'. *Hindustan Times*. 13 May.

[5] Based on World Bank estimation 2013.

the government to play a protective role, in helping the poor to avoid dramatic deterioration of income and to provide some protection against shocks. At the same time, the capability of the workforce to work productively—whether in field, factory, office, or home—is critical, since a productive workforce fit for the purpose is both a pillar of growth and a solution to poverty in the long term. While India has no shortage of young able-bodies, their employability is a question. The private and non-profit sectors each play a critical role in building this human resource and strengthening the economy as they adapt and innovate to turn the crisis into an opportunity. Urbanization, with its concentrated markets and infrastructure, expands the scope of livelihood options for rural people across the country.

The global economic meltdown of 2008 and subsequent turbulence affected the Indian economy far less than most other countries in the world. The current discourse is that the diverted hurricane has returned with a vengeance. What is the truth in this fear? Or is the situation rather the result of lack of reforms and 'policy paralysis'? What are the opportunities, embedded within, which provide the means to tackle the situation? The present chapter discusses these questions. First, we reflect on the past to get a fresh view of the present, by revisiting some of the tenets of economic nationalism—growth and industry, poverty and welfare, the role of the state versus the market, and local democracy—built by the post-Independence leaders. Second, we review the macroeconomic situation, the status of investment and the policy jam that has surrounded it, and some of the critical political challenges faced by the Indian state in overcoming crisis. Third, we discuss the foundations—education, health, infrastructure, and finance—which underlie industrial and private sector growth. Finally, we introduce the other five chapters of this report.

2. Revisiting economic nationalism

Before Independence, the nationalist leaders shared an integrated, interrelated picture of the Indian economy, its sicknesses, the remedies to be applied, and its relation to alien rule.[6] With this 'economic nationalism', they approached the problem of economic development holistically rather than by separating growth from human development and one sector from another. The focus was on socio-economic, industrial, and infrastructural development to improve the material status of the people, and on equal representation of all classes.

The 'abject and stark' poverty of so many Indians was a core preoccupation and the analysis of economic woes showed a strong understanding of the reality of poverty. For example, while debating the linkages between increasing food prices and other consumer goods, they agreed that the cause was not the improved purchasing power of the poor but the falling production, increased exports, and increased hoarding by middlemen.[7] We can observe similar arguments in the milieu of activist and civil society organizations (CSOs), but the level of consensus and shared values on such points, is much less today than earlier.

Today, economic development is near synonymous with economic growth. The neo-liberal view that growth will fund education and health over time[8] is not well borne out more than 20 years after liberalization.

---

[6] Chandra, Bipan. 1966. *The Rise and Growth of Economic Nationalism in India.* New Delhi: People's Publishing House Pvt. Ltd.

[7] Naoroji. 1887. *Essays, Speeches and Writings*, edited by C.L. Parekh, Bombay and it is cited in Bipan Chandra. 1966. *The Rise and Growth of Economic Nationalism in India*, People's Publishing House Pvt Ltd, New Delhi.

[8] Bhagwati, Jagdish and Arvind Panagariya. 2013. *Why Growth Matters: How Economic Growth in India Reduced Poverty and the Lessons for Other Developing Countries.* USA: Public Affairs.

Nearly 70 years after Independence, the debate is divided, and a shared vision which would provide the impetus for policymaking, implementation, and nation-building, seems further than ever. With this lens, this section reviews current debate and evidence on those topics which India's postcolonial leaders prioritized: poverty and inequality, welfare, economic growth, sustainable development, and local democratic representation.

2.1 Poverty and inequality

Poverty eradication is the ultimate goal of all social policy. Poverty estimates are constantly debated, while the latest estimates of the Planning Commission have proved particularly controversial.[9] The estimate of 'headcount' is crucial because so many benefits and schemes hang on it. According to the newly defined poverty line, those with a monthly per capita income of less than ₹1,000 in urban and ₹816 in rural areas (or ₹33.3 and ₹27.2 per day, respectively) fall below the poverty line. Based on this new line, 13.7 per cent of urban and 25.7 per cent of rural population are poor. Using the new figures, the overall poverty ratio (proportion of poor in total population) is said to have declined from 37.2 per cent in 2004–05 to 21.9 per cent 2011–12, an impressive 15.3 per cent point fall over only seven years.

With general elections on the cards, the government is, of course, keen to claim impact for its social policies. But the figures are challenged by economists, media, and CSOs who question how the estimates were made.[10] They argue that the Planning Commission simply applied the new price indices to the old 'consumption basket' on which the original poverty line (1973–74) was based. Thereby, the whole issue of what kinds of costs and needs—in the contemporary context—should fall into the basket was sidestepped. For example, what should be a minimum nutritional diet today? What are the other manufactured necessities, utilities, rents, transportation, health, and education costs which are, today, in the basket of essential expenses basket of a poor person? When such expenses are added, the poverty ratio for 2009–10 actually goes up to 75.5 per cent from 69.5 per cent in 2004–05.

The government came out with another set of poverty figures soon after releasing the Planning Commission estimates, based roughly on those to be covered under the new National Food Security Ordinance (NFSO). According to NFSO, nearly 67 per cent of the population needs subsidized foodgrains. Derived from 2012–13 consumption expenditure, the estimates put the poverty line significantly higher, at per capita ₹1,506 per month (₹50 a day) for rural and ₹1,850 per month (₹62 a day) for urban. This figure is very close to the World Bank's poverty line of US$2 (purchasing power parity [PPP]) corresponding in 2011–12 to ₹45 in rural and ₹57 in urban, per capita per day.[11] In the prevailing economic turbulence, the politics of poverty

---

[9] Methodology of Suresh Tendulkar Committee to estimate poverty rate used the National Sample Survey Organization (NSSO) consumption expenditure data for 2011–12. Poverty line divides the poor from the non-poor, puts a price on the minimum required consumption levels of food, clothing, shelter, fuel, and health care, etc. Tendulkar's estimation does not consider the expenditure on health and education, both of which are expected to be provided by the state. But, now 80 per cent of the health care is with private and education is increasingly moving to the private.

[10] Tendulkar Committee methodology used the Consumer Price Index (CPI) of agricultural labourer weighted by the consumption pattern of the rural people at the national level for 1973–74 for rural areas and a simple average of the index of the industrial workers weighted by the consumption pattern of the people and the CPI for urban non-manual employees for the urban areas used to update the urban poverty line (Report of the Expert Group on Estimation of Proportion and Number of Poor, Planning Commission, New Delhi, 1993).

[11] http://www.thehindu.com/news/national/beyond-the-debate-govt-accepts-65-indians-are-poor/article4948698.ece?ref=relatedNews (5 August 2013).

headcount is disturbing because it detracts from serious analysis of what works and what does not work to reduce poverty (if evidence of poverty reduction can be jumped up by statistical gimmicking, then why bother with real evidence)?

The evidence of recent shifts in real wages in India is mixed. Increasing prices, especially of food, eliminates much of the nominal gain in wages, and this is reported by the International Labour Organization (ILO) as the major cause of shrinking purchasing power of workers.[12] The ILO further reported that India's real wages fell 1 per cent between 2008 and 2011 while its productivity grew at 7.6 per cent over the same period. The relationship between wages, productivity, and skill is examined in more detail in Chapter 6.

The ILO report contrasts with evidence from the National Sample Survey Organization (NSSO) rounds (employment survey) which reports that salaried and casual workers' earnings increased by 150 per cent in the five years between 2004–05 and 2009–10. How much these increases are explained by growth and higher productivity in industry, versus the inflationary pressure on wages brought about by high agricultural production and the expansion of the National Rural Employment Guarantee Scheme (NREGS) is a matter of debate.[13]

The increasing wages on a base of National Rural Employment Guarantee Act (NREGA) and growth in the informal and agricultural sector, contrasts with the corporate sector's very slow creation of decent employment. While the number of poor people may have declined between 61st and 66th NSSO rounds (2004–05 to 2009–10), inequality[14] rose for the first time in 35 years in rural areas (from 0.26 to 0.28), and increased at a faster pace in urban areas. Rising inequality is also reflected in divergent consumption pattern.[15]

2.2 Social-economic rights and welfare

One-third of the world's hungry live in India. Over 230 million Indians sleep hungry every night. Over 7,000 Indians die of hunger every day. On the global hunger index India ranks 66th out of 88 countries. According to United Nations Children's Fund (UNICEF), one in every three malnourished children in the world lives in India and every second child is malnourished. In India, about 50 per cent of all childhood deaths are attributed to malnutrition.

Hunger and malnutrition is 'a shame', said Prime Minister Manmohan Singh in February 2012. On the other hand, India experiences impressive growth and is one of the major producers of food items.[16] If India produces enough food to combat hunger, then why do millions live and die in hunger?

There are several factors which have stalled the expansion and the profitability of agriculture in India. Among these are: the decline in agricultural investment since the 1980s, the liberalization of food imports through World Trade Organization (WTO) agreements, increasing input costs particularly in phosphate fertilizer and fuel for irrigation, and high losses in the supply chain. These factors are discussed in more detail in Chapter 4.

---

[12] *Global Wages Report*, 2012–13, International Labour Organization.

[13] Gulati, Ashok, Surbhi Jain, and Nidhi Satija. 2013. 'Rising Farm Wages in India—The "Pull" and "Push" Factors'. Discussion Paper No. 5, Commission for Agricultural Costs and Prices, Department of Agriculture & Cooperation, Ministry of Agriculture, Government of India (GoI). New Delhi, April.

[14] Measured by the Gini coefficient. The coefficient ranges from zero to one, with zero representing perfect equality and one showing perfect inequality. Hence, the more the coefficient, the more the inequality.

[15] The spending and consumption by the richest 5 per cent shot up by over 60 per cent between 2000 and 2012 in rural areas while the poorest 5 per cent witnessed only an increase of 30 per cent. In urban areas, it is 63 per cent and 33 per cent, respectively.

[16] Food and Agricultural Organization of United Nations, The State of World Fisheries and Agriculture, 2010.

The relationship between agriculture's health and profitability, and food security, is close, but not complete: food security also depends on smoothening supply and ensuring entitlement to the poorest. Food security is itself fundamental to the equitable development envisaged by post Independence leaders, being a base on which other human development depends. This view is reflected in the contemporary Right to Food Campaign,[17] which argues that any spending on food security needs to be viewed as an investment in growth and development. With the National Food Security Act (NFSA), just passed by Ordinance in the Lok Sabha, the government renews its commitment to address food security and hunger. It will be discussed briefly in Chapter 2 and in more detail in Chapter 5.

2.3 The shape of growth: Investment

The level of investment in an economy is determined by gross capital formation (GCF),[18] an indicator of the economy's ability to produce income. It is one of the expenditure components of gross domestic product (GDP), together with final consumption and net exports. Proper and equitable distribution of capital formation promotes economic welfare and eradicates poverty.

There is a clear correlation between the overall economic growth and investment growth. When the economy grew at 9 per cent, investment was around 35 per cent of GDP. The private sector (household and corporate, respectively 14 per cent and 11 per cent of GDP) constitutes the major investor in India. Domestic savings[19] (30.8 per cent of GDP in 2011–12) is the major contributor to capital formation. As a result

of the global meltdown and the decline in corporate but also household savings, the gap between saving and investment has widened, leading to negative growth in the net capital formation (see Table 1.1). This gap climaxed in 2011–12, but has since declined since foreign investment has also plummeted.

Table 1.1: Declining net capital formation

Years	Savings (% of GDP)	Capital formation (% of GDP)	Net capital formation	GDP growth
2007–08	36.8	38.1	–1.3	9.3
2008–09	32	34.3	–2.3	6.7
2009–10	33.7	36.5	–2.8	8.6
2010–11	34	36.8	–2.8	9.3
2011–12	30.8	35	–4.2	6.2

Source: Economic Survey 2013–14.

Sector-wise investment shows that industry (47.8 per cent) and services (44 per cent) dominate. Agriculture—still employing more than 50 per cent of the workforces—struggles to raise investment and to modernize production and supply chain, a topic examined more closely in Chapter 4. On the other hand, manufacturing and services which contribute more than 85 per cent of the GDP get the maximum share of investment, while employing less than half the workforce. This indicates that the higher growth and capital formation in these sectors have failed to transfer a significant proportion of the workforce from low-productive activities to high-productive activities. The employment outcomes of sector growth are discussed more in Chapter 2.

2.4 The shape of growth import-export

Indian foreign trade has witnessed drastic change in the last two decades. The growth model followed since reforms has focused on expanding exports while discarding the import substitution model followed since Independence. India's exports grew from

---

[17] http://www.righttofoodindia.org/

[18] GCF was earlier known as gross domestic investment and also referred to as 'capital stock'.

[19] It generates through bank deposits, small saving schemes, mutual funds, equity market, insurance, corporate bonds which gets channelled to private and public enterprises which then use it for investments.

US$50 billion in 2002–03 to US$300 billion in 2012–13, but imports grew at an even greater pace, from US$61 billion to US$492 billion, leading to widening of the current account deficit (CAD). India now accounts for 1.44 per cent of exports and 2.12 per cent of imports for merchandise, and 3.34 per cent of exports and 3.31 per cent of imports for commercial services, worldwide.

The foreign trade basket of India shows an interesting pattern. Petroleum products constitute the largest forex earning commodity (US$60 billion), followed by gems and jewellery (US$43 billion), and transport equipments (US$18 billion) during 2012–13 fiscal. From its export of services, India gained US$144 billion. On the other hand, petroleum and crude oil constitute nearly 32 per cent of total imports in 2012–13, while gold (US$54 billion), electronic goods (US$31 billion), machinery (US$29 billion), and precious and semi-precious stones (US$23 billion) are the other major import items. This indicates that the sectors that received heavy support and subsidy from reforms during the liberalization period (i.e. services and manufacturing) hardly made any significant improvement in the export commodity basket. The contribution of traditional and labour intensive sectors to exports is still significant, and they continue to perform with fewer incentives than those of the new economy.

The lessons of the last few years is that high CAD and depleting forex both result from inappropriate increases in the import of goods and services, which in turn threatens the value of the rupee and growth overall. Another fact clearly emerging is the need to focus on capital formation or investment in agriculture and boosting of exports in this most inclusive of sectors.

2.5 Environment and sustainable development

Since the 1980s, sustainable development has been mainstreamed in development economics. Globally, the conduct of unbridled corporates as well as state socialist regimes in exploiting and consolidate control of resources brought environmental sustainability to the fore. The climatic volatility and extremes experienced with growing frequency in many parts of the globe is the backdrop to this. The goals for the post-2015 period are now formulated, based on a framework of balanced and sustainable growth, by the United Nations in its Rio + 20 summit, June 2012.

Thanks to the efforts of CSOs and activists in India and internationally, the Twelfth Plan (2012–17) has foregrounded the issue of environmental sustainability.[20] The government has set up a committee to develop a framework for 'Green National Accounts', measuring economic well-being on the basis of a comprehensive definition of wealth covering natural and human capital, rather than GDP alone.[21] India leads the international negotiations under the United Nations Framework Convention on Climate Change (UNFCC) and has agreed to reduce the carbon emission intensity of its GDP by 20–25 per cent of 2005 levels by 2020.[22]

In the 2013–14 Union budget, the government promoted alternative energy especially solar. In the last 10 years, the government has further come out with various policies, such as the Joint Forest Management Act, Green Rating for Integrated Habitat Assessment, Coastal Regulation Zone, a clean energy drive through eco-labelling and energy-efficiency labelling and fuel efficiency standards. Implementation of many such policies is delayed and diluted so that results are weak. In the case of the Forest Management Act and Coastal Zone Regulations, for example, the community

---

[20] This is well reflected in this year's Economic Survey, 2012–13.

[21] Address by Dr K.C. Chakrabarty, Deputy Governor, Reserve Bank of India (RBI), at the Yes Bank–GIZ–UNEP Sustainability Series event on Environment and Social Risk Management on 23 April 2013 at Mumbai.

[22] This was agreed at the UNFCC meeting held in Doha in December 2012.

has been inadequately consulted, resulting in public agitation in many places.

2.6 A place for public and private

The Twelfth Plan document proposes public–private partnerships (PPP) in almost all sectors, from social to infrastructure. PPP has been robustly promoted in the last 10 to 15 years, as a neo-liberal model for development. But some Indian states used PPP effectively much earlier, as early as the 1960s. The role of PPP is often viewed as ambivalent because it exempts the government from responsibility, while gaining ground and support in inverse relation to the decline of public service delivery: the worse public services, the more support for PPP models.

The record of achievement under PPP is mixed. Generally, achievement has been considerably less than projected goals and implementation, while inclusiveness (reach and price to consumer) have also been poorer than expected.[23] PPP clearly works better where profits are assured, while it often inflates prices, thereby curbing access.

One of the problems is the paucity of monitoring or analysis of different PPP models. The poor accountability of many PPP projects, even those in essential services such as health and water, has been criticized by CSOs, government audit agencies, courts, and media. Neither installation costs nor service quality is adequately monitored or regulated. There is also poor transparency in the PPP contracting process, with social audit mechanisms not properly installed.

On the other hand, effective installation of PPPs in fields such as infrastructure development and supply chain development can ensure a higher standard of provision and broaden the scope for employment. Appropriate regulation of PPPs needs strong political will and capacity, and there is some distance to travel before the government is willing or able to provide this.

2.7 Local elected bodies: 20 years of Panchayati Raj

The Acts of 73rd and 74th Constitutional Amendments, passed in 1992, established three tier rural local governments and converted municipalities into self-elected governments. These bodies were mandated to serve people not only with municipal services but also to initiate participatory social and economic development. The Constitutional Amendments asked the state to devolve functions, functionaries, finance, and freedom to these local governments. Further, it mandated that elections should take place every five years and ensure reservation for women, Scheduled Castes (SCs), and Scheduled Tribes (STs). Central and state finance commissions were mandated to allocate funds to these local bodies and to transfer to these entities the powers of taxation. Finally, the Constitutional Amendment created a new entity, the *Gram Sabha* (village council) with powers to be decided by the states.

There are two clear achievements of these Amendments. First, elections to these local governments have become regular and reliable. Second, the reservation of women, SCs, and STs has been consistently ensured. India can be proud that it has 1.2 million elected women representatives, more than the rest of the world combined!

Unfortunately, the successes are limited to these two. Overwhelmingly, most states have failed in delivering other constitutional provisions. For example, an analysis of the devolution of the '3Fs' (finance, functionaries, and functions) across the country by the Indian Institute of Public Administration reveals that overall devolution is only 33 per cent (report of the expert committee

---

[23] Most of the expressway/national highway toll fees are set in such a way that the builder will receive the investment within the first five to 10 years, but the collection of fee will go on till the end of the lease period or agreed period which in some cases went up to 99 years. Available at: http://newindianexpress.com/cities/chennai/article545416.ece?service=print (20 August 2013).

2013).[24] While central funds transfer to local governments is more or less regular, the quantum remains tiny relative to demand and needs, while state government transfers hardly feature at all.

Local governments have the mandate to work on 29 subjects as per the Eleventh Schedule of the Constitution, of which, 13 are directly related to livelihoods. What have the local governments done on these subjects? The only answer we get is that local governments are implementing some of the central government's schemes. Not a single local government in India has formulated its own programme on any of the 13 subjects of livelihoods. George Mathew summed it up thus, 'Although panchayats got constitutional status twenty years ago, politicians have managed to subvert the decentralization of power, out of fear of the emergence of rival political forces. So Panchayati Raj remains a pipe dream, while bureaucracy's writ runs large'.[25]

The apathy and reluctance of state and central governments to empower local governments with authority and resources couples with the local governments' dependency on the state-level political and bureaucratic forces. From a livelihoods perspective, this has taken its toll in the continued gap in essential public services of water, sanitation, roads, housing, health care, nutrition, and school education.

3. Policy jam, prices, and populism

When the economic growth declined to 4.4 per cent in August 2013 and inflation and rupee depreciation touched new extremes, the lack of supportive policy reform was cited as the main cause of the problem. International rating agencies such as Standard & Poor downgraded India, citing lack of reforms which were blamed for reducing the pace of economic growth. While focusing on its defence around the various scams and corruption charges unraveling around it, the government ignored or delayed many critical policy decisions for which it is now paying the price. This section focuses on the macroeconomic and sectoral issues which have felt the cost of these delays and indecisions, and explores their effects on the livelihood opportunities of the people.

3.1 Macroeconomic challenges

Inflation and volatility in the rupee along with depleting forex reserve are the major macroeconomic challenges that the government is grappling with in the last one year. These issues are highly interlinked and have multiplier effects on the economy, politics, and the livelihoods of the poor.

Inflation

Since 2008, the Indian economy has undergone severe inflationary conditions. Food inflation was averaged around 10 per cent from 2008 to December 2012. As a result, 50 per cent of the income of an average Indian household is now spent on food items and the figure is more than 60 per cent in the case of poor households.[26] Food inflation is explained by production shortfalls, the propping up of the Minimum Support Price (MSP), the quantum of the Public Distribution System (PDS) versus open market sales, and the rising cost of imports as the rupee declines. Open liberal economies use monetary policy to address inflation: money supply is tightened, credit becomes costlier, and disposable income declines. Credit crunchiness is affecting almost all sectors

[24] Report of the Expert Committee. 2013. *Towards Holistic Panchayati Raj: Twentieth Anniversary Report of the Expert Committee on Leveraging Panchayats on Efficient Delivery of Public Goods and Services*, Volume I, Policy Issues, 24 April, pp. 16–17.

[25] Mathew. 2013, 'Panchayati Raj or Collector Raj'. *Times of India*. 15 April, Page 10.

[26] Report on Key Indicators of Household Expenditures in India, 2009–10, NSSO 66th Round, 2011.

that generate employment, such as real estate, automobile, cement, steel, durable goods, transportation, and hospitality.

The brief respite in early 2013 was reversed by July 2013 as price inflation rose to 5.79 per cent. In this regard, it is evident that monetary policy has not delivered any significant impact and the constantly falling rupee adds more woes. In contrast to its intervention in monetary policy, the state has abandoned intervention in the supply chain activities of food and other essential items. The PDS—limited on a macro scale—is the only mechanism that the government can use, and the transformation of this scheme through the National Food Security (NFS) will be discussed in more detail in Chapter 5.

Depreciation of rupee and depleting forex reserves

India's forex reserves are once again fast declining (Figure 1.1). The rise in the international crude oil price and the appreciation of the US dollar due to the recovery of the US economy is now cited as the reason. The CAD has gone up to 4.8 per cent of GDP, much worse than in 1991 (when it was 2.5 per cent). India's debt burden is, furthermore, in an alarming condition at 35 per cent of current account receipts and 3.7 per cent of the GDP.[27]

Declining rupee is a major economic issue as it inflates the already inflating economy (Figure 1.2). The policy to restrict investments and remittances abroad to reduce the out flow of dollar has not worked. Meanwhile, India continues to increase its capital goods imports which increased by 79 per cent during 2008–12. Although increasing capital goods imports is considered to be an indicator of economic growth, it is also cited as a major reason for widening CAD. It indicates, on the one hand, an unprecedented growth in the import of foreign

Figure 1.1: Declining forex reserve

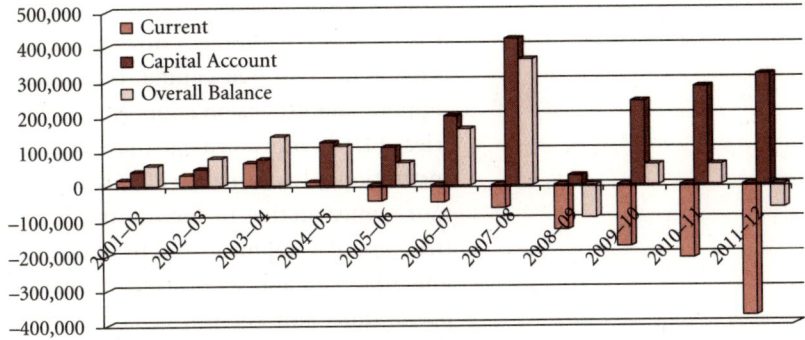

Source: Various Years Union Budget, Ministry of Finance, Government of India.

Figure 1.2: Value of rupee against US dollar

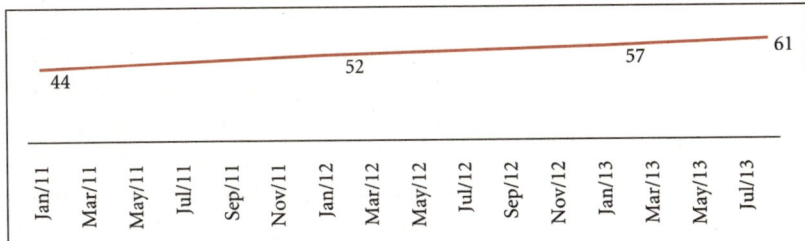

Source: Monthly Monitory Reports, Reserve Bank, Government of India.

manufactured goods, alongside a sharp decline in production on the other.[28] This answers why we escaped from the global slowdown in the post-2008 period and why we are getting into crisis at present.

It is imperative that policymakers intervene to restrict the import of goods on a priority basis. Reduction in CAD should be the core priority with sufficient improvement in the creation of domestic demand and supply. To tackle the present crisis, the government must address itself to the domestic market rather than focus on external markets. The size and the multi-dimensionality of the Indian economy and rapid growth of the middle class all offer wide opportunity. The government and other critical stakeholders need to focus on policies and programmes that support expansion of the domestic market.

---

[27] Finance Minister P. Chidambaram's statement in the Parliament on 11 August 2013. In 1991, India's debt was 21 per cent of current account receipts.

[28] Production measured in terms of the Index of Industrial Production (IIP) which details out the growth of various sectors in an economy.

3.2 Foreign Direct Investment (FDI) emerging trends

It is expected that foreign investment will provide the required capital, technology support, and expansion support to industries. FDI is more crucial than Foreign Institutional Investment (FII), since it is more constructive in facilitating infrastructural development and technological upgradations, and less linked to market perceptions and volatilities. Since 1991, the FDI inflow to the country has grown from US$1billion to a cumulative FDI of US$299.2 billion in June 2013. Table 1.2 illustrates the sectors that attracted higher inflows and the countries that took lead in investing in India. The service sector, including hotels and tourism and trade, bagged more than 50 per cent of the total investment between 2000 and 2013. Notably, more than 50 per cent of the investment came from countries generally known as tax havens (Mauritius, Singapore, etc.). This means the FDI is essentially the return of black money originating in India, after 'whitening' overseas.[29]

While the macro-level prospects for FDI look encouraging, from 2011–12 to 2012–13 India's net FDI declined from US$15.7 billion to US$10 billion. During the current fiscal (April–June 2013), the net FDI declined to an alarming condition to US$3.9 billion (inflow—US$7.6 billion and outflow—US$11.2 billion). This indicates that while the government takes measures to attract FDI, the outflow of foreign investment is taking place at a high pace.

FDI in infrastructure development (construction of roadways, ports, and telecommunications) multiplies growth in other sectors and promotes the movement of people and goods. As many argue, FDI in retail will boost the domestic production of manufacturing, agricultural, and allied enterprises. This would have far more impact on the livelihood options of people in the country. But the dilution of the clause which earlier demanded minimum 30 per cent of procurement from the domestic market will lessen this impact. Investors' insistence on this dilution belies their intent to promote imports into India. Another concern is that although the investment has taken place and many sectors experienced improvements in its production process at international standards, such standards have not always translated into more decent labour standards as per the articles of ILO.

3.3 Sectoral growth patterns

Although the growth of industry and service sectors provides a major push in the overall economic growth, the growth of agriculture, on the other hand, ensures the sustainability in terms of equity, employment, and food supply. The contribution of agriculture and allied activities in the GDP accounted for 13.7 per cent (at constant prices 2004–05) in 2012–13,[30] but it still provides employment to nearly 52 per cent of the population. Although this indicates very low productivity of the sector, it is still the major source of income for every second worker in the

Table 1.2:   Sector-wise inflow of FDI—April 2000 to June 2013

Sectors	FDI in US$	% Share of total FDI
Service Sector	38,189	19.22
Construction—Real estate	22,247.5	11.2
Telecommunications	12,865.83	6.48
Computer Software/Hardware	11,862.37	5.97
Drugs & Pharmaceuticals	11,318.32	5.7
Chemicals	8,993.12	4.53
Automobile	7,620.73	4.43
Power	7,953.93	4
Metallurgical Industries	7,620.73	3.84
Hotel & Tourism	6,731.89	3.39
Petroleum & Natural Gas	5,406.7	2.72
Trading	4,063.79	2.05
Information & Broadcasting	3,406.19	1.71

Source: Department of Industrial Policy and Promotion, Government of India, June 2013.

---

[29] Department of Industrial Policy and Promoting.

[30] Advanced Estimate of Central Statistical Organization tabled in the Parliament on 7 February 2013.

country. On the other hand, agriculture grew at an average rate of 3.6 per cent during the Eleventh Plan and is expected to grow at an average rate of 4 per cent during the Twelfth Plan. These issues are discussed in more detail in Chapter 4.

In 2012–13, India ranked 10th in global agricultural and food exports, and agricultural products account for 10 per cent of the total export earnings (Economic Survey 2013). Agricultural and Processed Food Products Export Development Authority (APEDA) forecasts that export of agricultural products will cross US$22 billion by 2014 and will account for 5 per cent of the global total. Currently (2012–13), it is US$20.74 billion. It is crucial for the government to sustain as well as increase the production as the NFSA 2013 will be in implementation in the current year across the country.

Agriculture's resilience and capacity to withstand macroeconomic crisis is well known. Thus government investments potentially have more impact here than elsewhere. The economic slowdown resulted in few jobs lost in the food and agriculture sectors.[31] In particular, jobs involved in the production, procurement, transport, storage, processing, and retailing of cereals, oilseeds, and pulses, remained intact. On the other hand, India may need to revisit its pricing regime and international trade agreements in order to enhance agricultural production to meet the increased demand from NFSA. Table 1.3 shows the relative subsidy in India compared to other key countries and regions. It shows the vulnerability of Indian farmers in the global market. India has taken an active stance in challenging the practices under WTO and any wins in India's negotiations would definitely provide a fillip to the entire agriculture sector in India.

Table 1.3: Comparative figure of agricultural subsidies

Country	Subsidy amt/hector	% agriculture subsidy to total subsidy	% of population depend on
EEC	$82	37	8
USA	$32	26	5
Japan	$35	72	4
China	$30	34	24
S. Africa	$24	61	18
India	$14	2.33	52

Source: WTO Report, 2012.

Services constitute 64.8 per cent of the GDP in 2012–13 (Advanced Estimates). The services sector includes the most sophisticated fields such as telecommunications, satellite mapping, and computer software to simple services such as carpentry, plumbing, to highly capital intensive aviation and shipping, to labour-intensive activities such as tourism and hotels, to infrastructure-intensive activities such as roadways and ports, and social sector activities such as health and education. Service sector growth is closely linked to growth in urbanization. New generation economic activities such as courier services, security services, and hospitality services are now absorbing unskilled rural labour on a large scale into urban areas. Government policy and private initiatives are further discussed in Chapter 6.

Indian manufacturing industry is largely driven by low-cost, skilled labour, adequate land laws, and reasonable cost of capital. The better performance of the manufacturing sector during 2007–09 worked as a shock absorber against the global economic crisis domestically. According to an estimate of McKinsey and Co., Indian manufacturing sector has the potential to create up to 90 million jobs by 2025, almost double the present capacity of 45 million. In this, 80 per cent will be in the unorganized segment. Even in a gloomy environment, Indian manufacturing industry ranked as the fourth most competitive manufacturing nation,

---

[31] Shah, Deepak. 2012. 'Implications of Economic and Financial Crisis for Agricultural Sector of India', MPRA Working Paper No. 39298. Available at: http://mpra.ub.uni-muenchen.de/39298/1/MPRA_paper_39298.pdf (6 August 2013).

behind China, the US, and Germany[32] and it positioned as the second highest after China in the Global Manufacturing Competitiveness Index, 2013.[33] All these indicate the capacity of Indian manufacturing to generate employment during the crisis days.

Considering the positive aspect of fall in rupee value (a boost for global demand and export in the coming days), these sectors, manufacturing and services, should gear up to produce more employment. To facilitate this, the government is announcing multiple reforms and policies. Some of the key policy measures include establishment of National Investment Manufacturing Zone (NIMZ) in Prakasham District of Andhra Pradesh which will lead to total 13 NIMZs in the country, National Policy on Electronics 2012 aims to have investment of US$100 billion by 2020.

3.4 Conflict and extremism

The intensity of internal political, social, and communal conflict has increased in India in the last 20 years. The number of districts where extremist forces are active have been expanded from one district in West Bengal in the late 1960s to nearly 180 districts in 14 states at present.[34] Over the years, statutory enactments and institutional mechanisms for addressing the various aspects of deprivation have been brought into being. But the experience has been that the discontent and unrest continue to surface notwithstanding such measures.

The government approach to address this issue as a law and order problem has impeded the role of socio-economic development. Development deprivation prevails in these regions and has played a major role in aggravating the situation. Social service delivery channels are increasingly defunct. Besides, the frequent fights and counter fights between extremist groups and security forces have limited and even destroyed livelihood options of the people. The issue of livelihoods in civil strife regions emerged as a key development issue as these regions report high rates of internal displacement. Further, there is a high geographical congruence between poverty, Adivasi populations, and civil strife.

The civil strife areas are, in general, rich in natural resource deposits. The movement to install Maoist principles of revolution, while it may be led from the top by ideologues and follows in a long tradition of Adivasi revolt against the state, also takes place in the context of wider conflicts between corporate industry and indigenous people over land and resources. These are coveted for livelihood sustenance of the indigenous people; these regions meet natural resources needs of corporate interests and are also preferred locations for energy and power requirements. This, in general, results in the displacement of the local communities in favour of private capital that gives very limited attention to the sustainability of the environment and the livelihoods of the people. The Land Bill which is making its way into policy is discussed in detail in Chapter 3. The shift in the land usage or non-voluntary displacement creates an issue of livelihood security. Simultaneously, there is lack of opportunity to update skills to adapt to the requirements of the new capital-based industries. The challenges of skilling and the government's skills policy are discussed in detail in Chapter 6.

4. Foundations of growth and development

This section is about the factors which ensure growth and its equitable distribution, about removing its impediments and structuring it to be more pro-poor and poverty-elastic. The section will cover the key human development and supporting

[32] Deloitte's Global Index, 2013.

[33] Based on a survey of chief executive officers (CEOs), executives, and other officials of 550 global manufacturing companies.

[34] Expert Group Report. 2008. *Development Challenges in the Extremist Affected Regions*, Planning Commission, GoI.

sectors which are required to ensure a high poverty impact of growth: education and skills, health, financial inclusion, infrastructure, and urban services.

4.1 Education and skill development

Education is the most important tool for socio-economic mobility since it is a requisite for many new opportunities and openings and a key way through which ascriptive social identities can be overcome and transformed. It provides skills and competencies as it equips people with the relevant knowledge, attitudes, and skills to adapt to the requirements of the rapidly evolving labour market and the opportunity for social mobility. It also enhances the negotiation power of the labour.

India made significant progress in improving access to education in the first decade of the 2000s. The mean years of schooling of the working population (those over 15 years) increased from 4.19 years in 2000 to 5.12 years in 2010. Enrolment of children at the primary education stage has now reached near-universal levels. Youth literacy increased from 60 per cent in 1983 to 91 per cent in 2009–10 and adult literacy improved from 64.8 per cent in 2001 to 74 per cent in 2011. It is estimated that emerging economies such as China will face a shortage of highly skilled workers by 2020, while, based on current projections of higher education, India is likely to see a surplus. Thus, India could capture a higher share of global skilled work, if there is focus on higher education and its quality is globally benchmarked.

The Twelfth Plan identified four main priorities for education policy: access, equity, quality, and governance. A major thrust of the Plan is on improving learning outcomes and rendering secondary education more job-relevant through skill training within schools. For this, higher investments will be needed to equip secondary schools with facilities (workshops, machines, computer equipment, etc.) and teachers/trainers who have technical skills.

When it comes to fund allocation to achieve these goals, education still receives only 3.3 per cent of GDP, far below the 6 per cent suggested by Kothari Commission in 1960s. It is envisaged that in the Twelfth Plan it will go up to at least 4 per cent if the fund allocation for school education enhances as per the norms of Right to Education (RTE) Act.[35] Till the end of 1980s, school education was largely in the public sector. Currently, the share of public sector has declined to nearly 80 per cent of the schools and 27 per cent of children access private school education. According to Annual Status of Education Report (ASER) statistics,[36] demand for private school education is increasing in urban India at such a high rate that 50 per cent of Indian children are expected to attend private school by 2020. Unfortunately, this shift doesn't necessarily reflect the quality improvement as there is no regulation to monitor the teaching and learning quality standards.

As per the review document of the Eleventh Plan, two-third of higher education is already in the private sector.[37] In the Twelfth Plan, although government proposes growth in the Gross Enrolment Rate (GER) of higher education at 25.2 per cent by 2017–18, government intervention is limited and gives extreme thrust to the private sector which is unregulated and operating on for profit principles. To address affordability, the government has provisioned for educational loan schemes in the last Budget.

As per the plan document, India is expected to enhance its skilled labour force from 12 per cent at present to 25 per cent by 2017 through vocational training, when around 70 million skilled people will enter

---

[35] To maintain minimum quality standards in school infrastructure, teachers' training, and recruitment of teachers under Sarva Shiksha Abhyan (SSA).

[36] Annual Status of Education Report (ASER). 2012. Published by ASER, New Delhi.

[37] In Eleventh Plan period, the private sector grew at 64 per cent and the public sector at 50 per cent.

into the workforce. As already mentioned, vocational education and skill training is increasingly a critical component to develop an employable workforce. In the last few years, several interesting initiatives have taken place in this regard, by a largely private set of skills providers and investors. In an India where only 12 per cent of the total enrolled children in the primary school reach the university level for higher education, the dropout could be absorbed by vocational education. But close dovetailing to industry job roles and requirements is essential to deliver this shift in employability. These issues are further discussed in Chapter 6.

4.2 Health

The size of the working population in the age group of 15–59 years in India is expected to increase from 58 per cent to 64 per cent by 2021. For India to reap the benefit of a young and huge workforce, it should be healthy, as well as skilled.

Health issues spread across nutrition, reproductive, maternal, and child health (RMCH),[38] diseases, and public health issues such as safe drinking water and sanitation. The nutritional aspect of adolescent girls, pregnant women, and children are critical as there is a cyclical pattern involved in the healthy development of the population.[39] The Twelfth Plan document has identified availability (access), quality, and affordability as the core issues of the health sector in India in achieving universal health-care goals. To achieve these goals, the government has to increase the allocation for the health sector from 1.04 per cent of GDP in the Eleventh Plan to 3 per cent of GDP by the end of the Twelfth Plan as suggested by the High Level Expert Group (HLEG).[40]

The number of hospital beds has to be increased to 2.8 million by 2014 to match the global average of three beds per 1,000 population from the present 0.7 beds[41] and to ensure the availability of the health workers at the minimum requirement of 250 per lakh of population, India needs to add another 2.6 million health workers.[42] In addition, there is a significant gap in the number of health care systems in rural, semi-urban areas. According to the Census 2011, India faces a shortfall of 35,762 sub-centres, 7,048 primary health centres, and 2,766 community health centres. These are very critical to address the core of the health care system of the poor households in the country.

The plan of public investment in health is limited. Instead, PPP interventions are promoted at various levels of health care including imparting skill training. According to the National Family Health Survey-3 (NFHS-3), the private sector dominates the health care service in both urban (70 per cent) and rural (63 per cent) areas. The Indian health care sector expects to touch US$280 billion by 2020. The hospital services market alone will be worth US$81.2 billion by 2015. This reflects in the FDI flow to the sector: while hospitals and diagnostic centres received US$1,395.82 million, medical and surgical appliances received US$523.54 million, and drugs and pharmaceuticals received US$9,659.26 million. In addition, government promotes

---

[38] Reproductive, Maternal, and Child Health.

[39] Malnutrition among the adolescent girls will lead to malnutrition among young pregnant mothers. This will result in the child survival and birth of underweight children. In case the child is underfed and didn't receive nutrition in the 0–6-year period, the probability of the child to grow as a malnourished person is very high which will lead to the another cycle of malnutrition.

[40] GoI. 2012. Report of High Level Expert Group (HLEG) on Health, Planning Commission.

[41] India needs 100,000 beds each year for the next 20 years.

[42] This does not indicate the optimum situation. For that the ratio should be increased to 354 health workers per lakh of population by 2017 (Human Resources for Health: Overcoming the Crisis, 2004, Joint Learning Initiative). This number includes doctors, nurses, auxiliary nurse midwives (ANMs), and accredited social health activists (ASHAs) or community health workers.

health tourism by incentivizing it and, as the rupee falls, the sector should benefit.

All these indicate that through achieving the health sector goals, India should not only achieve a healthy population, but also gain major employment as well.

4.3 Financial inclusion

The priority sector lending (PSL) prescriptions to India's banks are a key pillar of support to livelihoods. PSL broadly includes advances to agriculture, small-scale industries, weaker section, exports, education, and self-help groups (SHGs). The revised guidelines issued by the Reserve Bank of India (RBI) on 20 July 2012, mandate commercial banks to tender 40 per cent of their advances towards priority sector, while for foreign banks the limit is at 32 per cent of their total advances. The total outstanding of the priority-sector advances of Public Sector Bank (PSB) reported a 10.6 per cent growth during 2011–12 period, but declined in the last fiscal. The consolation is that during 2012–13, the lending to agriculture sector was higher than the target. The banks' credit to the small and medium enterprises (SME) sector registered a growth of 29.8 per cent in 2012–13 over the previous year. Though the Non-performing Assets (NPA) and decline in credit flow adversely affect the banking sector, the PSL to agriculture and SME give a scope for breath. They play a critical role in supporting the livelihood development of the rural sector and the banking policy should promote livelihood credit.

Microfinance was a ₹400-billion industry in 2010. Over a period of two decades, the SHG Bank Linkage Programme (SBLP) incrementally accelerated to reach out to rural poor through 8 million SHGs, maintained a balance of ₹65 billion in the savings accounts with the banks, while they are estimated to have harnessed savings of over ₹220 billion, of which nearly ₹150 billion was for internal lending. Over 4.4 million SHGs are regularly availing credit facilities

from the banks.[43] On the other hand, the entrepreneur-led microfinance institutions (MFIs) grew significantly in the last one decade. Along with growth complexities, a disastrous crisis evolved in Andhra Pradesh in 2010, resulting in the dramatic shrinkage of the sector. Loans disbursed through MFIs came down to ₹226 billion in 2011–12 from ₹350 billion in 2010–11. Various measures have been taken by RBI and other stakeholders to bring the sector back on track, directing greater transparency, customer protection, and adherence to the code of conduct within the sector. Towards this, RBI issued guidelines for Banks' lending to the MFIs and introduced a new category of Non-Banking Financial Company (NBFC)-MFIs in December 2011. It also deferred the implementation of asset classification and provisioning norms for NBFC-MFIs to 1 April 2013, and put in place a unified code of conduct for the sector and its implementation.

In this context it is imperative to look at the status of financial inclusion in the country. The banking penetration in India remains low at 58.7 per cent of the total population and only 55 per cent have deposit accounts. According to the Ministry of Finance (2012), only 5 per cent of the villages in the country have banks and nearly half of the districts in the country are under-banked. Government of India has accepted financial inclusion as a key strategy to improve the livelihood of the people in India, and in 2004, RBI set up the Khan Commission for this purpose. Accordingly, RBI relaxed the banking norms with the following measures: permitted 'no-frills' bank accounts for holders with annual deposits of less than ₹50,000, relaxed know your customer (KYC) norms, issued general credit cards (GCCs) to the poor and the disadvantaged with a view to

---

[43] Microfinance Status Paper, National Bank for Agriculture and Rural Development (NABARD), 2012.

help them access easy credit, and permitted commercial banks to make use of the services of non-governmental organizations (NGOs)/SHGs, MFIs, and other CSOs as intermediaries for providing financial and banking services.[44]

As the result of the financial inclusion campaign, states or union territories such as Puducherry, Himachal Pradesh, and Kerala announced 100 per cent financial inclusion in all their districts and over 62,000 villages have been covered by bank branches or business correspondents by January 2012. RBI also aims to open nearly 600 million new customers' accounts and service them through a variety of channels by leveraging on new technologies by 2020. Since financial education is considered as an impediment to achieve financial inclusion objectives, the RBI launched the National Strategy for Financial Education with a vision to build 'a financially aware and empowered India' on 16 July 2012. With the help of Credit Rating Information Services of India Limited (CRISIL), the rating agency, RBI and Ministry of Finance started a financial inclusion monitoring system, CRISIL Inclusix (see Box 1.1).

Box 1.1: *CRISIL inclusix index of financial inclusion 2013[45]*

To monitor the status of financial inclusion activities in India, CRISIL created a tool that would help policymakers, regulators, and financial sector intermediaries at large in measuring the extent of financial inclusion, both at a broader and disaggregated level as their corporate social responsibility (CSR) intervention. CRISIL Inclusix measures financial inclusion by evaluating the penetration of banking services. The first report analyzed the financial inclusion metrics based on data collected from 165 banks in 632 districts of the country over a three-year timeframe (2009–11). Some of the key findings of CRISIL Inclusix are as follows:

1. Deposit penetration (DP) is the key driver as the number of savings bank accounts, at 624 million, is near four times of the number of loan accounts at 160 million.

2. Enhancement of branch presence and credit availability are very critical. The bottom 50 scoring districts have only 4,068 loan accounts/100,000 population, which is nearly one-third of the all India average of 11,680. There are only three branches/100,000 population, against 7.6 branches/100,000 population at an all-India level.

3. CRISIL Inclusix score improved over the past three years to 40.1 in 2011, from 37.6 in 2010 and 35.4 in 2009.

4. Wide disparities exist across India in terms of access to financial services. Six largest cities have 11 per cent of the country's bank branches. While, four districts in the North-Eastern region have only one bank branch each.

5. High performing top 50 districts continuously improved in deposit and branch penetration (BP). Their DP score increased by a significant 9.3 in 2011, over 2009. Also, they added 2,824 branches in this period, nearly one-fourth of the total branches added in the country.

6. Branch efficiency that the number of savings deposit accounts per branch has improved by 20 per cent to 6,073 in 2011 from 4,919 in 2009 and the number of incremental saving deposit accounts growth at 35 per cent in the districts at the bottom.

Source: Government of India and RBI, 2013.

---

[44] These intermediaries could be used as business facilitators or business correspondents by commercial banks.

[45] GoI and RBI. 2013. 'CRISIL Inclusix: An Index to Measure India's Progress on Financial Inclusion'. An initiative by CRISIL developed with support from Ministry of Finance, GoI and RBI in June 2013. Available at: http://crisil.com/pdf/corporate/CRISIL-Inclusix.pdf (20 August 2013).

4.4 Infrastructure growth

Infrastructure growth is instrumental in transforming India in many ways. Transportation and technology (which includes information technology and telecommunication) are revolutionizing the life and livelihoods of the people of India. Investment in infrastructure development, hence, should be considered as the channel for trickle down in the neoliberal period, as it increases the access to services, connectivity (both physical and virtual), facilitates quick access to information, increases access to markets (both labour and commodity), and helps strategize production plans according to the weather conditions and external market scenarios.

The huge investment in infrastructure development in the country in the last two decades was largely focused on the requirements of industry and service sector. The investment for rural and agricultural sector declined substantially.[46] Infrastructure investments arguably need to be revived in these two sectors, as the economy gets deeper into a challenging period. This investment will not only boost employment opportunities in rural and semi-urban areas, but also improve the quality of critical services.

Investment in transportation and information communication technology is a great livelihood facilitator. It helps people to opt for the best livelihood choice as per the available information. The internal migration patterns in India in the last few years are very clearly linked with access to information on labour markets and increased capability to respond to this using improved transportation facilities. For example, road transportation received good investment in the last one decade in which the national highways attracted FDIs. The national highways cover 2 per cent of total roads but cater to 40 per cent of transport and attract more than 50 per cent of the investment. The rural road system in the country is also receiving more policy attention and fund allocation in the Twelfth Plan.

Considering the livelihood challenge that might affect the country in the present scenario, pumping more money into infrastructure development will enhance the livelihood options of people by widening their access to and broadening markets for their products. It will also facilitate the movement of people from one location to another for livelihoods and education, for example. Unlike the policymakers of the post-Independence period who sidelined growth while shaping economic priorities, present-day policymakers must combine growth with development.

4.5 Urbanization and livelihoods

Urban centres are known as the engines of economic growth. Urban centres attract inflows of people from rural and semi-urban areas. Patterns of 'step migration' and seasonal migration[47] are visible throughout India, from rural to urban areas. In absolute terms nearly 377 million Indian live in 7,935 towns. One-third of the urban people were poor in 2011.

The urban-oriented sectors (secondary and tertiary) report impressive growth in income and employment generation during the post-2008 period. Sectoral employment

---

[46] The financial requirements of Ministry of Human Resource Development (MoHRD) to meet the infrastructure requirements as per the Right to Education (RTE) Act and the suggestions of the HLEG on health to increase the availability of health care facility in rural India and district/block levels, including training centres, has been declined by the Planning Commission while finalizing the Twelfth Five-Year Plan document.

[47] Recent studies on Indian internal migration reveal clear step pattern to migration whereby people move initially from one rural area to another during the harvest/cultivation period; then they shift to rural to semi-urban areas that have manufacturing units. Finally, they have become semi-permanent migrants to urban areas. Seasonal or circular migration refers to perhaps the 100 million Indians who spend between four to 10 months in a year working away from their villages but have no fixed abode during this time, returning annually for the farm season (Deshingkar, Priya and Shaheen Akter. 2009. *Migration and Human Development in India*, Human Development Research Paper 2009/13, United National Development Programmes, India).

performance is discussed in more detail in Chapter 2. In the last two decades, urban India witnessed an amazing diversification in the semi-skilled and unskilled occupations. Most of these activities (security guard services, courier services, florists, housekeeping services, and domestic services) require basic literacy. Meanwhile, basic service delivery in urban areas such as housing, water supply, sanitation, solid waste management, and public transport is still inadequate. In case these sectors receive sufficient funds for infrastructure development, their potential to provide employment is huge.

To sustain inclusive growth in the urban environment, it is essential to address the basic needs of the urban poor by equipping them with necessary skills to take advantage of the growth process and, at the same time, reducing institutional dysfunctionalities that hamper inclusive and sustainable development of urban conglomerations. The Twelfth Plan documents on urban development suggest a multi-pronged strategy to meet the following objectives:

1. Accelerate the rate of job creation in urban areas.
2. Impart relevant skills to urban poor.
3. Facilitate self-employment for urban poor wherever viable.
4. Proactive and mandatory creation/allocation of spaces within city boundaries to ensure livelihood opportunities to the urban poor.
5. Provide basic services to the urban poor, especially through rehabilitation of slums.
6. Ensure financial inclusion of urban poor.
7. Ensure legislative inclusion of urban poor.
8. Facilitate the transition of the urban poor from the informal sector to the formal one and extend the provisions of social security.

The Plan is expected to fund programmes and projects to achieve these objectives mainly through the flagship programme, Jawaharlal Nehru National Urban Renewal Mission (JNNURM).[48] The fund allocation raises some concerns as during the Eleventh Plan JNNURM has received ₹123,711 crore, while it is now reduced to ₹101,917 crore in the Twelfth Plan. The other major initiative to address urban poverty by employment promotion is the National Urban Livelihoods Mission (NULM). This will provide policy and programmatic attention on the issue of urban livelihoods in a structured way. This will replace the existing Swarna Jayanti Shahari Rozgar Yojana (SJSRY) from the beginning of the Twelfth Plan. NULM will be target oriented with specific focus on the primary issues pertaining to urban poverty such as skill upgradation, entrepreneurship development, and employment creation through wage employment and self-employment opportunities opened up by the emerging markets in urban areas using a mission approach. The vision of these two flagship programmes is very encouraging, but the budget allocation to achieve the mission goals needs to be increased.

Considering the growth of urban areas in the country, it is essential to increase the capital formation in the urban infrastructure development in a huge way. This will help reduce the burden of agriculture in one way and, on the other hand, promote the inclusive growth that is envisaged by the policymakers.

---

[48] Jawaharlal Nehru National Urban Renewal Mission (JNNURM) is a massive city-modernization scheme launched by the GoI under the Ministry of Urban Development in December 2005. The scheme was meant to improve the quality of life and infrastructure in the cities. Initially, it was launched for a seven-year period (up to March 2012) to encourage cities to initiate steps for bringing phased improvements in their civic-service levels. The government has extended the tenure of the mission for two years, i.e. from April 2012 to 31 March 2014 and it is likely to continue under the Twelfth Five-Year Plan as well.

5. Introduction to chapters

Each State of India's Livelihoods (SOIL) report is part of an annual series, a digest of evidence, debates, and events which have taken place during the year. But it is also a collection of unique papers and accounts which explores specific themes selected for their particular pertinence to livelihoods at that time.

This year's report reflects—to an extent—the structure of earlier recent reports. Chapter 2 (Statistical Atlas) uses the latest round of NSSO data to provide an update of key livelihood-related indicators, and to review and discuss trends, at state level across India. In particular, the nature of the workforce and its distribution across kinds of work is discussed. This is followed by a closer look at agriculture, its share, and the changing land-ownership patterns. Then we review progress in the reduction of poverty using the 'headcount' figures (the most recent ones being still hotly debated), and we end with a review of the capability-oriented Human Development Index (HDI). Chapter 3 (Policy Initiatives and Policy Paralysis) provides our annual update of progress in government policy which affects the livelihoods of the rural and urban poor. As in previous SOIL reports, we cover the budgeting process, the commencement of implementation of the Twelfth Plan, and a myriad of legislations at different stages of progress. While some legislation is at an advanced stage of becoming installed as policy, other remains at the level of debate and first presentation.

In a departure from recent SOIL reports, Chapters 4, 5, and 6 explore sectors or themes of wide-reaching relevance to poor people's livelihoods. Each theme is treated at the level of policy, programme implementation, the configuration of state and market (public and private) operating in the sectoral space, and, above all, ramifications of trends and interventions, for livelihoods.

Chapter 4 (Agriculture and Livelihoods) returns to the agricultural sector which we last reviewed in detail in SOIL 2010. Agriculture's relatively healthy growth, coupled with the heightening public and policy debate on food prices, food security, and land use, warrants a detailed review of its health and the shifting trends for the poor. The chapter reviews the evidence of positive trends, in growth, wage rates, and expansion of horticulture. It also highlights key areas of concern such as the growing overuse of fertilizer, uneven yields across states, high wastage, and decreasing farm size. The second part of the chapter takes a broad sweep at the range of initiatives underway across the country to address these areas of concern, including aggregation, tenancy reform, new models for extension support, building stronger supply chains, advocacy towards a sustainable agriculture policy, finance to farmers at different levels, and interventions in support vulnerable farmers: women and agricultural labour.

Chapter 5 (Social Protection and Livelihoods) reviews the government's rapidly extending role in providing benefits and transfers to the poor. India's changing welfare regime has direct implications for livelihoods: for people's ability to secure their income and protect themselves from shocks, their appetite for certain kinds of risks, and even their motivation to work when state benefits are becoming more readily available at home. The chapter reviews India's recent trend towards a social protection floor. It then looks at specific schemes which make up the welfare environment in rural and urban areas respectively, schemes which secure income, on the one hand, and protect from shocks, on the other. The chapter concludes by arguing that India must move towards market and mutual solutions and avoid a slide into umbrella benefits in perpetuity.

The final chapter, Chapter 6 (Skilling India) turns to India's skills development sector, recently reborn under the Eleventh Plan and flush with funds and energy from government and private skills providers.

The chapter traces the evolution of the new policy on the base of the old and, through a review of evidence from training providers and learners, discusses what we can learn so far about the policy's ramifications and effectiveness. The chapter then takes a deeper dive into the root causes of some of the problems and shortcomings emerging from the new policy, including the weak schooling base, the inattention to experiential and on-the-job learning, the need to better understand the connection between skilling, productivity, and decent work, and the scope for going beyond certificates and competencies, to capabilities for lifelong employability.

Suggested readings

Government of India. 2012. Draft Twelfth Five-Year Plan (2012–17) Document, Volume I, Faster, More Inclusive and Sustainable Growth, Planning Commission.

———. 2013. Economic Survey 2012–13, Ministry of Finance.

———. 2013. Union Budget 2013–14, Ministry of Finance.

———. 2012. Report of the Working Group on 'Effectively Integrating Industrial Growth and Environment Sustainability', Twelfth Five-Year Plan (2012–17), Planning Commission.

———. 2013. Strategy Document Part 1 and 2 of Twelfth Five-Year Plan, Planning Commission.

———. 2012. Review of Eleventh Five-Year Plan, Planning Commission.

Websites

Planning Commission
Ministry of Finance
Ministry of Rural Development
Ministry of Human Resource Development
Ministry of Small Scale Industries and Micro-Enterprises
Ministry of Labour
Census of India
Reserve Bank of India
National Bank for Agriculture and Rural Development (NABARD)
Various newspapers
India Together
World Bank
UN Agencies

A Statistical Atlas of Livelihoods

Tara Nair

Chapter 2

1. Introduction

Attempting to capture the livelihood context of India is a complex exercise largely because of the diversity of resource conditions as well as development dynamics across regions. This chapter is an attempt to illustrate some of the major indicators of the status of livelihoods, especially rural livelihoods, with the help of disaggregated data at the state level. The analysis draws upon the conceptual understanding of livelihood security as a multifaceted phenomenon that combines elements of means of earning a living, ownership of and control over assets, capabilities, and the ability to stake claims. More specifically the chapter will analyze the changes in a range of indicators relating to (i) employment, (ii) assets (land holding), (iii) capabilities (human development index), and (iv) poverty over the last two decades.

The chapter is organized into four sections. Section 2 examines in detail the trends in employment across rural and urban populations, males and females and across states. Section 3 analyzes the changes in the structure of the agricultural sector, the sector that supports majority of the country's workforce. Section 4 discusses the shift in the poverty ratios since the mid-1990s, while the human development achievement of the country is looked at closely in Section 5.

2. How many get to work in India?

For a country that accommodates a large majority of its population in informal economic activities, particularly, agriculture, a livelihood is essentially about finding an opportunity to do something which brings in income. Close to 40 per cent of the country's overall population is in the labour force, available or looking for such work. About 39 per cent are indeed able to find work, either as their usual and principal activity or as a subsidiary activity. As per the official statistics about 2 per cent of the population tends to remain unemployed. This figure does not, however, reflect the extent of underemployment in the informal economy. That much of the growth that India experienced in the last two decades came without any rise in employment (captured by the phrase 'jobless growth') indicates that underemployment is prevalent in the economy.

The livelihood opportunity is structured differently for men and women, in rural and urban areas. Thus about 54 per cent of male population in rural and urban sectors found work in 2011–12 as against one-fourth of the women in rural and 15 per cent of women in urban sectors (see Figure 2.1). While the rural male workforce participation rate (WPR) remained more or less at that level through the 1990s and 2000s, the urban ratio

Figure 2.1:   Ratio of workforce to population[1]

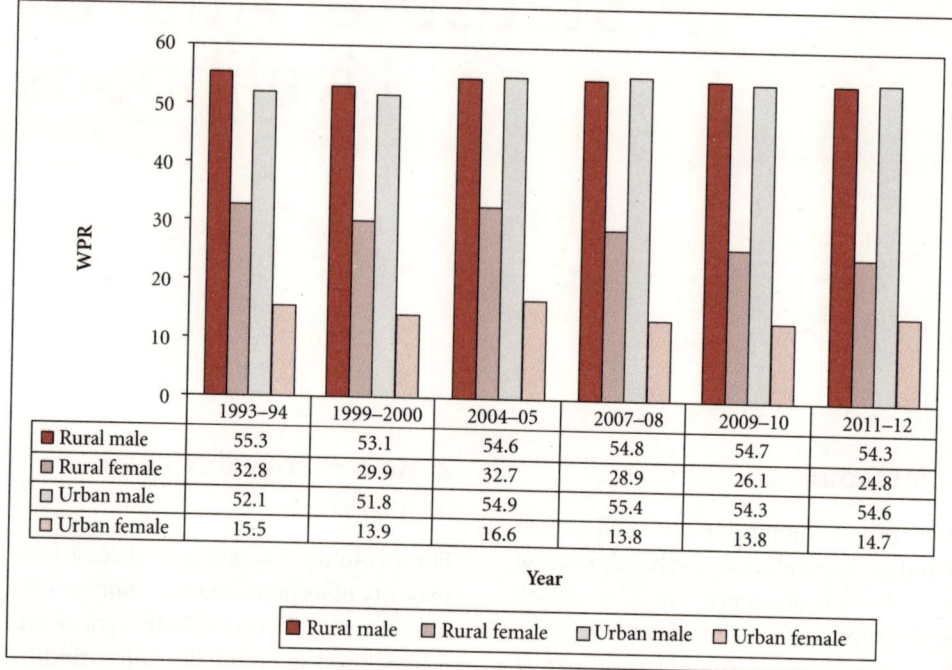

	1993–94	1999–2000	2004–05	2007–08	2009–10	2011–12
■ Rural male	55.3	53.1	54.6	54.8	54.7	54.3
■ Rural female	32.8	29.9	32.7	28.9	26.1	24.8
▫ Urban male	52.1	51.8	54.9	55.4	54.3	54.6
▫ Urban female	15.5	13.9	16.6	13.8	13.8	14.7

Year

■ Rural male   ■ Rural female   ▫ Urban male   ▫ Urban female

Source: Himanshu. 2011. 'Employment Trends in India: A Re-examination', *Economic and Political Weekly*, 46 (37): 43–59 and NSSO Report of 2013.

shows a definite increase from what it was in the 1990s. Less and less women in the rural areas are part of the workforce since the late 1990s, while the urban women appear to engage with employment off and on. What accounts for such changes? We will explore this later in the chapter.

What are the trends in terms of the opportunity to work? Between the early 1990s and the late 2000s, overall employment increased in absolute terms by 75 million from 398 million to 473 million. This included the 47 million male workers in the rural sector and 45 million male workers in the urban sector. However, the overall gain in employment was marred by the contraction in the rural women workforce since the mid-2000s. Though the number of rural female workers registered an expansion

between 1993–94 and 2004–05, it was more modest compared to males—about 19 million. In 2011–12 the female rural workforce in the country was 22 million short of what it was in 2004-05. In fact, the most striking aspect of work participation in the country is the perennially low share of women. And it is disturbing to note that the gender differential in work participation has been on the increase since 2004–05. Figure 2.2 depicts these changes. We have used index numbers to better capture the direction of change since 1993–94.

The trends in the status of employment would help us comprehend the changes delineated above. Employment status is analyzed broadly by classifying employment into self-employment, regular wage or salaried employment, and casual work. Such a classification conveys the larger dynamics of livelihoods—regularity of earnings, security of work, and overall vulnerability to shocks and stresses.

As shown in Tables 2.1 and 2.2, the absolute size of the self-employed male

---

[1] Himanshu. 2011. 'Employment Trends in India: A Re-examination', *Economic and Political Weekly*, 46 (37): 43–59; NSSO. 2013. *Key Indictors of Employment and Unemployment in India 2004–05, NSS 66th Round (July 2011–June 2012)*, Ministry of Statistics and Programme Implementation, June.

Figure 2.2:   Change in total male and female workforce

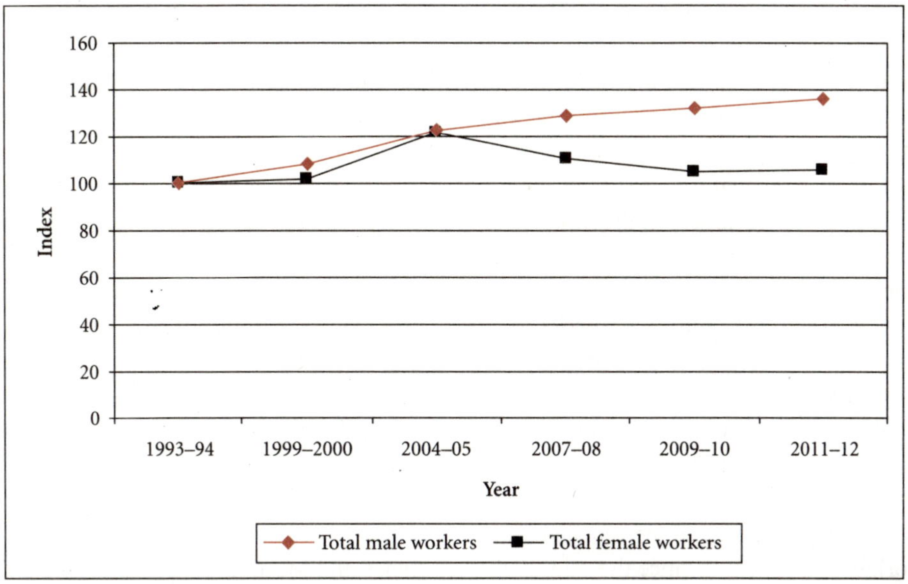

Source: Himanshu. 2011. 'Employment Trends in India: A Re-examination', *Economic and Political Weekly*, 46 (37): 43–59 and NSSO Report of 2013.

Table 2.1:   Rural workforce by status of employment: 1993–94 to 2011–12 (in million)

Year	Rural males				Rural females				All workers
	Self-employment	Regular work	Casual work	Total	Self-employment	Regular work	Casual work	Total	
1993–94	108.7	15.6	63.5	187.8	61.3	2.9	40.5	104.7	292.5
1999–2000	109.2	17.5	71.9	198.6	60.6	3.3	41.9	105.8	304.4
2004–05	127.2	19.7	72.0	218.9	79.0	4.6	40.4	124.0	342.9
2007–08	126.0	20.7	80.7	227.4	66.1	4.6	42.6	113.3	340.7
2009–10	124.3	19.7	88.3	232.3	58.4	4.6	41.8	104.8	337.1
2011–12	127.9	23.5	83.3	234.6	60.4	5.7	35.7	101.8	336.4

Source: Himanshu. 2011. 'Employment Trends in India: A Re-examination', *Economic and Political Weekly*, 46 (37): 43–59 and NSSO Report of 2013.

Table 2.2:   Urban workforce by status of employment: 1993–94 to 2011–12 (in million)

Year	Urban males				Urban females				All Workers
	Self-employment	Regular work	Casual work	Total	Self-employment	Regular work	Casual work	Total	
1993–94	26.9	27.1	10.5	64.5	7.9	4.9	4.4	17.2	81.7
1999–2000	31.3	31.4	12.7	75.4	8.2	6.1	3.9	18.2	93.6
2004–05	40.5	36.7	13.2	90.4	11.7	8.8	4.1	24.6	115.0
2007–08	41.7	41.0	15.0	97.7	9.3	8.3	4.4	22.0	119.7
2009–10	41.2	42.0	17.0	100.2	9.4	9.0	4.5	22.9	123.1
2011–12	45.5	47.4	16.3	109.2	11.7	11.7	3.9	27.3	136.5

Source: Himanshu. 2011. 'Employment Trends in India: A Re-examination', *Economic and Political Weekly*, 46 (37): 43–59 and NSSO Report of 2013.

workforce in the rural sector remained more or less the same since the mid-2000s at around 127 million. The number of rural women who are self-employed showed an increase till the 2004–05 NSS Round, and has fallen thereafter. The latest estimates (2011–12) show that the size of the women self-employed workforce in the rural sector is the same as its level in 1999–2000. All types of urban male employment—self-employed, regular employed, and casual workers—increased steadily through the 1990s and the 2000s. As for urban women, excepting for regular employment, the growth in numbers has not been steady. The size of women self-employed workers in 2011–12 is the same as in 2004–05, whereas the female casual workforce has shrunk since the mid-2000s by about 500,000.

By the end of the decade of the 2000s, some changes are visible in the distribution of worker population across types and location. For one, there is a rise in the population of self-employed and regular wage/salaried workers among both men and women in both rural and urban sectors. At the same time, there has been a decline in casual workforce among all categories. The rise in self and regular workers more than compensates for the decline in casual workers for all men and urban women. However, in case of rural women, the fall in casual workforce is more than the increase in the other two, tempting one to argue that amidst high economic growth and overall expansion in workforce, a significant population of rural women seems to have disappeared from the employment scene. Where have they gone? What does this mean to the livelihood strategies of rural households?

A comparative analysis of the shares of men and women across employment types and location of residence (see Table 2.3) provides us with useful insights into the structure of employment. The major changes are the following:

1. The share of both male and female workers in rural self-employment (accounting for the largest segment of

Table 2.3: Share in overall workforce by status of employment

	Rural males			Rural females		
	Self-employment	Regular work	Casual work	Self-employment	Regular work	Casual work
1993–94	29.0	4.2	17.0	16.4	0.8	10.8
1999–2000	27.4	4.4	18.1	15.2	0.8	10.5
2004–05	27.8	4.3	15.7	17.3	1.0	8.8
2007–08	27.4	4.5	17.5	14.4	1.0	9.3
2009–10	27.0	4.3	19.2	12.7	1.0	9.1
2011–12	27.0	5.0	17.6	12.8	1.2	7.6

	Urban males			Urban females		
	Self-employment	Regular work	Casual work	Self-employment	Regular work	Casual work
1993–94	7.2	7.2	2.8	2.1	1.3	1.2
1999–2000	7.9	7.9	3.2	2.1	1.5	1.0
2004–05	8.8	8.0	2.9	2.6	1.9	0.9
2007–08	9.1	8.9	3.3	2.0	1.8	1.0
2009–10	9.0	9.1	3.7	2.0	2.0	1.0
2011–12	9.6	10.0	3.4	2.5	2.5	0.8

Source: Himanshu. 2011. 'Employment Trends in India: A Re-examination', *Economic and Political Weekly*, 46 (37): 43–59 and NSSO Report of 2013.

the workforce—52 per cent in 2011–12) declined since 1993–94.

2. While the share of men (both rural and urban), who are casual workers, in the overall workforce does not show any perceptible change, women's share in casual work has secularly declined.

3. Share of regular workers has increased among all categories. But regular work supports only about 4 per cent of women overall.

It may be noted that the relatively greater fluctuations in female employment have been discussed in earlier analyses.[2] In the specific context of India, women's participation in the labour force is found to be influenced by economic conditions. They tend to join the labour force in times of economic distress and withdraw during prosperity.

At the state level, Andhra Pradesh, Karnataka, and Tamil Nadu had the highest worker population ratio (WPR) for rural males in 1994–95 and 2004–05 indicating these states' capacity to generate employment. In 2011–12, Karnataka recorded the highest rural male WPR (61.2) while Gujarat rose (59.9) to replace Tamil Nadu as the third state at the top. As shown in Table 2.4, the states that have improved their employment capability since the mid-1990s, apart from Gujarat, are West Bengal, Kerala, Odisha, and Punjab. The data shows that Andhra Pradesh and Tamil Nadu have lost some of their potential for employment creation for rural males over the years. Also, it is disturbing to note the decline in WPR in the case of Rajasthan, Bihar, and Uttar Pradesh.

As for rural females, the states of Andhra Pradesh, Tamil Nadu, Maharashtra, and Rajasthan who had the highest WPRs in 1994–95, are found to have experienced a decline in the values (Table 2.5). On the

Table 2.4: Change in rural male WPR of major states[3]

Major states where WPR for rural males improved	1993–94	2004–05	2011–12
West Bengal	55.7	57.4	58.6
Kerala	53.7	55.9	56.5
Odisha	56.6	58.6	59.2
Gujarat	57.4	59.3	59.9
Punjab	54.6	54.9	56.6
Major states where WPR for rural males declined			
Himachal Pradesh	59.0	55.5	54.1
Rajasthan	54.0	51.0	49.5
Bihar	51.1	47.7	47.3
Uttar Pradesh	52.2	49.6	49.1
Andhra Pradesh	63.1	60.5	60.2
Tamil Nadu	60.2	59.7	59.5

Source: NSSO Reports of 1997, 2006, and 2013.

Table 2.5: Change in rural female WPR of major states

Major states where WPR for rural females improved	1994–95	2004–05	2011–12
Odisha	31.7	32.2	41.2
Kerala	23.8	25.6	37.7
Punjab	22.0	32.2	39.2
Uttar Pradesh	21.9	24	33.3
West Bengal	18.5	17.8	39.2
Major states where WPR for rural females declined			
Andhra Pradesh	52.1	48.3	47
Tamil Nadu	47.8	46.1	44.3
Maharashtra	47.7	47.4	43.1
Rajasthan	45.7	40.7	40.0
Karnataka	43.0	45.9	42.3

Source: NSSO Reports of 1997, 2006, and 2013.

other hand, Odisha, West Bengal, Kerala, Punjab and Uttar Pradesh improved the WPR consistently through the late 1990s and the 2000s.

---

[2] Himanshu. 2011. 'Employment Trends in India: A Re-examination', *Economic and Political Weekly*, 46 (37): 43–59.

[3] National Sample Survey Organization (NSSO). 1997. *Employment and Unemployment in India 1993-94, NSS Fiftieth Round (July 1993 – June 1994)*, Ministry of Statistics and Programme Implementation, March; ———. 2006. *Employment and Unemployment Situation in India 2004–05, NSS 61st Round (July 2004–June 2005)*, Ministry of Statistics and Programme Implementation, September; ———. 2013. *Key Indictors of Employment and Unemployment in India 2004–05, NSS 66th Round (July 2011–June 2012)*, Ministry of Statistics and Programme Implementation, June.

Obviously, such data cannot help us find useful answers to the question of employment quality. For instance, the high male WPR in states such as Andhra Pradesh, Karnataka, and Tamil Nadu in the earlier period may be explained by the boom in the information technology sector. But a part of the rise may also have come from the increased absorption of low-skilled workers in the burgeoning urban informal sector in these states. As for the rural sector, there has been noticeable growth in non-farm employment since the mid-1990s through the 2000s. While this may have been triggered by the fall in employment opportunities in the agricultural sector,[4] there is evidence now to show that productive opportunities drive this process. This is contrary to the earlier thesis that non-farm employment diversification is driven mainly by distress.

In short, the last two decades have not witnessed any substantive shifts in the structure of employment in the country despite some changes in the distribution of workers across different categories. Self-employment still accommodates more than half of the country's workforce. A large chunk of this is accounted for by the agricultural sector, though there has been a sharp fall in the share of agricultural workers after 2004–05 (from 60 per cent to 48.5 per cent in 2011–12). Agriculture continues to be a major employer in all the states. Its role in employment provision is relatively more prominent in the poorer states such as Chhattisgarh, Bihar, Madhya Pradesh, and Odisha (see Figures 2.3 and 2.4). A few states including Kerala, Tamil Nadu, and Punjab, on the other hand, appear to have diversified their employment base. The share of agriculture and landholding size are discussed more in the following section, and an in-depth review of the sector is in Chapter 4.

About one-third of the workforce still lacks regularity of work and security of

Figure 2.3:   Distribution of all workers by industry: 2011–12[5]

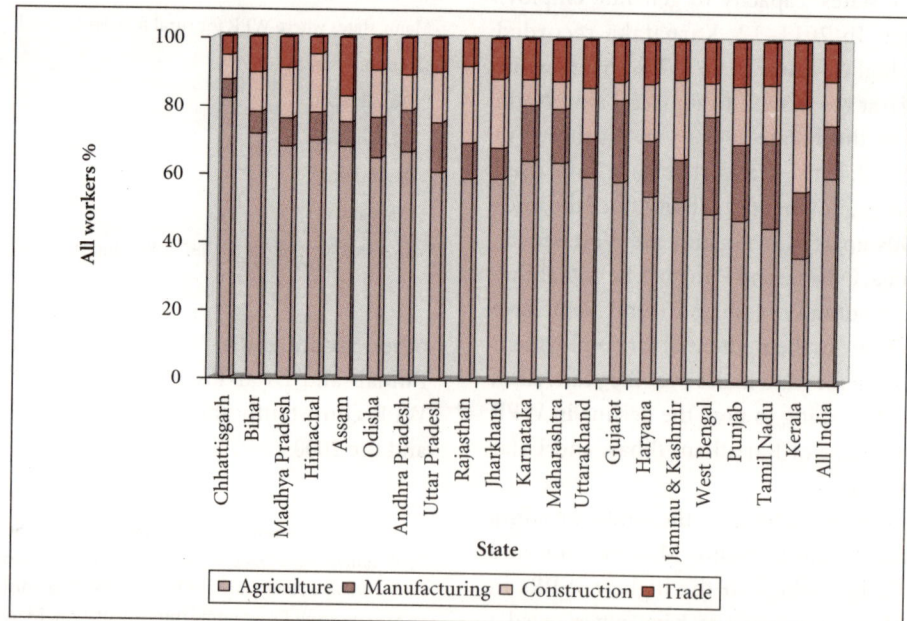

Source: NSSO Report of 2013.

[4] Papola, T.S. and Partha Pratim Sahu. 2012. 'Growth and Structure of Employment: Long-Term and Post-Reform Performance and the Emerging Challenge', ISID Occasional Paper Series 2012/01, Institute for Studies in Industrial Development, New Delhi.

[5] NSSO. 2013. *Key Indictors of Employment and Unemployment in India 2004–05, NSS 66th Round (July 2011–June 2012)*, Ministry of Statistics and Programme Implementation, June.

Figure 2.4: Distribution of rural workers by industry: 2011–12

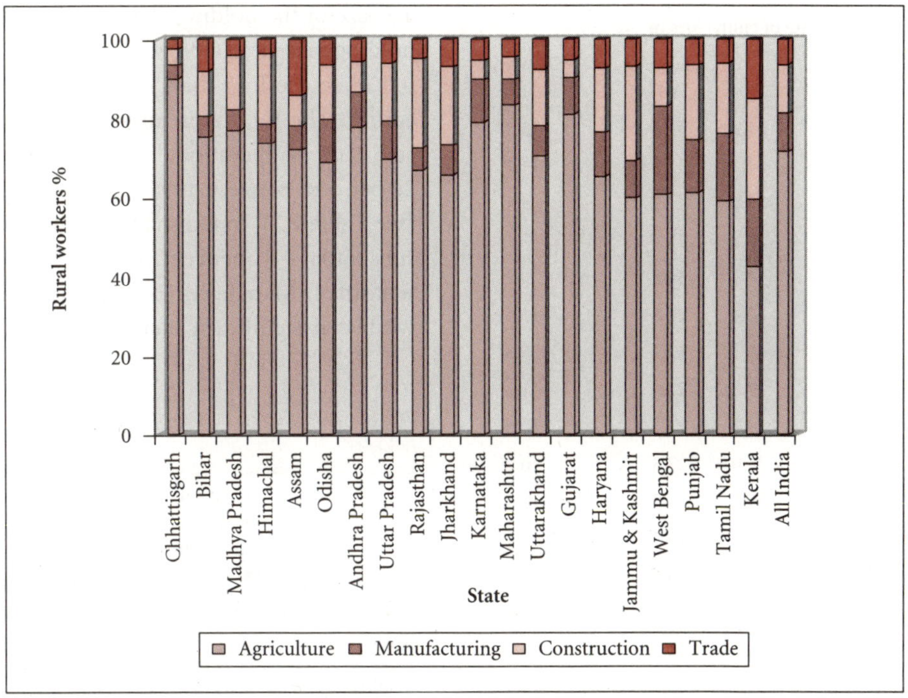

Source: NSSO Report of 2013.

earnings as they are employed 'casually' without any contract, security, or wider benefits. There has, however, been a gradual rise in the share of regular workforce, a trend that should perhaps be associated with the rising shares of workers in secondary and tertiary sectors. Between 1993–94 and 2011–12 the employment share of the secondary sector rose from 15 per cent to 24 per cent, and of the tertiary sector from 21 per cent to 27 per cent. But this cannot continue unabated as the productive activities increasingly shift towards less formal and more flexible regimes.

3. Agriculture and rural livelihoods

The predominance of agriculture in supporting rural livelihoods makes it imperative for us to examine some of the major trends in the sector more closely. The most striking observation about the sector is the all-India decline in the population of cultivators between 2001 and 2011 from 127.3 million

to 118.6 million.[6] It must be noted that the number of cultivators had increased by about 27 million between 1991 and 2001. The population of agricultural workers, on the other hand, increased consistently from 74.6 million to 106.8 million and further to 144 million over the three census periods. The share of cultivators in total workers in rural areas came down from 40.2 per cent in 2001 to 33 per cent in 2011 and that of agricultural workers rose from 26 per cent to 30 per cent.

The fall in the population of cultivators has been more pronounced in the case of Uttar Pradesh, Bihar, Madhya Pradesh, and Odisha (see Table 2.6). In absolute terms, the cultivator population declined

---

[6] Census of India. 2011. *Primary Census Abstract,* http://www.censusindia.gov.in/2011census/hlo/pca/pca_data.html (accessed 1 August 2013); Government of India. 2012. *Agricultural Statistics at a Glance 2012,* Directorate of Economics and Statistics, Department of Agriculture and Cooperation, Ministry of Agriculture.

Table 2.6: Share of cultivators in worker population

State	Absolute change in the no. of cultivators	% share of cultivators in workers			Change in % share
		1991	2001	2011	
Rajasthan	5,437,358	58.8	55.3	45.6	13.2
Chhattisgarh	4,004,796		44.5	32.9	11.7
Jharkhand	3,814,832		38.5	29.1	9.4
Maharashtra	2,397,265	32.8	28.7	25.4	7.4
Uttarakhand	1,580,423		50.1	40.8	9.3
Jammu & Kashmir	1,245,316		42.4	28.8	13.6
Himachal Pradesh	936,751	63.3	65.3	57.9	5.3
Gujarat	743,872	33.4	27.3	22.0	11.4
Karnataka	665,016	34.2	29.2	23.6	10.6
Haryana	651,271	38.8	36.0	27.8	10.9
Assam	502,510	50.9	39.1	33.9	17.0
Punjab	17,301	31.4	22.6	19.5	11.9
Kerala	−345,730	12.2	7.0	5.8	6.5
Odisha	−494,511	44.3	29.8	23.4	20.9
West Bengal	−728,305	28.4	19.2	14.7	13.7
Andhra Pradesh	−1,399,645	27.7	22.5	16.5	11.3
Tamil Nadu	−1,415,633	24.8	18.4	12.9	11.9
Uttar Pradesh	−2,973,293	53.3	41.1	29.0	24.3
Madhya Pradesh	−3,059,682	51.8	42.8	31.2	20.6
Bihar	−3,968,293	43.6	29.3	20.7	22.9
India	7,990,294	38.7	31.7	24.6	14.1

Source: Census of India (various years).

obviously suggests a decline in the average size of the holding. A typical marginal holding measured 0.38 hectare in 2010–11, 0.02 hectare less than its size a decade earlier. The total area under the smallest size class of operational holdings rose by 26 per cent between 1995–96 and 2010–11 (see Table 2.7). In Odisha the increase was substantial—81 per cent. Madhya Pradesh, Rajasthan, Maharashtra, and Gujarat also witnessed significant increase in the area

Table 2.7: Area under marginal operational holdings[8]

State	Marginal operational holdings (area '000 hectare)		Absolute change	% Change
	1995–96	2010–11		
Odisha	1,064	1,922	857.9	80.6
Madhya Pradesh $	795	2,868	1,072.6	59.7
Rajasthan	780	1238	457.9	58.7
Maharashtra	2,087	3,186	1,099.3	52.7
Gujarat	562	857	294.8	52.4
Karnataka	1,248	1,851	602.7	48.3
Andhra Pradesh	2,904	3,727	822.8	28.3
Assam	621	775	153.6	24.7
West Bengal	2,399	2,891	491.9	20.5
Himachal Pradesh	230	272	41.8	18.2
Bihar	3,871	4,433	562.0	14.5
Uttar Pradesh	6,266	7,007	740.6	11.8
Tamil Nadu	2,210	2,292	81.7	3.7
Jammu & Kashmir	402	416	13.9	3.5
Kerala	912	886	−26.4	−2.9
Haryana	404	360	−44.2	−10.9
Punjab	122	101	−21.4	−17.5
Total	27,881	35,082	7,201.5	25.8

Source: Government of India. 2012. *Agricultural Statistics at a Glance 2012*, Directorate of Economics and Statistics, Department of Agriculture and Cooperation, Ministry of Agriculture.
Note: $ includes Chhattisgarh.

by about a crore in these states. The number would go up to 1.4 crore if one adds states such as Andhra Pradesh, West Bengal, and Tamil Nadu, which also registered absolute reduction in cultivators. It may be worth noting that some of these states report high incidence of indebtedness among farmers.

At the same time, there has been a consistent increase in the number of and area under marginal operational holdings (<1 hectare). The percentage share of marginal holdings in all holdings increased from 62 per cent to 67 per cent between 2000–01 and 2010–11.[7] But they accounted for only 22 per cent of the total area in 2010–11. This

[7] GoI. 2012. *Agricultural Statistics at a Glance 2012*, Directorate of Economics and Statistics, Department of Agriculture and Cooperation, Ministry of Agriculture.

[8] GoI. 2012. *Agricultural Census 2011–12*, Ministry of Agriculture, New Delhi.

under marginal holdings suggesting further fragmentation of agricultural land. The sustainability of these farms is a crucial factor that shapes the livelihood environment of rural areas. Some of the challenges faced by small and marginal farmers according to NCEUS (2008)[9] are

> imperfect markets for inputs/product leading to smaller value realizations; absence of access to credit markets or imperfect credit markets leading to suboptimal investment decisions or input applications; poor human resource base; smaller access to suitable extension services restricting suitable decisions regarding cultivation practices and technological know-how; poorer access to 'public goods' such as public irrigation, command area development, electricity grids; greater negative externalities from poor quality land and water management, etc.[10]

At the macro level, the percentage share of agriculture to gross state domestic product (GSDP) across major states (see Table 2.8) has declined steadily over the years as the structure of the overall economy moved in favour of services. Over the period 2004–05 to 2011–12 the decline has been more drastic in the case of states such as Punjab, Himachal Pradesh, Uttarakhand, Kerala, and Uttar Pradesh. States including Tamil Nadu, Maharashtra, Madhya Pradesh, Chhattisgarh, and Gujarat have witnessed modest decline in agricultural GSDP over the period. Apart from the structural transformation logic, i.e. the progressive movement of growing economies towards secondary and tertiary activities, there are also reasons that are specific to the agricultural sector such as deterioration of soil health and over exploitation of

water resources. Lack of adequate capital investment in agriculture (irrigation works, command area development, land reclamation, afforestation and development of state farms, etc.) by the public sector has been identified as a major bottleneck in this regard. A recent media report quotes the government sources to point out that capital investment in agriculture and allied sectors has risen from 13.5 per cent of the GDP in 2004–05 to 20.1 per cent in 2010–11.[11] If this is so, the effect of such investment will be seen in the years to come.

Table 2.8: Percentage share of agriculture to GSDP

| State | % share of agriculture to total state GSDP | | | % share to total state GSDP of | |
	2004–05	2008–09	2011–12	Manufacturing 2011–12	Services
Punjab	31.12	25.39	21.56	21.19	45.54
Uttar Pradesh	26.90	22.96	20.38	13.46	53.26
Bihar	26.58	23.80	20.92	5.14	61.03
Madhya Pradesh	24.39	21.51	21.68	12.60	47.78
Jammu & Kashmir	22.34	19.04	16.90	8.40	53.87
Haryana	21.89	18.49	15.42	18.69	54.95
Rajasthan	21.85	18.48	18.51	12.98	45.45
Assam	21.70	19.56	18.97	6.50	55.91
Andhra Pradesh	20.58	18.22	15.48	12.30	55.60
Himachal Pradesh	19.72	15.54	11.09	15.79	44.19
West Bengal	19.18	15.60	13.85	10.61	61.61
Odisha	18.79	14.84	14.19	17.23	50.53
Uttarakhand	16.60	9.21	7.99	25.83	54.67
Karnataka	15.87	13.41	12.84	17.86	57.74
Chhattisgarh	14.75	12.12	14.37	18.37	39.17
Kerala	14.24	10.16	7.61	8.23	69.20
Gujarat	13.15	11.29	10.84	27.41	45.70
Jharkhand	11.37	14.54	11.45	19.04	47.16
Tamil Nadu	9.60	7.84	7.21	20.74	60.99
Maharashtra	8.29	6.81	5.79	19.83	61.66
All India	16.04	13.36	12.02	15.70	58.39

Source: http://planningcommission.gov.in/data/datatable/2504/databook_51.pdf (accessed 28 August 2013).

---

[9] National Commission for Employment in the Unorganised Sector (NCEUS). 2008. *Report on Conditions of Work and Promotion of Livelihoods in the Unorganised Sector*, New Delhi: Academic Foundation.

[10] Dev, Mahendra S. 2012. 'Small Farmers in India: Challenges and Opportunities', WP-2012-014, Indira Gandhi Institute of Development Research, Mumbai, June, p. 7.

---

[11] *The Economic Times*, 'Capital Formation in Agriculture up 87% in Last 6 Years: Official', 10 April 2012. Available at: http://articles.economictimes.indiatimes.com/2012-04-10/news/31318702_1_gross-capital-formation-agriculture-capital-investment (accessed on 10 August 2013).

Table 2.9: Status of the MSME sector: 2005–06

State	No. of enterprises (lakh)			Employment (lakh)			% share of unreg. sector in total workers
	Reg. sector	Unreg. sector	Total	Reg. sector	Unreg. sector	Total	
Uttar Pradesh	1.9	42.2	44.0	7.6	84.8	92.4	14.0
West Bengal	0.4	34.2	34.6	3.6	85.5	85.8	24.7
Tamil Nadu	2.3	30.8	33.1	14.3	80.8	81.0	24.6
Maharashtra	0.9	29.8	30.6	10.9	69.8	70.0	14.2
Andhra Pradesh	0.5	25.5	26.0	3.8	70.6	70.7	17.9
Kerala	1.5	20.6	22.1	6.2	46.6	49.6	42.7
Gujarat	2.3	19.5	21.8	12.5	43.9	47.7	19.3
Karnataka	1.4	18.8	20.2	7.9	40.5	46.7	16.8
Madhya Pradesh	1.1	18.3	19.3	3.0	22.8	33.7	10.7
Rajasthan	0.6	16.1	16.6	3.4	27.4	30.8	10.3
Odisha	0.2	15.5	15.7	1.7	33.0	33.2	18.9
Bihar	0.5	14.2	14.7	1.5	26.8	28.3	8.1
Punjab	0.5	14.0	14.5	4.2	22.6	26.8	27.1
Haryana	0.3	8.3	8.7	3.8	15.0	18.8	21.1
Jharkhand	0.2	6.6	6.8	0.8	5.0	12.9	9.9
Assam	0.2	6.4	6.6	2.1	12.8	14.3	11.9
Delhi	0.0	5.5	5.5	0.6	19.2	19.8	35.5
Chhattisgarh	0.2	5.0	5.2	0.8	8.9	9.5	7.8
Uttarakhand	0.2	3.5	3.7	0.8	6.2	7.0	18.0
Jammu & Kashmir	0.2	2.9	3.0	0.9	4.9	5.8	13.3
Himachal Pradesh	0.1	2.8	2.9	0.7	4.0	4.7	13.1
Goa	0.0	0.8	0.9	0.3	−10.6	1.9	32.6
Puducherry	0.0	0.3	0.4	0.2	−3.2	1.0	10.7
India	15.64	346.12	361.76	93.09	712.16	805.25	16.7

Source: www.dcmsme.gov.in
Note: 'Reg.' and 'Unreg.' denote 'Registered' and 'Unregistered' respectively.

Table 2.9 reveals an interesting relationship between reduced engagement of the population with agriculture and the growth of the industry sector. The states that rank high in number of micro, small, and medium enterprises (MSMEs) have all witnessed an absolute reduction in the population of cultivators.

4. Changing poverty levels

Notwithstanding the controversies around the measurement of poverty, the estimates do help us understand the relative position of regions with respect to livelihood insecurity. In other words, these estimates, in a comparative perspective, throw light on the regional capability/vulnerability in ensuring security of livelihoods.

Table 2.10 presents poverty ratios across states based on NSS data. As per these estimates in 2011–12, Chhattisgarh and Jharkhand are the poorest states in India with 40 and 37 per cent overall population below the poverty line. They also have the highest percentage of rural poor. Bihar, Odisha, Madhya Pradesh, and Uttar Pradesh are the other states with relatively higher incidence of poverty. Goa, Kerala, Himachal Pradesh, Punjab, and Andhra Pradesh have

Table 2.10: Poverty headcount ratio

	Poverty headcount ratio								
	2011–12			2004–05			1993–94		
State	Rural	Urban	Total	Rural	Urban	Total	Rural	Urban	Total
Andhra Pradesh	11.0	5.8	9.2	32.3	23.4	29.9	48.1	35.2	44.6
Arunachal Pradesh	38.9	20.3	34.7	33.6	23.5	31.1	60.0	22.6	54.5
Assam	33.9	20.5	32.0	36.4	21.8	34.4	54.9	27.7	51.8
Bihar	34.1	31.2	33.7	55.7	43.7	54.4	62.3	44.7	60.5
Chhattisgarh	44.6	24.8	39.9	55.1	28.4	49.4	55.9	28.1	50.9
Delhi	12.9	9.8	9.9	15.6	12.9	13.1	16.2	15.7	15.7
Goa	6.8	4.1	5.1	28.1	22.2	25.0	25.5	14.6	20.8
Gujarat	21.8	10.1	16.6	39.1	20.1	31.8	43.1	28.0	37.8
Haryana	11.6	10.3	11.2	24.8	22.4	24.1	40.0	24.2	35.9
Himachal Pradesh	8.5	4.3	8.1	25.0	4.6	22.9	36.7	13.6	34.6
Jammu & Kashmir	11.5	7.2	10.4	14.1	10.4	13.2	32.5	6.9	26.3
Jharkhand	40.8	24.8	37.0	51.6	23.8	45.3	65.9	41.8	60.7
Karnataka	24.5	15.3	20.9	37.5	25.9	33.4	56.6	34.2	49.5
Kerala	9.1	5.0	7.1	20.2	18.4	19.7	33.9	23.9	31.3
Madhya Pradesh	35.7	21.0	31.7	53.6	35.1	48.6	49.0	31.8	44.6
Maharashtra	24.2	9.1	17.4	47.9	25.6	38.1	59.3	30.3	47.8
Manipur	38.8	32.6	36.9	39.3	34.5	38.0	64.4	67.2	65.1
Meghalaya	12.5	9.3	11.9	14.0	24.7	16.1	38.0	23.0	35.2
Mizoram	35.4	6.4	20.4	23.0	7.9	15.3	16.6	6.3	11.8
Nagaland	19.9	16.5	18.9	10.0	4.3	9.0	20.1	21.8	20.4
Odisha	35.7	17.3	32.6	60.8	37.6	57.2	63.0	34.5	59.1
Pondicherry	17.1	6.3	9.7	22.9	9.9	14.1	28.1	32.4	30.9
Punjab	7.7	9.2	8.3	22.1	18.7	20.9	20.3	27.2	22.4
Rajasthan	16.1	10.7	14.7	35.8	29.7	34.4	40.8	29.9	38.3
Sikkim	9.9	3.7	8.2	31.8	25.9	31.1	33.0	20.4	31.8
Tamil Nadu	15.8	6.5	11.3	37.5	19.7	28.9	51.0	33.7	44.6
Tripura	16.5	7.4	14.1	44.5	22.5	40.6	34.3	25.4	32.9
Uttar Pradesh	30.4	26.1	29.4	42.7	34.1	40.9	50.9	38.3	48.4
Uttarakhand	11.6	10.5	11.3	35.1	26.2	32.7	36.7	18.7	32.0
West Bengal	22.5	14.7	20.0	38.2	24.4	34.3	42.5	31.2	39.4
All India	25.7	13.7	21.9	41.8	25.7	37.2	50.1	31.8	45.3

Source: Government of India. 2009. Report of the Expert Group to Review the Methodology for Estimation of Poverty, Planning Commission, November; Government of India. 2013. Press Note on Poverty Estimates 2011–12, Planning Commission, July.

the lowest overall levels of poverty—less than 10 per cent.

An earlier study carried out by Chaudhuri and Gupta argued that the disparity in poverty at the sub-state level is more serious than the disparity between states. They found that in both rural and urban sectors in almost all the states, some districts have higher intra-district inequality compared to the level of inter-state inequality. Through a detailed analysis of 20 major states, this study has brought about valuable insights as to how to identify 'pockets of impoverishment' by extending enquiries beyond the state level.

The study highlights the high degree of variance in monthly per capita expenditure (MPCE) even among the best districts in the country. The MPCE of the best districts vary between ₹540 per capita per month in Dhanbad, Jharkhand to ₹1,559 per capita per month in Gurgaon, Haryana. Similarly, MPCE of the worst districts range between ₹218 in the case of Dantewada, Chhattisgarh to ₹656 in Kannur, Kerala. Paradoxically, Dangs, the poorest district in the country—with 88.4 per cent of the population below the poverty line—is located in Gujarat, the state that also houses the district that claims the fourth position in MPCE in the country (Gandhinagar with MPCE of ₹1,012). In Gujarat, one finds districts that have 'zero poverty' (Junagadh, for instance) and districts with more than 75 per cent poor population.[12]

5. Human development index

Livelihoods are not only about employment, enterprise, and income. Capability deprivation is a critically important consideration in understanding poverty and in preparing a public policy to promote livelihoods. The central argument behind the capability approach as propounded by Sen is that

> standard economic approaches to welfare—based on utility or access to resources—exclude a great deal of relevant information and provide unreliable guides to poverty and well-being. The solution to this problem is to view poverty and well-being in terms of human capabilities or opportunities to achieve positive freedoms, such as being able to live long, be well nourished, achieve

literacy, take part in community life and achieve self-respect.[13]

There are many different kinds of capabilities that are closely linked to human well-being. The HDI captures the importance of three critical human capabilities—achieving knowledge, longevity, and a decent standard of living. The HDI combines normalized measures of life expectancy, literacy, educational attainment, and GDP per capita for distinct regions. Table 2.11 presents the HDI for the year 2011 of 19 states in India along with their relative ranks.[14]

Table 2.11: Human development index of select states: 2011

State	HDI	Rank
Kerala	0.625	1
Punjab	0.569	2
Himachal Pradesh	0.558	3
Maharashtra	0.549	4
Haryana	0.545	5
Tamil Nadu	0.544	6
Uttarakhand	0.515	7
Gujarat	0.514	8
West Bengal	0.509	9
Karnataka	0.508	10
Andhra Pradesh	0.485	11
Assam	0.474	12
Uttar Pradesh	0.468	13
Rajasthan	0.468	14
Jharkhand	0.464	15
Madhya Pradesh	0.451	16
Chhattisgarh	0.449	17
Bihar	0.447	18
Odisha	0.442	19
India	0.504	

Source: Suryanarayana et al., 2011.

---

[12] Chaudhuri, Siladitya and Nivedita Gupta. 2009. 'Levels of Living and Poverty Patterns: A District-wise Analysis for India', *Economic and Political Weekly*, 45 (9): 94–110.

[13] Clark, David and David Hulme. 2009. 'Poverty, Time and Vagueness: Integrating the Core Poverty and Chronic Poverty Frameworks', *Cambridge Journal of Economics*, Advance Access published online on 3 March 2009. DOI:10.1093/cje/ben046.

[14] Suryanarayana, M.H., Ankush Agrawal, and K. Seeta Prabhu. 2011. *Inequality-adjusted Human Development Index for India's States 2011*, United Nations Development Programme (UNDP), New Delhi.

6. Conclusion

This chapter attempted to compile some important data relating to the overall context in which livelihoods, particularly rural livelihoods, need to be understood. The analysis of the major trends over the past two decades indicate that the livelihood base of rural population in the country has been transformed significantly due to the workings of a multitude of forces. An important aspect of this transformation is that the structure of the economy of almost all the states has shifted away from agriculture towards other sectors. While the shift has largely been towards services, some states such as Gujarat, Tamil Nadu, Punjab, Maharashtra, and Haryana also registered higher share of manufacturing income. These include some of the land consolidating states too. The challenges to livelihood diversification are particularly serious for the poorest states—Jharkhand, Chhattisgarh, Madhya Pradesh, Bihar, and Odisha—as they lag behind others in terms of human development achievements also. Initiatives to promote livelihoods in these states hence need to be anchored effectively on the goals of expansion of economic opportunities, alleviation of human poverty, improvement of capabilities, and reduction of inequalities.

Policy Initiatives and Policy Paralysis

Ashok Kumar Sircar

Chapter 3

1. Introduction

If you ask a member of the main opposition in Indian parliament, 'How would you describe the year 2012–13', you will most likely get a reply something like this, 'The year of scandals and policy paralysis.' Indeed, this is the first time in Independent India that five cabinet-level ministers had to be pulled for corruption charges. The political paralysis is evident with the non-functioning of parliament taking its toll as important bills such as the Food Security Bill, Land Acquisition Bill, Street Vendors Bill, and the Manual Scavenger Bill are being repeatedly deferred. The Companies Amendment Bill could pass through the Lok Sabha, but had to wait for more than six months, and just got passed in the Rajya Sabha in August 2013. Yet some policies continue to be made overcoming the policy barriers that confront them. On the other hand, some policy decisions are taken very quickly, from political compulsions and other factors.

The public debate on livelihoods in the last year focused heavily on the food security bill that promises to deliver various food distribution programmes as a package of entitlements. The discussion has centered on the Bill's economic feasibility, with the two sides arguing polemically rather than debating constructively how to arrive at a more efficient and higher impact solution than the current food security policy.[1] The government failed in its attempt to get the bill through the parliament and finally, keen on 'gifting' this entitlement to India's poor, the government put out an ordinance on 1 August 2013, just a week before it was placed in the parliament once again.

The other major discussion has been on the pros and cons of cash transfer, conditional or unconditional, linked with the Aadhaar card. Proponents of cash transfer are primarily the government and the Planning Commission, while a section of the academia and civil society have reservations about its efficacy. The Planning Commission's affidavit in the Supreme Court on the number of BPL families drew criticism at all levels. The issue of who is and is not categorized as poor continues to be controversial, as is clear from the response to the recent publication of the NSSO report which showed drastic reduction in poverty levels in its latest sample survey. Mihir Shah, a member of the Planning Commission, in an attempt to quell the controversy, wrote on 5 August 2013:

> In fact, the Twelfth Plan clearly acknowledges that even if the figure of people below

---

[1] For a discussion on the feasibility of the food security programme, please see Sinha, Dipa. 2013. 'National Food Security Ordinance: Nothing but Expensive', *Economic and Political Weekly*, July 27 (web exclusive edition).

the consumption poverty line were to fall to zero, removing poverty in India will remain a challenge till every Indian has access to safe drinking water, sanitation, housing, nutrition, health and education. That is the challenge we need to focus on, rather than splitting hairs over the singular estimation of poverty.[2]

From the poor people's perspectives, the most important event last year was perhaps the long march of 60,000+ landless labourers and marginal farmers to Delhi, that resulted in a 10-point agreement signed by Ministry of Rural Development (MoRD) with the Ekta Parishad, promising 10 decimals of land for all landless families as a legal entitlement, and a new national land reform policy. One desired outcome of this event would be to bring back pro-poor land reform to the fore of the public agenda. Similarly, thanks to sustained efforts of the forest rights activists, the Ministry of Tribal Affairs finally sent out the revised rule in September 2012, reinforcing the centrality of the forest dwellers' rights as promised in the Forest Rights Act (FRA), 2006.

As in the past two years, we have structured our discussions in four capsules: (i) discussion on the current union budget, (ii) analysis of the Twelfth Five-Year Plan, (iii) ongoing policy initiatives, and (iv) new policy initiatives. As in the past, we have considered a policy in its various forms: an act or bill, a policy directive, a programme initiative, and the like.

Framing an appropriate definition of livelihoods policy is always a tricky exercise. Indian policymaking does not categorize any intervention as a livelihoods policy with the sole exception of the National Rural Livelihoods Mission (NRLM). This makes it difficult for us to define the principles we should apply in selecting a particular intervention as one aimed at livelihoods. We have applied the principle that any policy intervention that impacts the capacity of the poor to earn a living and the wider

economic well-being of individuals and families will be taken for discussion in the context of this chapter. Well-being here is defined as income and assets but also capabilities and one's ability to make claims and assert rights.

Two years ago, we made an attempt to identify whose livelihoods we are concerned about. We added a few categories in the last year's report, and this year we would like to add one more. Table 3.1 shows these categories.

Table 3.1: Categories of people facing livelihood challenges*

	Description	% of population and numbers
1	Persons below the poverty line	25.7% of rural population (Rural)[3]
2	Forest dwellers of India	93 million[4]
3	Absolutely landless families	18–20 million[5]
4	Street vendors	10–12 million[6]
5	Manual scavengers	1.0 million[7]
6	Single women	25.9 million[8]
7	Women farmers	90 million[9]
8	Number of disabled persons	21 million[10]
9	Seasonal and casual workers in informal sector or informal jobs in the formal sector	140 million (29% of total workforce)
10	Vulnerable workers (as per ILO definition)[11]	80 million (17% of total workforce)

Source: Please see notes 3 to 10.
Note: *These numbers are overlapping, for example, a section of manual scavengers and single women may be part of the BPL population. The numbers are relevant to planning and policymaking, and hence given separately.

---

[2]Shah, M. 2013. 'Understanding the Poverty Line'. *The Hindu*, 5 August, p. 6.

[3]Planning Commission. 2013. Available at: http://planningcommission.nic.in/news/pre_pov2307.pdf, accessed on 10 August 2013.

[4]Ministry of Tribal Affairs. 2013. Available at: http://www.tribal.nic.in/WriteReadData/CMS/Documents/201305300323522984783TribalProfile.pdf, accessed on 9 August 2013.

[5]Rawal, Vikas. 2008. 'Ownership Holding of Land in Rural India', *Economic and Political Weekly*, 43 (10, March): 45 (projected with rural households on Indian Census 2011).

This chapter is divided into the following sections. We start with a brief analysis of the budget, followed by an overview of the Twelfth Plan. A discussion on those policies which are already at the stage of becoming installed follows. This includes bills long in the public debate which are passed (or likely to be passed), such as the Street Vendors Bill, Manual Scavengers Bill, Women Farmer's Bill, Food Security Bill, and Land Acquisition and Resettlement and Rehabilitation (LARR) Bill and the Mining Bill follows. It also includes a couple of programmes underway where new policies are being introduced, to improve implementation, such as the FRA and the NRLM.

The new policy debates that came to the fore during the year, and for which new bills are drafted, such as FDI in retail, decontrol of sugar, the new CSR component of the Companies Act, the draft National Land Reform Policy, and direct benefit transfers, are discussed in the following section. We conclude with our overarching observations and concerns.

---

[6]Bhowmick, S. 2005. 'Street Vendor in Asia: A Review', *Economic and Political Weekly*, 40 (22–23): 22–62.

[7]Report of the Subgroup on *Safai Karmachari*s. 2007. Submitted to Working Group on Empowerment of Scheduled Castes for the Eleventh Five-Year Plan, New Delhi, p. 9.

[8]Census of India. 2001. Available at. http://censusindia.gov.in/Census_And_You/age_structure_and_marital_status.aspx, accessed on 15 August 2013.

[9]Census of India. 2001. Available at: http://censusindia.gov.in/Census_And_You/economic_activity.aspx, accessed on 15 August 2013.

[10]Census of India. 2001. Available at: http://censusindia.gov.in/Census_And_You/disabled_population.aspx, accessed on 15 August 2013.

[11]The ILO defines 'vulnerable workers' as own-account workers as well as those who contribute to family enterprises. This now forms part of the sub Millennium Development Goal, 'Achieve full and productive employment and decent work for all, including women and young people', which itself forms part of Goal 1, 'Eradicate extreme poverty and hunger'. See http://mdgs.un.org/unsd/mdg/Metadata.aspx?IndicatorId=0&SeriesId=760 (accessed on 1 September 2013).

2. Budget analysis

The annual union budget reflects the government's approach to improving the economy, including specific allocations to improve livelihoods of the population. A central challenge in analyzing the union budget from a livelihoods lens is what budgetary support should be categorized as livelihoods support? A second challenge is the cut-off point: budgetary allocations through schemes, missions, and programmes run into hundreds and, therefore, we must make a selection of those most relevant to our criteria.

We have defined livelihood as one's ability to earn a living as well as the wider economic well-being of individuals and families (refer previous section). Budgetary provisions which support these means of making a living and wider well-being are therefore categorized as livelihood support, including provisions of human resource and other capitals. We restrict ourselves to major schemes, missions, and programmes—major in terms of inputs (while their assessment in terms of outputs or impact is a more difficult process).

The most usual way of looking at the union budget is to compare it with the past allocation to determine whether the allocation shows an upward or a downward trend. Such budgetary trend analysis is often done without consideration of what an upward trend might imply, or if a downward trend is a reflector of shifting priorities and if such shifts are justified with respect to a reduction in actual need.

Unfortunately, neither the economic survey that precede the budget nor the budget analysis, conducted as independent and often commendable initiatives, analyze the budget of the past in the mirror of its outcomes and the lessons and gaps thus revealed. The budget is analyzed only in terms of utilization, allocation, and estimate of funds. Independent budget analysis shows whether an increase is an inflation adjustment or real, and the per-capita allocation. The economic survey discusses performance of the sector. Both kinds of analysis fall short of discussing what impact the budgetary allocation had in terms of performance, and, therefore, what a fresh budget allocation could do for impact in the future performance in a sector or programme.

Table 3.2 shows budget allocations for the last three years for major programmes that are meant to positively impact livelihoods. Apart from agricultural credit that is primarily provided by the banks, all other expenditures are from the state exchequer. The figures shown here are the contribution the union government makes towards these programmes. In addition, the state governments contribute their share. Fundsharing formulas differ from programme to programme and even have geographic variations. For example, the NREGA funds are shared by the centre and the state on a 75:25 basis; Indira Awas Yojona funds are shared on a 50:50 basis; Mid Day Meal Programme is shared on a 75:25 basis. In the case of North Eastern states, the fund sharing between the centre and the state is always on 90:10 basis.

The most distinguishing feature of the budget allocation in 2013–14 is that while there has been a modest increase in allocations for most programmes, the increase disappears when sums are adjusted for inflation. NREGA, is shockingly, having no increase at all. Another shocking feature is the very small increase to NRLM, indicating its slow progress so far.

Using the detailed response the Centre of Budget Governance and Accountability (CBGA) has provided to the current year's union budget, we look at the budget allocation in the light of a few specific categories of population. Notwithstanding the crudeness and limitations of such an exercise, we present the per capita allocations in Table 3.3, which provide a revealing picture. For example, per capita allocation to an Indian child below 18 years, taking into account

Table 3.2: Budget allocation in three consecutive years for existing programmes (in ₹ crore)

Key areas	2013–14	2012–13	2011–12	Constituency
Agricultural credit	700,000	575,000	475,000	Farmers
Drinking water & sanitation	15,260	14,000	11,000	Mostly rural population
Rastriya Krishi Vikas Yojana (RKVY)	9,954	9,217	7,860	Farmers, associated people
Bringing Green Revolution to Eastern India (BGREI)	1,000	1,000	400	No clarity on constituency
Integrated Child Development Services (ICDS)	17,700	15,850	10,032	Children in the age group of 0 to six, pregnant and lactating mothers
NRLM	4,000	3,914	2,921	70% of rural women
National Mid Day Meal Scheme	13,215	11,937	10,564	All children of six to 14 years attending school
National Social Assistance Programme (NSAP)	9,541	8,447	6,165	Old age, disabled people
Right to Education/Sarva Siksha Abhiyan (SSA)	27,258	25,555	20,998	All public schools
National Health Mission (previously National Rural Health Mission [NRHM])	21,239	20,822	18,115	Everyone dependent on public heath care
NREGS	33,000	33,000	31,000	125 million job cardholders
Food Security subsidy	90,000	75,000	72,823	75% of rural and 50% of urban population
Total	241,167	218,742	191,338	

Source: Compiled by the author from SOIL report 2011, 2012, and budget highlights on 2013.

Table 3.3: Per capita allocation of selected categories of population

Key constituencies	2013–14 (₹ in crore)	2012–13 (₹ in crore)	Population (crore)	Expenditure in ₹ per capita
Children	77,236	77,251	50.40	1,532
SCs	41,561	37,113	19.92	2,086
STs	24,598	21,710	10.32	2,386
Muslim Minorities	3,530	3,152	16.08	219
Disabled	701	651	2.52	278
Women	97,134	88,143	58.74	1,653
Old age people, widows, disabled, destitute	9,541	8,447	9.6 + 4.24	691
Forest Dwellers			10.0	
*Safai Karmachari*s			0.12	
Street Vendors			1.2	
Single Women	200		3.6	55.5

Source: Compiled by the author from Response to Union Budget 2013: CBGA, March 2013, pp. 7–13.

education, health, nutrition, and others is roughly about ₹1,530 in a year. Even if we consider that only 50 per cent of Indian children need the state's support for their education, health, and nutrition, the figure is just about ₹3,060. Similar is the per capita allocation for women considering all conceivable budgeted expenditures. The per capita annual allocation for SCs and STs is ₹2,086 and ₹2,386 respectively. On the other hand, there are categories of population such as the forest dwellers, street vendors, and manual scavengers who still await budget allocation.

Every budget announces new programmes (see Table 3.4), the progress on previously announced and initiated programmes is not reported while constructing the next and subsequent years' budgets. New programmes appear more as the outcome of new compulsions rather than evidence of past programmes. For example, this budget announced three new programmes for women: the *Nirbhaya* Fund, Women's Bank, and an unnamed programme under the Department of Women and Child Development (DWCD) for single women. There is no doubt that these came about in response to the large scale popular protests that erupted last year around the brutal rape of a young student in the heart of national

capital. Even now it is not clear which ministry will handle the *Nirbhaya* Fund. A task force has been set up to advise on the institutional mechanism of use of this fund. The Women's Bank, reports the *Indian Express*, will start operations in six cities and will have 25 branches in the first year, followed by a gradual rise to 300 branches in five years.[12]

Table 3.4: New programmes announced in the union budget 2013–14 (₹ in crore)

Nirbhaya Fund (Women's Bank)	1,000
Rashtriya Uccha Siksha Abhiyan (National Higher Education *Abhiyan*)	400
Crop Diversification Programme	500
National Livestock Mission	307
National Women's Bank	1,000
Unnamed scheme for single women and widows	200
Credit Guarantee Fund for Small Farmers Agri-Business Corp	100
Direct Benefit Transfer Scheme	

Source: Budget Highlights 2013–14.[13]

[12]*Indian Express.* 2013. May 8. Available at: http://www.indianexpress.com/news/womens-bank-to-begin-operations-in-november/1112768/, accessed on 15 August 2013.

[13]Budget Highlights. 2013. Available at: http://indiabudget.nic.in/ub2013-14/bh/bh1.pdf, accessed on 10 August 2013.

Box 3.1:   Nirbhaya *Fund*

Cities are centres of economic power and connectivity, generating opportunity for female employment, especially in commerce and services. But urban public spaces can be hostile to women, adversely affecting their free and safe movement. As the number of girls and women circulate in the public sphere, for education, work, and leisure, the violence against them also increases. The law and order system is constantly challenged by the growing number of sexual and physical assaults on girls and women.

Realizing the need to increase the safety and security of women and girls, the Union Budget 2013 announced the ₹1,000-crore *Nirbhaya* Fund. Under the scheme, the Ministry of Women and Child Development provides financial assistance for interventions such as working women's hostels, shelter homes and short-stay homes, and microcredit facilities.

Source: Budget highlights 2013–2014.

The other important new programme announcement this year is the direct benefit transfer scheme. The new element in this scheme is that it envisages replacement of various subsidies given in kind, such as essential commodities through the PDS, to cash equivalents. Yet another important new programme for livelihoods is the National Livestock Mission. Livestock-rearing is the main livelihood of nearly 30 per cent of India's rural poor; interventions in improving the quality and productivity of livestock contribute directly to livelihoods and well-being.

The budget process is partly open and partly opaque. The finance minister and his team meet a huge variety of stakeholders between the months of November and January. These stakeholders include: chambers of commerce, industry associations, trade unions, professional associations, civil society groups, politicians, and media personnel. The same team meets almost every ministry to discuss their allocations. Once these consultations are closed, a departmental process gets underway which is extremely opaque and the results of which become known only on the budget day.[14]

A scan of the coverage of budget issues in various business dailies reveals a few key trends in the public debate: (i) There is a shrill cry to reduce personal income tax, a clamour from the rising Indian middle class, (ii) much debate hovers around import duties, excise duties, and export subsidies on various products, a reflection of the demands made by exporting communities who feel their leverage increasing as India is once again faced with the spectre of forex shortage, (iii) demands from the business press to liberalize labour laws, FDI, investment clearances, and the like, (iv) the trade union press demands improved social security, (v) demands from the banking sector for budgetary support to special development-oriented credit lines, and finally, (vi) women's associations demand a deepening gender focus—rather than mere lip service—in the budgeting process.[15]

The opacity of the intra-departmental process which follows broad-based consultations means we know little what considerations finally determine the various allocations. The existing analytical literature provides scant analysis of the demands of the various sectors and how each finally found its place in allocations of new programmes, or changing course of existing programmes.

---

[14] A good account of who the finance minister meets is available in, 'How the Dice Rolled: Response to Union Budget', CBGA, March 2013, p. 14.

[15] These trends were visible in budget discussions published in the *Economic Times* and *Business Line* from December 2013 to February 2014.

3. Twelfth Five-Year Plan

A remnant of the state socialism to which India's early post-Independence leaders aspired, the Five-Year Plans draw out central and state governments' strategic priorities in improving the economy, generating growth and employment, and reducing the barriers to overall development. As the country embraced economic liberalization, many of the earlier features of 'command and control' planning gave way to greater involvement of the private sector and CSOs in the planning and execution processes.

Before every Five-Year Plan, an elaborate exercise is made to develop an 'approach paper' to the plan. The approach paper can be said to be the 'philosophy and ideology' of the plan. For each sector and some sub-sectors, working groups are formed comprising bureaucrats, academia, civil society activists and experts, and private sector representatives. These working groups hold public discussions, conduct desk research, and write their part of the plan with recommendations. These are collated and after elaborate discussions, the Planning Commission finalizes the document. The draft plan is placed in the National Development Council (NDC), a body of all the chief ministers and central ministers. NDC's approval makes the plan operational. Civil society's involvement in the planning process is a recent phenomenon, and members of CSOs have been included in a number of working groups, and sub-groups mostly in the social sector planning.

The Twelfth Plan was supposed to have commenced from 1 April 2012. However, at the time of writing SOIL 2012, the plan document was not ready, so our discussion was limited to that of the approach paper to the Twelfth Plan. The plan document is now available for discussion. As we did for the brief discussion of the budget, we will follow the same procedure to look at how Twelfth Plan wishes to address the issue of livelihoods. The Twelfth Plan envisages 25 plan indicators that it intends to monitor over the next five years. Of these 25 indicators, we identify 14 that can be construed to have direct impact on livelihoods. These 14 indicators are given in Table 3.5. While there were 27 such indicators in the Eleventh Plan, we see that 11 indicators continue as monitorable targets in the Twelfth Plan as well.

Between the two Plans, there is, therefore, continuity in investing in those parameters

Table 3.5: Twelfth Plan indicators directly connected to livelihoods

Indicators that can directly impact livelihoods in terms of earning a living and enhanced well-being	To be achieved by the end of the Twelfth Plan	Eleventh Plan promises	Actual achievements so far
1. Reduction of poverty	10% points from now	10% points of consumption poverty	7.5–8.0% points during the Eleventh Plan
2. Job creation in non-farm sector	50 million	58 million	Less than half
3. Mean years of schooling	7 years	No promise	
4. Additional seats in higher education in each age cohort	2 million	Increase in each cohort by 15%	
5. Gender gap and gap between SCs/STs/ Muslims versus others	Zero	10% points	
6. Infant mortality	25 per 1,000	28 per 1,000	47 per 1,000 in 2010
7. Child sex ratio	950 per 1,000	935 per 1,000	
8. Under nutrition of 0–3 children	Half of NFHS-3	Half of existing level	
9. Rural electrification	To all villages	Same and additionally to all BPL families	Just over 50% households use electricity as per 2011 census
10. All weather roads	To all villages	To 1,000 + habitations and 500 + habitation in hill areas	
11. Piped water supply	50% of all villages	Clean drinking water to all by 2009	
12. Banking services	90% of Indian households	No promise	
13. All major subsidies and welfare payment	Cash transfer	No promise	
14. Increase in vegetation cover	1 million hectare every year	Forest and tree cover by 5% points	

Source: Compiled by the author from Overview of Twelfth Plan, Volume I, pp. 34–35 and Eleventh Plan Document, pp. 23–24.

which most directly impact livelihoods. Out of the 14 parameters, 11 continue through both Five-Year Plans. Of the three plan indicators that appear new in the Twelfth Plan, banking services (financial inclusion) and major subsidies and welfare payments (social protection through direct cash transfers) are the two that deserve attention.

The key challenge in discussing the Plan indicators is the lack of data on actual achievements in the earlier plan period. What is surprising is that the plan document does not make any serious attempt to declare what has been achieved in the previous plan period before announcing the new set of plan indicators. For example, malnutrition data is available on the basis of National Family Health Survey-3 for 2007, at the beginning of the Eleventh-Plan period. We have to wait until the end of this year to know the current status. There is no data in the public domain showing how much forest and tree cover has increased in the last five years against a promise of one million hectares every year. All we know is that the forest cover has increased by 3 million hectare in the last decade.[16] The same situation arises with data on all-weather roads and rural electrification. This lack of data is a key limitation to accountability with respect to plan implementation. Connected with this is the lack of a national tracking mechanism of plan commitments, state by state and district by district, so that performers and non-performers can be easily distinguished. Plan after plan has passed by, without such a national monitoring mechanism to track progress and hold public offices accountable. What exists instead is a mid-term appraisal of the Five-Year Plan that does not always track the plan indicators, but instead tracks inputs and growth. Further, plan indicators are not divided into yearly

traceable indicators, nor into specific state responsibilities.

The other concern with the Twelfth and previous plan documents, is that analysis, on the one hand, and operational details (inputs, outputs, and outcomes) on the other, are mixed up in the narrative. While each of these components is necessary they should be clearly separable. In the present format, the analysis is reasonably strong, while the management part is weak. None of the plan indicators find an appropriate level of discussion in the respective sectoral chapters. For example, reading the chapter on energy, one cannot get a sense of how the national promise of 'electrification of all villages' would be achieved.

While sectoral and sub-sectoral objectives are identified in the Twelfth Plan, not all such sectors have monitorable indicators and clear strategies to achieve these. Adding a monitorable indicator section to each sectoral objective would strengthen the accountability of the plan.

Our final comment is about the structure of the data presented in the plan. The plan documents are a rich source of near current and aggregate data. But reading the data presents two kinds of challenges. First, the data is in absolute numbers without referring to appropriate denominators, so that figures are not comparable; second, the lack of appropriate inflation adjustments necessary to make sense of the monetary figures presented in the text.

4. The installation of policy

Indian lawmaking is an elaborate process that travels long miles involving a large number of stakeholders. While technically, any member of parliament, legislature or political group represented in the parliament or legislature, can place a bill for consideration, it is the government's bills that form the bulk of all the laws made in India. How are the bills made? If we look at the bills that have affected the development

---

[16] Kothari, Ashish. 2013. 'Development and Ecological Sustainability in India: Possibilities for Post 2015 Framework', *Economic Political Weekly*, 48 (30, July): 146.

sector in the last decade and a half, most came from civil society. The RTE, Forest, Rights, Right to Information, Food Security, those addressing disabilities or domestic violence…In all cases, one sees the central role of the civil society in such lawmaking.

There are perhaps four stages to lawmaking: the formative phase, the departmental phase, a cabinet phase, and a parliamentary phase, though the four phases may not always proceed in this sequence. At the initial phase, the draft is negotiated and framed through discussions with a variety of stakeholders. Each bill has a nodal ministry to take it forward. Once a draft is prepared, the departmental phase begins where at least three interdepartmental reviews take place—by the law ministry, by the finance ministry, and by another ministry that might have relevance to the content of the draft. Sometimes, a bill may affect a number of ministries; so a group of secretaries must review the bill. Thereafter, the cabinet phase begins, when the modified bill is placed with the cabinet. If the cabinet cannot come to a decision on the bill, it refers the bill to a group of ministers (GoM) to review collectively. The cabinet gets the bill back with GoM's review and suggestions.

Once the cabinet passes the bill, it is ready to be placed in the Parliament by the concerned ministry. The parliament phase then begins, whereby the bill is referred to the parliamentary standing committee. The parliamentary standing committee conducts public consultations and prepares a detailed review with suggestions. Typically, the bill again goes back to the cabinet or the ministry for modification. With the cabinet's decision on the standing committee's recommendation, the bill again comes back to the Parliament, and this back and forth between the standing committee, cabinet, and Parliament can happen any number of times. Finally, the Parliament debates the bill and passes it, with or without amendments. Once the Parliament passes the bill, it goes for presidential assent. In case of substantive financial involvement, the bill must be passed by both houses of the Parliament.

We will discuss here the bills that are already installing themselves as policy and/or have become a law since last year. Continuing from last year's policy chapter (SOIL 2012), we focus first on those bills that continue their journey, and thereafter, those bills that finally became law in 2012–13. We will also cover two policies which are already well installed and where we wish to review and assess progress. These are the FRA (passed in 2008) and the NRLM.[17]

4.1 Manual Scavenger Bill[18]

Manual scavengers remove human excreta from private and public toilets which are not connected to sewage lines. This population is low caste, mostly illiterate and treated by the Indian society as outcaste. Despite the decline in such toilets over the last few decades, the practice still continues in every state with varying degrees. The Indian Railways is still the single largest employer of manual scavengers, who clean the waste dropped directly from open toilets onto the tracks.

In 1993, a central law[19] was passed to end the practice and enforce replacement of dry with sewage-linked toilets. The law was not enforced partly due to its weak design, and its misdirected provisions for rehabilitation of the *karmachari*s. At the time of writing

---

[17] NRLM is a huge and composite programme. Here we will discuss the core…excluding NREGA and skills components which are covered in other chapters of this report (Chapter 5 and Chapter 6 respectively).

[18] A fuller treatment of the history of this bill can be found in SOIL 2012 (pp. 39–41).

[19] The battle to eradicate manual scavenging started in 1993 with the enactment of The Employment of Manual Scavengers and Construction of Dry Latrine (Prohibition) Act, 1993. It soon became clear that the Act and the rehabilitation scheme which evolved from it lacked teeth. In 1995, the Safai Karmachari Andolan (the union of manual scavengers) sought new stronger legislation. See the report of the parliamentary standing committee at http://www.prsindia.org/uploads/media/Manual%20Scavengers/SCR%20Manual%20Scavengers%20Bill.pdf, accessed in October 2013.

SOIL 2012, the bill named The Prohibition of Employment as Manual Scavengers and their Rehabilitation Bill 2012 was waiting to be placed in the Parliament. This was finally achieved on 3 September 2012, and it was then immediately referred to the parliamentary standing committee. In its report dated March 2013, the Committee mostly accepted the Bill, but recommended the addition of the phrase 'national shame' to the preamble. The committee also recommended that the Bill commit in its text to have a GoM monitor the progress of implementation. Further, the committee sought central and state funding for the upgrading of latrines in a time bound manner, while not specifying a deadline. In the same vein, the committee sought to reduce the penalty clause for non-compliance in the stipulated time. Rather, the committee recommended the insertion of a penalty clause for the implementers designated in this Bill for any delay caused by them.

The parliamentary standing committee's report was taken up for consideration by the union cabinet on 1 May 2013. The cabinet note circulated by the Ministry of Social Justice and Empowerment did not accept the committee's recommendation to declare the phenomenon as a national shame, but in general accepted almost all other recommendations. The Cabinet cleared the Bill with standing committee's recommendations for submission to the Parliament. At the time of writing this report, the Bill had just been passed by the Lok Sabha but could not get through the Rajya Sabha, so manual scavengers will now have to wait until the winter session.

In spite of the claims of many state governments, the census 2011 showed that there are still about 1.0 million households in the country having insanitary latrines, over and above the open latrines in the 7,000 plus trains of Indian Railways.

4.2 Street Vendors Bill

There is barely any urban resident who does not use and enjoy the products or services of street vendors. Street vendors enjoy complete social legitimacy, but they are illegal. Their existence depends on paying 'rent' to the police and local thugs. Hundreds of thousands of street vendors work on railway tracks and platforms, paying 'rent' to railway officials to survive.

Street vendors, organized under the National Association of Street Vendors of India (NASVI), are fighting for legal recognition and legitimate space for conducting their business, as well as other benefits such as financial services from formal sector institutions.

The Street Vendors (Protection of Livelihoods and Regulation of Street Vending) Bill 2012 is in the making for several years. Following our report in SOIL 2012, the Bill was placed in the Parliament on 6 September 2012 and referred to the parliamentary standing committee for review. The parliamentary standing committee submitted its report to the Parliament on 13 March 2013, followed by the union cabinet's review which approved a modified version of the Bill on 1 May 2013. The Bill now awaits re-presentation to the Parliament. Here, we will discuss the observations of the parliamentary standing committee and the union cabinet.

First, the standing committee directed that the exclusion of Indian Railway's land from the purview of the bill must be revisited, since railway platforms and trains provide livelihood space and market for one of the most significant sections of street vendors and this group, it is argued, must also benefit from the Act. Second, the standing committee advised against the high degree of delegated power to central and state authorities charged with implementing 'schemes' for street vendors. The committee argued that such a large degree of delegation would defeat the purpose of a central bill.

Based on these and other more operational recommendations, the Ministry of Housing and Urban Poverty Alleviation has reworked the bill and presented it to cabinet, which cleared it on 1 May 2013.

This revised version will now be placed in the Parliament.

The Manual Scavengers and Street Vendors Bills illustrate how India's legislative process can jam and stymie policy creation even for the most uncontroversial bills that enjoy wide social legitimacy. While manual scavenging is accepted as a practice which must stop and alternative livelihoods built for the workforce, street vendors have broad-based support in their fight for an umbrella of legal protection. Even for these, the lawmaking process has already taken more than three years. And the legal framework is the lesser part of the battle; making the law work for the relevant population is the bigger part.

4.3 Women Farmers' Entitlement Bill

It is said that the deprivation of a rural woman in India starts when she is in her mother's womb, and does not end until she dies. The story of women farmers is relatively new, brought to the fore by Bina Agarwal's pioneering work, *A Field of One's Own* in 1994. Women today are the largest workforce in Indian agriculture and their share is growing due to male migration to towns and cities. However, since they do not own land, women are not recognized as farmers in India's Agricultural Policy. Only 9 per cent of rural women own land[20] and only a negligible number of Kisan Credit Cards are held by women. The women are also not recognized as farmers by their own natal and marital family. Unless her father or husband dies, she has no chance of getting the legal title, since she has no property rights under the marriage law.

During his tenure as a Rajya Sabha MP, M.S. Swaminathan drafted a private member's bill to remedy this situation. He proposed that by virtue of her marriage, a rural Indian woman be recognized as a farmer and be given an automatic right to her husband's land. Additionally, the bill proposed that support services (finance, technology, inputs, etc.) for women farmers be provided.[21]

The bill was never taken up for discussion; as Swaminathan's term in the Rajya Sabha came to a close in March 2013, the bill lapsed in the Parliament 'for technical reasons' at the end of the parliamentary session. This has killed, for the time being, the chance to probably make the most far reaching change in favour of Indian rural women which India has witnessed for decades. The future course now depends on the resolve of the Ministry of Women and Child Development to push the bill to fruition.

4.4 Food Security Bill/Ordinance

In 2001, the Supreme Court ruled that access to food is a fundamental right and part of the right to life enshrined in the Indian Constitution. It, thereby, made the state accountable for all deaths caused by hunger. One immediate effect of the ruling was the expansion of the ICDS services to all habitations of 500 people or more. The quantum of food and allocation increased for children as well as pregnant and lactating mothers. The Mid Day Meal Scheme was introduced soon after (initially in government-owned and sponsored schools) and the discussion on improving the failing PDS began. The Supreme Court's monitoring through court-appointed commissioners for nearly a decade kept the issue alive in the public sphere. Finally, 10 years later, these food provisions became an agenda of entitlement for which a National Food Security Bill was framed in 2011.[22]

Contrary to our expectations, the Bill was not passed in 2012–13. It underwent several drafts after being placed in the Parliament and a new version was placed specifically to ensure that it could not lapse due to technical reasons. At the time of writing, an ordinance

---

[20] Agricultural Census 2005–06. Available at: http://agricensus.nic.in/documents/ac0506/reports/chapter-6_2005-2006.pdf, accessed on 10 August 2013.

[21] SOIL 2012 (pp. 43–44) reported the trajectory of this bill introduced in the Parliament by M.S. Swaminathan.

[22] The trajectory of the Food Security Bill was traced more fully in SOIL 2012 Report (pp. 38–39).

had been promulgated and signed by the President of India on 5 July 2013. This ordinance is being placed before the Parliament as we write. While the details of entitlements under the Act are covered in Chapter 4 (Social Protection), here we limit the discussion to comments on operations and wider experience of entitlement-focused programmes.

The Act will constitute a State Food Commission to oversee its implementation. A variety of technology platforms will be used to improve efficiency, reduce leakage, and improve transparency and accountability. Successful large-scale technology adoption in Chhattisgarh, Andhra Pradesh, and pilots in Odisha has shown how this can be done. Technology measures coupled with institutional reform in Chhattisgarh, have reduced leakage, ensured better quality, and driven a remarkable increase in offtake by the poor. Social audits—increasingly a standard for rights-based legislations—are also provided for.

The Ordinance came into force from the month of August 2013. So, time will tell how it unfolds with the population it is meant to benefit. Nonetheless, a point can be made based on the experience of the similar entitlement-framed legislations.

As we have described, provisions for food security in the Act are all services in place for many years. ICDS is nearly 40 years old, PDS is no less, and even the Mid Day Meal is almost a decade old now. Delivery of these services presents a mixed picture: while some states deliver well, many do not. The nature of the institutions and processes delivering these services will not be changed by the virtue of the Ordinance or the Act. Therefore, what is the guarantee that the Act or an ordinance will make it work better? The experience of NREGA illustrates that the quality of delivery often depends more on the collective pressure of civil society than on legal fiat. It is a sad commentary on governance that the food insecure population must wait for a similar pressure from civil society to get the Act effectively enforced.

4.5 The Land Acquisition Bill

In the last 20 years, land acquisition has become one of the most contentious issues of development in India. Beginning with the Narmada Bachao Andolan and reaching a climax in West Bengal with the furore over Singur and Nandigram, anti-land acquisition struggles spread all over the country. The conflicts and debates centre around what should be the limits of LARR terms, the concept of eminent domain and its social contract, and the definition of public purpose. The following paragraphs will briefly capture the issues before proceeding to discuss the journey of the Bill.

One of the absolute powers of the state has always been to decide how land should be used. This is defined as eminent domain. The model of development followed in the last two centuries demanded land use to be shifted from agrarian and forest-based use to modern use by industries, mines, infrastructure, and other modern establishments including defence. While this model of development has increasingly come into question, the absolute power of the state to decide land use and acquire land accordingly has, until recently, been upheld without question. This is now changing. The power of eminent domain is closely linked to the idea of public purpose. Public purpose is not clearly defined in Indian law, except by examples of what are to be treated as public purpose. So acquiring land for the purpose of a private motor car company is a public purpose, as much as acquiring land for setting up a school or college. Considerable debate has been generated on the very idea of the public purpose. Thus there are two fundamental questions being asked: First, why should the state have this absolute power?[23] Second, what is public about a stated purpose, or what purpose can be called public?[24]

[23] Sampat, Preeti. 2013. 'Limits to Absolute Power: Eminent Domain and the Rights to Land in Indian', *Economic and Political Weekly*, 48 (19, May): 40.

[24] Ghatak, M. 2011. 'Land Acquisition Bill: A Critique and a Proposal', *Economic and Political Weekly*, 46 (41, October): 65.

The third question is under what circumstances this absolute powers need to be exercised, and what are its limits? The limits are imposed in consideration of other valued uses and functions of the land, for example, from the viewpoint of agriculture, ecology, environment, and socio-economic justice.

Finally, the critical question of fair compensation, resettlement, and rehabilitation, the debate which has taken up most of the public space. Two approaches have emerged: a pure compensation model and a rehabilitation model. The existing Bill is tilted towards a combination of both. There is little evidence of success of either model in India or elsewhere, so the approach settled on can only be based on reasoned conjectures.

The journey of this Bill appears never ending. A first draft appeared in the public domain in the form of a policy in 2007, followed by a bill that eventually lapsed. In 2011, a bill combining resettlement-rehabilitation and acquisition was placed in the Parliament, and then referred to the parliamentary standing committee that submitted its report in May 2012. The bill again went back to the cabinet, which could not agree on the draft and so referred it to a GoM headed by Sharad Pawar, the agriculture minister. The GoM referred it back to the cabinet. And, thereafter, the government has presented a series of amendments to the Bill in the Parliament on 17 December 2012. These amendments are worth discussing (see Table 3.6).

Table 3.6: Changes proposed by the government in the latest draft LARR Bill

	2011 Bill	2012 Bill
Name of the Bill	Land Acquisition, Rehabilitation, and Resettlement Act, 2011	Right to Fair Compensation and Transparency in Land Acquisition, Rehabilitation, and Resettlement Bill 2012
Public purpose	Defence, roads, railways, highways, ports built by government and public sector	Infrastructure projects as notified, agriculture-agro processing, cold storage, industrial corridors, mining, educational institutions, sports, health care, space programmes, and for PPP projects where land will belong to the government and private companies for the above except private hotels and educational institutions.
Mandatory consent	Eighty per cent of project affected people with certain excluded cases of acquisition by government	Eighty per cent of landowners, 70% of landowners for PPP
R&R provision for private purchases of land	Purchase above 100 acre in rural areas and 50 acres in urban areas	To be decided by the state government
Social Impact Assessment (SIA)	To be conducted in consultation with Gram Sabha to estimate socio-economic impact on families among other assessments. The SIA to be published in project area.	To be conducted in consultation with Gram Panchayat and municipality, scrap the socio-economic impact assessment of the displaced families, and instead substitute socio-economic impact assessment of the area. The SIA to be published at Gram Panchayat and municipality office.
Review of SIA by expert group	If the expert group recommends against the project, the project will be abandoned immediately.	Despite expert group decision, the government can go ahead and implement the project.
Constitution of the committee on LA	For LA of 100 acres or more, the government shall constitute a committee to look into all aspects of the project.	Proposes deletion of that clause
Food Security	Limit of LA of multiple crop area pegged at 5% of total land of the district.	To be decided by the government.
Public hearing and R&R scheme	If land is acquired in more than one Gram Sabha, public hearing to happen in each Gram Sabha.	Public hearing proposed only in those Gram Sabhas where more than 25% of the land is acquired.
Retrospective effect	All cases where no award is made when this Act comes to force will lapse.	Only in few cases, it will lapse.

(Continued)

(Continued)

	2011 Bill	2012 Bill
Determination of market value	Minimum land value specified in the Indian Stamp Act, 1899, for the (i) registration of sale deeds in the area where the land is situated or (ii) the average of the top 50% of all sale deeds in the previous three years for similar type of land situated in the vicinity or village.	The market value of the acquired land shall be based on the higher of (i) market value specified in the Indian Stamp Act for the registration of sale deeds or (ii) average of the top 50% of all the sale deeds in the similar type of land situated in the vicinity, or (iii) the amount agreed upon as compensation for acquisition of land for private companies or PPPs. While determining the market value of land, the compensation paid for acquisition of land under the provisions of this Bill shall not be taken into consideration. While determining market value and the average sale price, the collector shall have the discretion to not take into account any sale price which is his opinion is not indicative of the actual prevailing market value of the land.
Possession of land	Only after all R&R processes are over	Proposed to be deleted
Urgency clause and additional compensation	National defence, national security, natural calamity. Seventy-five per cent additional compensation to be paid to land losers.	Additionally any emergency defined by Indian Parliament, no additional compensation in case of sovereignty, integrity, and strategic relations of the state.

Source: Compiled by author from PRS research on official amendments to the draft LARR Bill 2012.[25]

The government proposed amendments to 33 different clauses of which we have selected only a few to illustrate the overall direction of the amendments. The author has heavily drawn from the comparison table made by PRS.[26] The overall direction of these amendments is aimed at smoothening land acquisition process by removing the more restrictive clauses. While the earlier version is clearly aimed at restricting land acquisition, the amendments proposed aim to facilitate it. It is interesting to observe the cabinet divide: the ministries of commerce and industries, civil aviation, highways, and others were on one end of the debate (the facilitators), while ministry of justice and empowerment, rural development, tribal affairs, housing and urban poverty alleviation were at the other end (the restrictors).

The Bill was finally passed on 29 August 2013 in the Lok Sabha, then in the Rajya Sabha the following week with a minor

amendment, to which the Lok Sabha agreed, on 5 September. It now goes to the President for his approval. Meanwhile, land acquisition is likely to remain a growing challenge for industry, as public resistance continues to deepen and spread across the country. Few of the affected or potentially affected people are likely aware of the legislative deliberations underway for the last six years, and their outcomes will depend on their collective voice rather than a better law to protect their interest.

4.6 Mining Bill

Mining extracts natural resources available beneath and on the surface of the earth for multiple uses. About 60 different minerals are mined in India. Ninety per cent of mining occurs in 11 states. About 30 mineral-rich districts are among the 150 most backward districts in the country. India's map of mines strangely coincides with its rich natural forests and Adivasi population. From a livelihoods perspective, it is this tribal population that concerns us.

Indian mining has become the locus for popular protests in a number of states, most notably Odisha, where Adivasis of the Niyamgiri Hills and Jagatsinghpur continue to protest against aluminum and iron ore mining. In parallel, widespread violations of

---

[25] PRS Research. 2012. Available at: http://www.prsindia.org/uploads/media/Land%20and%20R%20and%20R/Comparison%20of%20Bill%20and%20amendments.pdf, accessed on 10 August 2013.

[26]One can see the full comparison between earlier and current bills in http://www.prsindia.org/uploads/media/Land%20and%20R%20and%20R/Comparison%20of%20Bill%20and%20amendments.pdf (accessed on 1 September 2013).

mining laws have come to light in Karnataka, Chhattisgarh, Andhra Pradesh, and lately in Uttar Pradesh. Three voices or interest groups have pulled the public debate on mining in different directions: the voice of the mining lobby that wants mining to grow and increase its contribution to GDP, the voice of sustainable mining advocates who argue for limits and alternatives ways of mining, and the voice of the affected people who resist the taking-over of their land by large mining companies.[27]

Indian mining is regulated by The Mines and Minerals (Development Regulation) Act, 1957, though this Act has been amended several times since it was first passed. In 1993, the central government issued a National Mineral Policy. In 2006, the Hoda Committee was set up to examine this policy. The Committee observed that mining projects are high risk investments as they have a long gestation period and require large investments in exploration and other development activities before commercial production can begin.[28] Based on the committee's recommendations, the National Mining Policy was revised in 2008. The policy incentivizes private sector investment in exploration and mining, ensures transparency in granting concessions, and stresses sustainable mining practices to safeguard the environment and local population. Subsequently, the Mines and Minerals (Development and Regulation) Bill, 2011 was introduced in order to update and dovetail legislation with the new National Mineral Policy, 2008.

After the Bill's introduction in the Parliament, it was sent to the parliamentary standing committee on 5 January 2012. The standing committee took more than a year and submitted its report to the Ministry of Mines on 6 May 2013. It now awaits placement again in the Parliament. The slow progress of the Bill has again entered public debate after the suspension of a subdivisional magistrate in Greater Noida by the Uttar Pradesh government for her brave attempt to curb illegal sand mining.

We will briefly discuss the Bill's attempts to assuage the concerns of the tribal populations, since this is the key link to livelihoods.

- Compensation shall be paid to every person or family holding occupation or rights of the land surface for which a licence is granted. The holder of a mining lease will pay a specified amount of money each year to the District Mineral Foundation, a fund entity to be created by the government at the district level, which will be used for the benefit of persons or families affected by mining-related operations. This amount is equivalent to 26 per cent of profit in the case of coal and lignite, and is equivalent to the royalty paid during the financial year in case of other major minerals.
- Mining companies shall allot at least one non-transferable share at par to each person of a family affected by mining-related operations. The holder of a mining lease shall also be liable to provide employment in addition to other compensation payable to affected persons or families.

There are a number of new proposals in the Bill to improve the operational aspects of mining regulation and, thus, to ensure better enforcement. However, there are two major questions remaining. First, providing mineral concessions (permission to mine) to non-tribals as envisaged in the proposed bill is in direct conflict with the Supreme Court ruling in 1997 that no immovable property

---

[27] For discussion on different voices, the reader may consult, 'Unlocking the Potential of the Indian Minerals Sector', Strategy Paper for the Ministry of Mines, November 2011, Sustainable Development; 'Emerging Issues in the Mineral Sector', Institute of Studies in Industrial Development, New Delhi, 2012, 'Rich Lands, Poor People—Is Sustainable Mining Possible?' Centre for Science and Environment, 2008.

[28] Planning Commission. 2006. *National Mineral Policy: Report of the High Level Committee*, Planning Commission (Chairperson: Anwarul Hoda), 22 December.

can be transferred to a non-tribal in a 'fifth schedule' area.[29] Second, the Supreme Court further ruled on 8 July 2013 that subsoil materials belong to the same persons who are owners of the land above it. It has, thus, struck down Section 425 of the Mines and Mineral (Development & Regulation) Act of 1957 that bans any mining activity without licence. The Court has instead ruled that there is no law in the country that provides proprietary right to the state on subsoil materials. The court has also struck down similar clauses in other laws concerning mining.[30]

These questions present major challenges to the Bill and are most likely to send the bill back to the drawing board, for further deliberations. Meanwhile, one can always expect that what cannot be done legally can always be done illegally, thus illegal mining will continue the way it is now continuing.

4.7 The long road to implementing the FRA

The implementation of the FRA, 2006, is now in its fifth year (after the rules were notified in January 2008). The challenges in its implementation are best summarized by the new guidelines issued in July 2012:

> Over a period of last four years of implemen-tation of the Act, some problems impeding the implementation of the Act in its letter and spirit have come to the notice of the Ministry of Tribal Affairs, such as, convening of Gram Sabha meetings at the Panchayat level result-ing in exclusion of smaller habitations not formally part of any village, non-recognition of unhindered rights over the minor forest produce (MFP) to forest dwellers, non-recog-nition of other community rights; harassment and eviction of forest dwellers without settle-ment of their forest rights, rejection of claims by insisting on certain types of evidences,

inadequate awareness about the provisions of the Act and the Rules, etc.[31]

An Act that requires cooperation of three departments at the state level (forest, tribal affairs, revenue) can be expected to face a number of hurdles in its implementation. What is distressing is the failure to mitigate and design for these hurdles at the outset, and the long period taken before implemen-tation problems are brought to light.

Minor forest products (MFPs) include bamboo, brush wood, stumps, cane, *tussar*, cocoons, honey, wax, lac, *tendu* or *kendu* leaves, medicinal plants and herbs, roots, tubers, and the like. Traditionally, these products were gathered, processed, packaged, and sold by monopolistic, state-owned Forest Development Corporations (FDCs). While forest dwellers are allowed to collect, their status remains as labourers of the FDCs.

The FRA set out to change all this, by providing unrestricted rights of gathering, processing, packaging, and selling of all MFPs by cooperatives and other collectives of forest dwellers.

The guidelines issued during this year (see Box 3.2 for salient features of the guideline) respond to widespread evidence of implementation failure. Among the chal-lenges identified are—restrictions are being imposed on community rights; community forest resources are not demarcated leading to disputes between forest dwellers and for-est departments; and the powers of Gram Sabhas are not honoured by officials.

The guidelines do little more than reit-erate the rules which were clearly set out following the original Act, in January 2008. Section II (a, b, c, d, e) of the guidelines, for example, require the disbanding of FDCs and the scrapping of transit rules required for movements of MFPs. They highlight the

---

[29] We may note that almost two-third of the area under mining is 'fifth schedule area'.

[30] For a full discussion of the Supreme Court ruling, the reader may see the full judgement at: http://judis.nic.in/supremecourt/imgs1.aspx?filename=40542, accessed in October 2013.

[31] For full guideline see http://www.fra.org.in/new/document/FRA%202006,%20Amendment%20Rule%202012%20&%20Guideline.pdf (accessed on 29 October 2013).

rights of unrestricted use of MFPs by federations or cooperatives of forest dwellers, and the abolition of any fees or charges by the forest department. Further, the guidelines (Sections III [a, b, c, d] and IV [a, b, c, d, e]) call on state governments to recognize community rights of various kinds (*nister*, pastoralists, Primitive Tribal Groups…).

The key expectation that the FRA would encourage cooperatives and other business entities owned by forest dweller communities dealing in MFP has clearly not been met. The 2012 guidelines, therefore, seek to boost the chances of this outcome, by initiating a centrally sponsored scheme to provide minimum support price for purchase of a list of MFPs, thus taking on (once again) marketing and distribution responsibility while ensuring the forest dwellers a fair share of revenue. The scheme has just under ₹970 crore as central government share and ₹250 crore as the states' share for the current plan period. The scheme covers 12 MFPs not nationalized in states having Scheduled Areas and STs in accordance with Fifth Schedule of Constitution.

The efficacy of this programme will surely depend on how well the forest dwellers are able to respond with collective entities to make use of the provisions. The building of collectives who can handle logistics and sales as well as collection, is a complex process requiring external facilitation. Presently, this facilitation comes from forest rights groups that have been instrumental in bringing the law into being. But their expertise is more in advocacy than trade. The challenge will be the transition of the forest rights movement from *sangharsh* (fight) to *nirman* (build).

Reading the guidelines and amended rules, 2012, there is a sense of déjà vu from the FRA's original text. The new instructions and guidelines are so basic as if they are trying to discipline an incorrigible child who will just not listen to the rules.

4.8 Aajeevika: The NRLM*

The government commemorated completion of two years of NRLM (also known as Aajeevika) on 3 June 2013. Restructuring the erstwhile Swarnajayanti Gram Swarojgar Yojana (SGSY) scheme, NRLM's components are: formation, federation, and financing of women SHGs; livelihoods programme for rural women's farmers and agricultural labourers; value addition in non-timber forest produce in tribal districts; gender rights issues and various skills development programmes, namely Aajeevika Skills, Himayat, and Roshni. It aims to cover all the rural districts of the country in a period of eight years, in phases. The central outlay for NRLM for 2013–14 is ₹4,000 crore, barely an increase from the outlay of ₹3,915 crore in 2012–13.

Aajeevika has incorporated several key shifts from the earlier programme. First, it responds to demand from states. Second, it provides a professional support structure for programme implementation at all levels. Third, it has taken a 'saturation' approach to ensure maximum coverage of the rural poor. As the sole government programme with 'livelihood' in its title, Aajeevika takes a nuanced view that the poor have multiple livelihoods as a coping strategy, and as such, it aims to embrace the entire household

---

* This section has been contributed by Suryamani Roul, Senior Vice President, ACCESS Development Services.

portfolio. This shapes NRLM as a highly process-oriented programme.

During 2012–13, the Ministry of Rural Development's and Planning Commission's reviews of the programme have led to modifications in the guidelines. These are summarized as follows:

1. Improved targeting: In lieu of using the traditional criteria of 'BPL' to define inclusion in the programme, the Mission will introduce a new process of Participatory Identification of the Poor (PIP) to target its interventions. This is consistent with the programme's focus on building affinity groups which are not engendered by drawing persons from an externally prepared and incomplete BPL list. The PIP results will, furthermore, require approval from the Gram Panchayat. It is estimated that the new targeting system will add an additional 32 million to NRLM's net.

2. Interest subvention: Aajeevika provides loans up to ₹3 lakh at 7 per cent per annum to women's SHGs, while prompt repayers get an additional 3 per cent subvention. This provision will cover 150 districts (including the 88 Left-Wing Extremism (LWE)–affected districts)—in its first phase.

3. Pattern of financial assistance: The 'capital subsidy' earlier provided to the SHGs will be replaced by financial support (in the form of the Community Investment Support Fund) to SHG federations and livelihoods organizations which will then lend in turn to SHGs.

4. National-Level NRLM Society: An autonomous, adequately staffed, professionally managed, and empowered agency will be established to improve implementation. The National Rural Livelihoods Promotion Society (NRLPS) will act as the technical support unit of NRLM, continuously building capacities of the State Rural Livelihoods Missions (SRLMs). The Society structure will facilitate entry of high-quality profes-

sional support and offer flexibility to create partnerships.

The news on progress of NRLM so far gives a mixed picture. Reports from the field show:

- uneven mobilization of rural poor
- insufficient capacity building of beneficiaries
- low credit mobilization
- lack of dedicated professionals for implementation

These findings have led to the debate as to whether aspects of the design have influenced the slow start of the programme. The MoRD's Annual Report 2012–13, highlights the following priorities to address weaknesses:

- Need for sensitive support structure to induce social mobilization and grassroots institutions.
- Poor rural women, organized into SHGs, require repeated doses of finance at affordable rates.
- A strong system is formed when all the poor in the village are organized into SHGs and all the SHGs consolidate to form a federation.
- Alternate livelihoods must be present to overcome livelihoods risk.

Table 3.7 provides an update of statewise preparation and roll-out of the programme.

NRLM's progress depicts a poor show in the hills, not only in the North East but in Uttarakhand and Himachal Pradesh as well. A 'special package' is, thus, in planning to roll out before the general election.

One of NRLM's major thrusts is the installation of human resources to mobilize the community and deliver the project at every level. There is currently a wide divergence across states with respect to levels of approval and recruitment to fill these positions. Madhya Pradesh and Bihar lead, with Odisha, Tamil Nadu, and Maharashtra

Table 3.7: State-wise status of preparation and roll-out of SRLM

Parameters	Status of states
Set-up of SRLM and appointment of full-time SMD/CEO	Process completed in all 19 states except Uttarakhand and Goa. The SRLM is approved in Uttarakhand.
Identification of intensive districts/blocks	Process completed in all states except Uttarakhand and Goa.
Approval for recruitment of SRLM staff for intensive districts and blocks	Process completed in all 20 states except Goa.
SPMU core team in place	Except Uttarakhand and Goa, in all 19 states.
Preparation, submission, and approval of Annual Action Plan	The Annual Action Plan is approved for AP, Assam, Bihar, Chhattisgarh, Gujarat, Haryana, Jharkhand, J & K, Kerala, MP, Maharashtra, Mizoram, Odisha, Punjab, Rajasthan, Tamil Nadu, UP, and West Bengal.
Commencement of recruitment at state/district/block	All except Himachal Pradesh, Jammu & Kashmir, Uttarakhand, and Goa.
Completion of state-level recruitment	Except West Bengal, Himachal Pradesh, Jammu & Kashmir, Uttarakhand, and Goa
Completion of district and block-level recruitment	The recruitment is completed in AP, Chhattisgarh, Jharkhand, MP, Assam, Bihar, Kerala, Rajasthan, Odisha, Gujarat, Punjab, and Haryana whereas in other states the programme is in process.
Preparation, submission, and approval of SPIP	AP, Bihar, and Kerala have completed the process in SPIP while the other 18 states have yet to start
Status of financial management (FM) system	Tamil Nadu has full FM team at district level, and Jharkhand, Bihar, and Odisha have FM manual while other states are in the process of developing the manual. Jharkhand, Tamil Nadu, Maharashtra, Bihar, and Odisha have delegation of Financial Power rules.
Bimonthly workshop on procurement and financial management	So far three workshops have been conducted.
States where SLBC sub-committee of RSETI has been set up	Karnataka, Jharkhand, West Bengal, Assam, Chhattisgarh, UP, Maharashtra, MP, and AP.
States that have organized workshop on RSETI	Maharashtra, West Bengal, Bihar, Chhattisgarh, Jharkhand, Haryana , Rajasthan, and UP.
States which are ready to start NRLM work in 2013–14	Maharashtra, Odisha, Chhattisgarh, Jharkhand, Assam, Karnataka, West Bengal, Rajasthan, MP, UP, Gujarat, Tamil Nadu, and Bihar.

Source: http://aajeevika.gov.in/nrlm/PRC-NRLM%20Group%20I-%20Jan%202013.pdf (last accessed on 8 November 2013).
Note: SMD—State Mission Director; SPMU—State Project Management Unit; SPIP—State Perspective and Implementation Plan; SLBC—State Level Banker's Committee; RSETI—Rural Self-Employment Training Institutes.

following, while Chhattisgarh, Jharkhand, Karnataka, and UP are all very slow.

It is estimated that Aajeevika alone requires 70,000 professionals to reach out effectively to rural areas and promote community-based institutions, SHGs, and federations, in 6,000 blocks. Taking a lead from a cross-ministry note on skill development requirements of functionaries for social sector programmes prepared by the National Advisory Council (NAC), Aajeevika is considering how to address the gap in terms of demand and supply.

At the same time, in recognition of the complexity of its development and social transformation role, Aajeevika has partnered, on a new level, with CSOs. MoRD and Pradan have signed a memorandum of understanding (MoU) to carry out develop-mental activities in tribal and LWE-affected districts. The move is a recognition of the difficulties faced by government agencies in working in such regions and the comparative advantage of long-serving and apolitical CSOs. Aajeevika's work in these difficult regions is also likely to be supported by the extension of the Planning Commission's Integrated Action Plan (IAP). Currently implemented in 82 (expanding to 88) LWE-affected districts across nine states, the IAP provides public infrastructure and services such as construction of school buildings, *Anganwadi* centres, drinking water facilities, rural roads, community halls, livelihoods activities, skill development, minor irrigation works, electric lighting, health centres, and construction of toilets. IAP will continue for four more years with an annual allocation of ₹1,000 crore. The IAP funds are placed at the disposal of a committee headed by district collector and consisting of the superintendent of police and the forest officer.

Perhaps due to the reported slowness in progress, the National Rural Livelihoods Project (NRLP), part of the NRLM, has witnessed a scaling down of allocated resources from the World Bank, from the original US$1 billion to US$500 million. Notwithstanding this setback, 2013–14 shows greater prospects in almost all states as the Mission gears up its activities and disbursements. The Aajeevika team continues to be consultative and is looking for alternative ways and means to reach objectives, seeking views from practitioners and CSOs towards a road map under changing and challenging circumstances.

5. New policies: Debates and first steps

This section reviews some of the public debate which is pushing (or may push) its way to new policies. While we have seen that some policies take years to pass and begin to install themselves, others get through swiftly with worryingly little debate. This section will cover those which remain in the sphere of discussion (yet to be enacted, such as the land reform policy), those which are gradually being tested or piloted (such as FDI in retail and direct benefit transfers), and those which have 'crept up' on us and made it to legislation and rules relatively quickly (such as CSR for corporates and reform of the sugar sector). We have made the selection according to strength of linkages to livelihoods of vast number of population.

5.1 FDI in retail

Retail business in India refers to outlets that directly supply products to consumers (not for resale), and it typically covers food and related products, apparels, groceries, electronics-telecom products, leather products, stationery, and others. In the last 20 years, the retail business is steadily undergoing changes in favour of single and multi-brand retailers with branded and large format stores replacing a section of the *kirana* shops. But this transformation is occurring extremely slowly in India, partly—it is argued—due to shortage of investment. The debate on FDI in retail has polarized three sets of interests: the *kirana* shops that fear their customer will wither away; the pro FDI developers and investors who argue that greater organized retail will lead to employment and wealth creation, better prices for suppliers, and enlargement of overall market; and a third group, viewing the issue from the perspective of developed country markets, argues that multinational players may induce unfair competition at home.[32]

FDI in wholesale was first permitted in 1997 under the 'government approval' route, finally brought under the automatic route in 2006. Retail, rather than wholesale, was first opened to FDI in 2006, but capped at 51 per cent and permitted only for 'single brands'. In 2011, the cap was removed, while FDI in multi-brand retail remained withheld until 20 September 2012 when it was finally permitted with several conditions attached,[33] and capped at 51 per cent. To assuage political sensitivities, the government has left final decision-making with the state governments, leaving on them the option to allow or not, as well as the power to issue trade licence.

Supporters of organized retail argue that, with the help of FDI, the sector will bring

---

[32] A detailed discussion on the retail sector is available in Akhtar, Shahid and Ifthekhar Iquebal. 2012. 'Organized Retailing in India—Challenges and Opportunities', *International Journal of Multidisciplinary Research*, 2 (1, January): 281. ISSN 2231 5780.

[33] Conditions include a minimum investment of US$100 million; 50 per cent of investment must be to establish back-end infrastructure such as cold chain, processing and packaging; greater than 30 per cent of sourcing must be local and from small-scale units. Stores can be set up in a range of 53 cities and within 10 km of these cities as well.

several advantages to the consumer, such as fair weights (always an issue with the *kirana* shops), better quality (less adulteration), wider choice and the convenience of range under one roof, and some degree of price benefits of scale. It is further argued that, since 97 per cent of retail trade remains with the unorganized sector (which contributes 13 per cent of GDP and employs 6 per cent of India's workforce[34]) inflows of investment are unlikely to steal the existing share of *kirana* stores so much as to expand the size of the sector and the market. It is projected that organized retail can create an additional 10 million jobs for the retail sector and bring in nearly ₹30-lakh crore investment.[35]

Opponents of FDI in organized retail, on the other hand, have focused not only on the potential loss of livelihoods in the unorganized and small-scale sector, but also on the possibility of reduced choice and increased risk for farmers as retailers impose their monopoly power, price inflation for consumers, and even unfair labour practices for the workers of corporate retail firms.[36]

The vociferous lobby of small traders in India has ensured that the debate has focused on the two poles of *kirana* stores and large format corporate retailers. There are, of course, alternatives. Throughout the 1970s and 1980s, marketing cooperatives served city dwellers as effective multi-brand shops; several of them survive such as *Safal*

of the National Dairy Development Board (NDDB) or Chennai's *Subhiksha*. There are also successful private sector small-format chains such as Bengal's *Arambagh's*, and Tamil Nadu's *Nilgiris* and *Nallis*. South East Asian states invest in strong covered market infrastructure, providing convenience, choice, and price competitiveness to the customer, alongside space, custom, and security to small traders. The point is that diverse and middle paths exist inside and beyond India which have not yet been fully explored.

Left to make their own decisions as to whether to allow the entry of multinationals in retail, the states have been divided on the issue. Maharashtra, Haryana, Andhra Pradesh, Rajasthan, Jammu & Kashmir, Uttarakhand, Manipur, Assam, and Delhi, for example, supported the move towards 100 per cent FDI. On the other hand, Gujarat, Uttar Pradesh, West Bengal, Bihar, Tamil Nadu, Kerala, Chhattisgarh, and Odisha opposed the move.

Partly due to the polarity of the debate, there is a shortage of balanced research on the topic. While India-based research is lacking, the predatory practices of large multinationals elsewhere are well documented. Wal-Mart's unfair labour practices and pressure on suppliers to cut prices, for example, has created new intermediaries under their control, and pushed many small traders out of business.[37]

5.2 Partial decontrol of sugar

As a 'notified essential commodity', sugar's entire value chain is heavily administered and regulated by the government. In 2012, Government of India appointed a high-level committee, headed by C. Rangarajan,

[34] Kaushik, K.R. and Kapil Kumar Bansal. 2012. 'Foreign Direct Investment in Indian Retail Sector Pros and Cons', *International Journal of Emerging Research in Management & Technology*, ISSN 2278-9359, p. 7.

[35] Ibid.

[36] For discussions on FDI in retail, please see, Sarkar, A. 2013. 'Understanding FDI in retail: what can economic principles teach us', *Economic and Political Weekly*, 5 January; Teltumbte, A. 2013. 'FDI in retail and Dalit entrepreneurs', *Economic and Political Weekly*, 19 January; Chalapati Rao, K.S. 2012. 'Vaulting over India's retail FDI policy wall', *Economic and Political Weekly*, 17 November; Singh, S. 2011. 'FDI in retail: Misplaced expectations and half truths', *Economic and Political Weekly*, 17 December; and Swamy, Shekhar. 2011. 'The Pitfalls of FDI in Multi-brand Retailing in India', Madhyam Briefing Paper#3.

[37] For a detailed discussion on Wal-Mart's labour practices, see UNI Global Union. 2012. 'Wal-Mart's Global Track Record and the Implications for FDI in Multi-Brand Retail in India'. UNI Global Union is a union of 20 million workers in 900 trade unions of services and industries. It has produced a well-researched paper on Wal-Mart's practices, recommending several protective measures to ensure that such practices are not repeated on Indian soil.

to look into the feasibility of liberalizing certain aspects of these controls. Based on its recommendations submitted in October 2012, the Government of India has partially decontrolled the sector.

Tight government control over sugar since Independence was meant to ensure availability to all at reasonable prices (distributed through ration shops) and at the same time protecting the sugarcane producers, and to prevent monopolization. Every sugar mill has necessarily to buy sugarcane from a designated cane area, with a minimum 15 km distance between sugar mills. Prices of sugarcane are fixed separately by union and state governments (with wide divergences in these two pricing mechanisms) and sugar mills must surrender 10 per cent of their product to the government at the state government price (known as state advised price [SAP]) as 'levy sugar' for the PDS. Sale of the balance ('non-levy sugar') is heavily controlled by the union government which issues quarterly release orders to the mills. Furthermore, there are heavy restrictions on the use of by-products, exports and imports, requirement to use jute bags, and other issues. This tight control has made sugar a highly political commodity in India where mill-owners function in a tight nexus with major political parties. Control has also created a huge black market and encouraged hoarding. To check the price rise, the government's response has always been to import sugar.

The Rangarajan Committee recommended that market logic should gradually replace state control. For example, the cane area and distance restrictions imposed on mills and growers should be relaxed since neither gains, and the result is monopolistic practices, poor quality, not enough competition, and low investment. Second, the Committee also felt that the revenue generated out of the value chain in sugar should be fairly distributed between growers and millers. It computed and found that the value ratio between the farmers and millers should be 70:30, meaning sugarcane producers

would get 70 per cent of the value created, and the millers would get 30 per cent of the value. Third, the Committee recommended the revenue from sugar's three by-products be properly shared between the growers and millers.[38] The Committee recommended abolition of the monthly quarterly release mechanism, arguing that such controls are neither in the interest of the grower, nor of the millers and general consumers. It also argued the abolition of levy sugar and advised the states to buy the PDS from the open market.[39]

The cabinet committee (headed by the prime minister) accepted the report and, in its meeting in April 2013, abolished the levy system completely and dismantled the regulated release of sugar, allowing mills for the first time to sell in the open market. It decided that the states will now buy PDS sugar in the open market, and the difference between open market price and the union government price (known as the FRP) will be paid by the central government as a subsidy to the states. The subsidy burden is estimated around ₹2,700 crore. Please see Box 3.3 for salient feature of the sugar decontrol measures.

Box 3.3: *Decontrol of sugar at a glance*

1. Levy procurement of sugar abolished
2. System of regulated release of sugar in the open market dismantled
3. Cane dues to be shared between the farmers and millers on a 70:30 ratio and cane dues to include by-products as well
4. Cane dues to be released twice a year

Source: Compiled by author.

---

[38] The three by-products of sugarcane are bagasse (used to make pulp and biofuel), molasses (alcohol), and press mud (fertilizer). The 'cane dues', the Committee recommended, are to be paid to the farmers in two instalments and the states will declare the prices twice in a year.

[39] For details see Rangarajan Committee report available at: http://eac.gov.in/reports/rep_sugar1210.pdf, accessed in October 2013.

Press reports[40] show that the growers are divided in their views. Growers in Uttar Pradesh are sceptical that millers will share 'cane dues' fairly with them, as directed. The total cane arrear[41] in the country stands at ₹10,694 crore, of which Uttar Pradesh accounts for more than half amounting to ₹5,800 crore followed by Karnataka and Tamil Nadu. Growers in Maharashtra and Karnataka are more optimistic, confident that millers will pass on their share. The removal of the levy sugar is a popular measure with millers who will save about ₹3,000 crore.

To date, the price of sugar showed no signs of increase, although one was expected. Demand once again exceeds supply, in response to which the government has imported 2.74 million tons of sugar in June 2013. Further, the central government's commitment to pay states the price difference between market and FRP has helped keep the sugar flowing to the PDS. We will have to wait and see whether the government is resolved to drive further deregulation in the sector, as the Committee recommended, and what impacts this will have for growers and consumers.

5.3 Companies Act Amendment Bill

Jamshedji Tata's vision of the country's first steel company, TISCO, included a full township, with municipalities, schools, hospitals, drinking water, and basic sanitation.[42] At that time, it was understood as part of nation building.

But CSR today is associated with the period of liberalization. It follows the dictum that with the shrinking of the state in public life, the market will have to lead not only in creation of wealth and jobs, but also in the provision of social welfare and human development. As the government pushes forward with the modalities of how corporates will make these provisions, towards what kinds of ends, the larger political question remains: in the process of creating growth and even jobs, markets create new deprivations and inequalities, they marginalize livelihoods and destroy resources on which much well-being was built. If this is so, then will such a scheme be against the 'DNA' of business? Can it be anything more than an eyewash? Worse still, will it take our focus off the regulation which was already in place (labour law, environment law, etc.) to curb the negative impact of corporate activity?

In 2009, a voluntary guideline was issued by the Corporate Affairs Ministry. In 2012, the new Companies Bill[43] made clear provision for what it called CSR. The CSR envisaged is of the three types: First, companies can donate funds to the International Red Cross, UNICEF, the Prime Minister's Relief Fund, etc. Second, companies can contract NGOs to implement development projects as mutually decided. Third, companies can set up their own implementation arrangements. The companies that have a turnover of over ₹1,000 crore or have a net worth of ₹500 crore, or that have recorded a net profit of ₹5 crore in last three years, are expected to spend 2 per cent of their net profit of preceding three years on CSR. The Board is responsible for reporting its CSR spending to the Corporate Affairs Ministry. If company is not spending money for CSR, it'll have to *explain* why they are not doing so. Companies that *do not report* will face a penalty ranging from ₹50,000

---

[40] Kulkarni, Viswanath. 2013. 'Partial Sugar Decontrol: Cane growers divided over impact', *The Hindu Business Line*, 5 April.

[41] Cane arrears are the dues that accrue to farmers since the government permits the mills to sell not when they want but according to a regulated schedule of slow release.

[42] Fred Hariss, in his Biography of Jamshedji Tata writes, 'from the time of driving in the first stake, Tata Iron & Steel Company assumes the functions of a municipality, focusing on free health care, decent schooling, provision of safe water, and basic sanitation'. It was quoted in Dreze, Jean and Amartya Sen. 2013. *India: An Uncertain Glory* (India: Penguin, Allen Lane), p. 278.

[43] The new 2012 Companies Bill aims to replace the Companies Act, 1956, the longest and most complex bill in India's legal canon.

Box 3.4: *List of interventions to be recognized as CSR*

1. Eradicating extreme hunger and poverty
2. Promotion of education
3. Promoting gender equality and empowering women
4. Reducing child mortality and improving maternal health
5. Combating human immunodeficiency virus (HIV), acquired immunodeficiency syndrome (AIDS), malaria, and other diseases
6. Ensuring environmental sustainability

7. Employment-enhancing vocational skills
8. Social business projects
9. Contribution to the Prime Minister's National Relief Fund or any other fund set up by the central government or the state governments for socio-economic development and relief and funds for the welfare of the SCs, the STs, other backward classes (OBCs), minorities, and women

Source: Schedule VII of the Companies Act 2013.

---

to ₹25 lakh or even imprisonment of up to three years.

To guide companies towards acceptable activities, a 'Schedule VII' has been created in the Companies Bill, that stipulates what expenditures will be counted as CSR expenditures (see Box 3.4), most of which directly relates to livelihoods enhancements of Indian population—rural or urban.

The Bill has been passed by the Lok Sabha in December 2012, and placed in Rajya Sabha. Since the Parliament hardly functioned in the winter and the budget sessions, the Bill had to wait, and as we write the report, the Bill has just been passed in Rajya Sabha on 8 August 2013.

5.4 National land reform policy

In 2004–05, 10.21 per cent of the rural households were completely landless and another 31 per cent had no cultivable land.[44] The Gini Index of India's land inequality is as high as 0.76.[45] But land reform as a development agenda disappeared during the 1980s. Only recently have land rights issues again come to the fore, perhaps for three different reasons. First, the spread of LWE across the poorest states of the country has reinstalled land inequality as a core grievance. Second, resistance to land acquisition

and displacement has been growing, some of this in the form of Dalit and Adivasi social movements opposing large projects and connecting with the environment agenda. Third, the international price rise of food products and emerging concerns of food shortages and food security have also highlighted landlessness once more as a core deprivation.

As a result of all these developments, the discussion on issues of land has become popular, perhaps more among the researchers, international bilateral and multilateral institutions, and civil society, than government. On the other hand, various state governments such as Andhra Pradesh, Karnataka, West Bengal, and Odisha have started new experiments in land allocations. These new experiments include allocations of homestead land, reallocation through targeted purchases, providing legal aid to remove land insecurities of the poor, and regularizing squatters.

In 2008, the revived land redistribution movement showed its strength when nearly 25,000 landless people from seven to eight states marched to Delhi and pushed the union government to declare formation of a national committee to look into what was then described as 'unfinished tasks' in land reforms. The committee produced a report listing all the different types of unfinished tasks, but then failed to meet again. In September 2013, nearly 60,000 landless people took to streets and

---

[44] NSSO 64th Round (2004–05).

[45] Rawal, Vikas. 2008. 'Ownership Holding of Land in Rural India', *Economic and Political Weekly*, March: 47.

again started marching towards Delhi. The Rural Development Minister was quick enough to stop them at Agra where the Government and marchers—represented by Ekta Parishad—signed an agreement for a National Land Reform Policy (NLRP) and a National Rural Homestead Bill (NRHB) to entitle every landless family of the country to 10 decimals of land. Both of these are in the formative stage, while a draft of the NLRP has been published (see Box 3.5 for details of the NRHB).

Box 3.5:   *Salient features of NRHB*

1. Eighteen to 20 million rural landless households to be given 10 decimals of homestead land
2. Land may be obtained by purchase, from existing government land, land acquisition, and ceiling surplus land
3. In case of purchase, central government will share the costs with state governments on a 75:25 basis
4. Allocated land will be titled only in the name of the woman of the family
5. The SCs/STs, single women, minorities, tea tribes, etc., will be given priority in allocation

Source: Compiled by author.

The Draft National Land Reforms Policy aims at five policy prescriptions. First, the unfinished task of land distribution to the rural landless. Second, restoration of alienated lands to the Dalits and tribals. Third, mechanisms to protect the land of the Dalits and tribals including the Commons that they depend on. Fourth, liberalizing tenancy and leasing. And fifth, the land rights of women. Finally, the policy sets out a few means of how to achieve these prescriptions. See Box 3.6 for salient features of National Land Reform Policy.

Distribution of land to the landless

On the issue of land distribution among the landless, the policy prescribes the following:

Box 3.6:   *Salient features of the draft national land reform policy*

1. Lowering of ceiling to five to 10 acres for irrigated land and 10–15 acres for un-irrigated land
2. Fresh survey of all ceiling surplus land acquired but not distributed, take possession and distribute to the landless
3. Creating a land pool
4. Creating two special funds to protect distress sale of SCs/STs
5. Restoration of alienated land back to STs and SCs
6. Liberalizing tenancy laws in favour of the poor
7. Implementation of Hindu Succession Amendment Act, 2005, giving inheritance rights of agricultural land to women
8. All future land allocation of government to poor only in the name of woman of the family
9. Ten decimals of homestead land to all the landless as entitlement
10. Women groups to be entitled for land allocation along with the landless

Source: Compiled by author.

- Lowering of land ceiling limits to five to 10 acres per family for irrigated land and 10–15 acres per family on un-irrigated land (while current ceilings go up to 24 acres)
- Removal of ceiling exemptions now given to educational institutions, religious institutions, and industrial units, so they would be subject to the same limits as a family
- Computation of ceiling based on the tougher standard of operational holdings and not on ownership holdings
- Creating a land pool which includes the possession of *Bhoodan*[46] land, revenue wasteland, assignment land, and government land, and allocate those lands to the landless

There are several major challenges in realizing this land distribution. First, is the need to vest the ceiling surplus land and take physical possession of it. The challenges here begin with its demarcation, fight other claimants in court, and find means to keep it in the state's possession. Taking possession

---

[46] *Bhoodan* was a land gift movement initiated by Gandhians, in the late 1950s, in which large landowners were urged to voluntarily surrender land above the ceiling.

of the wasteland, assignment land, and *Bhoodan* land is another critical challenge, given the difficulties the government faces in taking and keeping possession of land. Second, previous land distribution efforts by government have not led to physical possession by the landless, land title, and land record. Third, the government's land records are not updated, leaving the new policy vulnerable to all possible malpractices on the ground.

To address these challenges, the policy proposes some measures (resurvey, updating of records, enlisting the help of the community, CBOs, Panchayats, etc.). But it is not clear that these measures will be adequate to overcome the huge challenges.[47]

Restoration of lands to Dalits and tribals

The second thrust of the policy is on the restoration of the land back to the Dalits and tribals that were alienated by unfair means, i.e. with respect to historical and *ryoti* lands, land allocated by the government where the intended communities could not take possession, land under the Panchayat (Extension to Scheduled Areas) Act (PESA)[48] that were alienated to private commercial interests, or the Commons encroached by the powerful local elites. The draft policy captures these challenges, and calls on state governments to take strong administrative actions to restore lands back to the Dalits and tribals. The policy depends on securing the participation of the poor and CBOs to identify those whose lands were alienated.

Protection of land belonging to Dalits and tribals

The third thrust of the policy is on protection of Dalit and tribal-owned land so that alienation should be minimized in future. The policy calls for the formation of a Land Protection Fund at the Gram Panchayat or SHG-federation level to provide soft loans to those families at risk of selling land. The policy also restricts the transfer of land from Dalits and tribals to other communities, and calls for creating a mechanism of land purchase by government at full market price. The policy calls for strong state legislation to empower Gram Sabhas to safeguard the land rights of tribals, and the policy suggests the creation of a Land Consolidation Fund to support Gram Sabha to buy land from tribals wanting to sell, and transfer it in the name of Gram Sabha. For land occupied by tribals in non-scheduled areas, the policy suggests fresh mapping and notification as a Scheduled Area.

Modifying tenancy laws

The critical issue of leasing is addressed in the draft policy. The leasing in farm land has become an important means for farm labour and marginal cultivators to increase income from agriculture. While leasing is promoted under many state and non-state programmes, it is officially banned or at best restricted, a hangover of the postcolonial reaction against the woes of *zamindarism* and exploitative tenancy. The policy recognizes the crucial livelihood function of leasing and advocates removing of legal restrictions.

Women's land rights

The draft policy recommends that all future land allocation by government be transferred only in the name of women, including land restored.[49] The policy takes note of the failure in implementation of the Hindu

---

[47] For the distribution of land to the landless there is a special section on homesteads as a part of land distribution. Homesteads serve multiple purposes of a house, animal shed, work shed, nutrition garden, fruit trees, and timber. The outline of the Homestead Bill is given in the Box 3.4.

[48] PESA, passed in 1996, extended to 'Scheduled Areas' (i.e. Adivasi regions) the provisions of local elected government which had been extended to the rest of the country through the 73rd Amendment to the Constitution in 1992.

---

[49] Furthermore, the policy recommends that 50 per cent of community forest rights should be in the name of women.

Succession Amendment Act, 2005 (giving inheritance rights to women on agricultural land), and calls for immediate proactive state action in this regard. Further, the policy recommends women's groups to be one of the target categories of land distribution.

To sum up, the policy has many desirable prescriptions and has achieved the major objective of bringing back pro-poor land reform as a key agenda in the public sphere. But it has several shortcomings. First, it has not considered what is politically feasible as the existing ceiling laws have not been implemented in most states, lowering the ceiling seems politically unrealistic. Second, land reform is a state subject and a national policy will have relatively little leeway. Rather than dealing with almost every aspect of the issue, pointing out a few key desirables to the state governments would have been politically wiser. Third, the draft does not give sufficient focus to the recent experiences of the states. In fact, what has worked in a number of states such as homestead land allocation and land legal aid to the poor find passing mention instead of foregrounding those in the policy.

5.5 Direct benefit transfers

Government of India and state governments together run hundreds of schemes for the rural and urban population providing a number of benefits in kind and cash. Often these subsidies are not directly passed to the target population, but to producers and traders that make these benefits available. For example, the subsidy on Liquefied Petroleum Gas (LPG) used by most middle class and lower middle class urban and rural homes is paid to the oil companies who are expected to cap the price to the consumer. Such subsidies paid by the Government of India to its poorer population amount to 5.8 per cent of the GDP. While the reduction of subsidy is a valid economic concern, a legitimate argument arises to directly transfer the subsidy in cash to the ultimate consumer. These direct cash transfer arrangements can be made directly through banks and post offices in all cases.

The political context of cash transfers is not about reduction in subsidy, therefore, but about more efficient targeting and plugging the leakage. For example, consider the story of PDS traders. They receive the subsidy (meant for targeted consumers) and divert a good part of the foodgrains to the open market through black market channels, thus depriving the state as well as the consumers.

The advantages of direct benefit transfers, from a livelihoods viewpoint, are manifold. First, the system aims to ensure money reaches the ultimate beneficiary without leakage. Second, it promises to deliver the money when one needs it. Third, the combined and encashed components of various schemes add up to substantial lump sums for one family that can positively impact family cash flow and opportunity. Fourth, the benefits in kind such as foodgrains and LPGs still remain available to access.

The challenges are equally daunting. First, banks and post offices (the points of disbursement) are often far from hamlets, and irrespective of their location, the capacity of these branches to handle additional several million accounts is in question. Second, it is not always clear that supply markets—for commodities and services slated for encashment—are sufficiently developed to ensure smooth access. Critics of cash transfers have cited the experience of states, such as Chhattisgarh, which have improved their PDS several fold without moving to a cash system.[50] Third, the government's ambition to tie disbursement to unique identification and biometric technology puts huge pressure on a complex and un-honed technology to deliver these benefits on which life and livelihood often depend. Similar improvements can be made

---

[50] For a discussion on the improvements Chhattisgarh achieved, see Dreze, J. and Amartya Sen. 2013. *Uncertain Glory: India & Its Contradictions* (India: Penguin, Allen Lane), pp. 206–09.

in other states too thereby making cash transfers redundant.

Cash transfers—the evidence for and against and the operational detail—are discussed in more detail in Chapter 5 (Social Protection).

6. Conclusion

Based on the above discussions we would like to make five key conclusions. Firstly, there seems to be a lot of emphasis in lawmaking to make livelihoods better for the target population. And the laws are envisaged to be rights-based, so that the state can be held accountable. While there cannot be any doubt that this is a laudable objective, rights-based laws are by no means enhancing the intrinsic capacity of the state to deliver. The institutions and processes remain almost the same as they were 50 years ago, while non-state and quasi-state mechanisms are constantly created to improve state's delivery. On the other hand, India's most radical experimentation in institutional reform, namely Panchayati Raj Institutions and urban local bodies turned out to be a non-starter; neither has been bestowed with powers and authority to make local governments work for the larger citizenry. Therefore, we are in a situation where more and more laws are made without revamping the institutions that are meant to deliver the promises. NREGA is a typical case in point, for example, while the programme aspects of the Act are working with mixed results, the legislative promises are surely not working, neither are they being tracked. NREGA has four fundamental legislative promises: job card within 14 days of application, work within 15 days of application, wages within 14 days, and unemployed allowance if job is not provided. None of these provisions of law are working; most of these are not even officially tracked. Right to Information (RTI) is another typical example; even after eight years of its passing, not a single public authority has become transparency friendly in its institutional processes. We would like to stress that lawmaking is only the beginning of fulfilling a promise; the fulfilment of the promise in India has always been a bigger challenge. Our country is notorious in making plethora of laws and not implementing them with any sincerity. The debate in the last decade seems to have shifted from fulfilling promises to making promises by making more laws.

The second conclusion is about the institutions' commitment and capacity. The unfulfilled promises of development can be reasonably classified into two categories. One is lack of institutional commitment, and the second is the lack of institutional capacity, and these two are interrelated. Lack of commitment is notorious: public expenditure in India on education in proportion to GDP is 3.3 per cent compared to China's 4.5 per cent, Brazil's 5.6 per cent, Russia's 4.1 per cent, whereas teachers' salaries in India are nearly three times than Organization for Economic Cooperation and Development (OECD) average.[51] Public expenditure in health care is only 1.2 per cent in proportion to GDP in India, whereas in China, its 2.7 per cent, Brazil 4.2 per cent, Russia 3.1 per cent.[52] A section of the policymakers are resistant to Food Security Act, for an additional expenditure of ₹27,000 crore, whereas the country forgoes customs duty on import of gold and diamond, used mainly for ornaments, to the extent of ₹57,000 crore.[53] The lack of commitment also shows up in other ways such as engagement of para-teachers (instead of full-fledged teachers), not increasing the number of ICDS staff to two despite several recommendations, not increasing Panchayat's staff and recruiting casual workers to support the Gram Panchayats in performing MGNREGA responsibilities, and the like.

[51] For a discussion on the improvements Chhattisgarh achieved, see Dreze, J. and Amartya Sen. 2013. *Uncertain Glory: India & Its Contradictions* (India: Penguin, Allen Lane), pp. 67–133.

[52] Ibid., p. 67.

[53] Ibid., p. 272.

The lack of institutional capacity is equally serious. The Mid Day Meal is one example. Despite being the world's largest school feeding programme, where 120 million children are daily eating meals in schools for approximately 160 days in a year, the lack of institutional capacity to cater to this need is appalling. From lack of storage space for foodgrains, lack of hygienic kitchen, lack of adequate washing facility, lack of eating space—all combine together to tell the grim story. This also reflects the institutional apathy towards the children of the poor in the country, an apathy that finds expression in many aspects of affirmative action.

The third conclusion we would like to draw is on the process of lawmaking itself. Most non-controversial laws, such as the Manual Scavengers Bill, are taking at least three to four years to become a law and with no certainty. The controversial ones, such as the LARR Bill is in the making for six years again with no certainty at all. Needless to say that laws should not be made in a hurry, the question what is the time frame between 'hurry' and 'delay' is increasingly becoming unclear.

Our fourth conclusion is about the nature of policymaking process. Policymaking requires extensive public discussions among the stakeholders to generate all the possible perspectives, and supported by extensive contemporary research to back up a policy proposal. Over and above, pilots too, provide a great deal of experience and knowledge informing policy. Over the years, the first aspect of policymaking in India has seen substantive and significant progress; the process has now become much more participatory, open, and discursive. This is partly due to strong civil society voice that has emerged in the last two decades who primarily champion the livelihoods and entitlement issues of the poor, and, also, partly due to multiplicity of local and regional political forces that stake claim in the policymaking. The proliferation of independent media has also substantively contributed to this

improvement. This is indeed absolutely laudable. The second and the third aspects of the policymaking, i.e. backing it up by contemporary research, particularly policy research and serious piloting have not seen similar improvements. Policy prescriptions, irrespective of its nature (a law, a scheme, a mission) are not backed up by adequate policy research and only in some cases by loose pilots to say the least. For example, the Twelfth Plan in its section on women clearly prescribes that land titling in all allocations of land to the poor should be titled exclusively to women, as joint titling, the prevalent practice has not worked.[54] There is no research in the public domain to support this policy prescription, nor has any pilot provided results to that effect. And such examples are not exceptions. It needs to be recognized that the nature of policy research is much different than impact research that evaluates programmes and missions that are necessary for mid-course corrections. Lack of such research-informing policy has become a pattern in Indian policymaking ambience.

Lastly, most often policies are made at the union level, and the state governments implement those policies. The central government's role is limited to funding, monitoring, and review. The states being sovereign entities, often decide priorities according to the dynamic of their local political economy, and not necessarily as desired by the centre. NRLM is a typical case of this kind, where this mismatch of priorities is quite visible thus impeding progress of the mission. And this is not limited to NRLM alone.

The poor, vulnerable, and the marginalized people of this country look forward to responsive governments that at least make sincere attempts to address their life concerns. They expect that policies are timely

---

[54] Planning Commission. 2012. Twelfth Five-Year Plan, Volume III, Social Sector, Section 23.25, p. 169.

made, made well, and most importantly executed well. The most important way to achieve this would be to conduct serious policy research, extensive deliberations on policy formations, serious pilots, and state-specific and region-specific strategies of scale-up, and then track policy implementation very closely on outputs and outcome levels. To make this happen, the most important intervention necessary is to conduct sweeping institutional reform, empowering local governments with authority and capacity. There is no country on earth that has progressed far without strong local governments, and there is no reason to believe India can be an exception.

Agriculture and Livelihoods

Adarsh Kumar

1. Introduction

India has a number of different agro-climactic regions and the regional context, dynamics, and problems faced by farmers differ significantly by region. The complex agricultural ecosystem and the multiple sets of problems faced by farmers mean that there are a wide number of variables to be considered when looking at agricultural livelihoods and a number of entry points for interventions by livelihood practitioners.

This chapter is aimed at providing livelihood practitioners a summary of the current state of the sector. Towards this end, the chapter reviewed information from a wide range of data sources (listed in section 2) with the objective of identifying key trends in the agricultural sector, highlighting vulnerable populations that need livelihoods support, and identifying key gaps and bottlenecks that need to be addressed to provide such livelihoods support. The SOIL report seeks to provide a contemporary snapshot of livelihoods, and this chapter focuses on data from the previous five years from 2007 to 2013, wherever such data was available. The chapter focuses on agricultural and horticultural crops and does not seek to cover allied sectors such as livestock, dairy, and fisheries.

2. Sources of data

The main data sources used in this chapter are as follows:

- 2011 census data on employment figures for the sector.
- Economic Outlook 2012/13 by the Economic Advisory Council to the Prime Minister.
- Twelfth Plan Document and Approach Papers to Twelfth Plan.
- Situational Assessment of Farmers as part of the National Sample Survey 59th Round in January–December 2003.
- Directorate of Economics and Statistics—Annual Statistics at a Glance 2012 based on self-reported data by states has been used for crop area, production, and yield information.
- The India Human Development Survey (IHDS) conducted jointly by the National Council for Applied Economic Research (NCAER) and the University of Maryland has been used for household income data. The first round of the survey was conducted in 2004–05.
- The NCAER's Agricultural Outlook and Situation Analysis Reports (AOSAR), the most recent of which was published in February 2013, collates a wide range of data from various government sources to identify key trends in the agricultural sector.

3. Overview and current status of agriculture

The SOIL report in 2010, focusing on agriculture, had flagged five key gaps and corresponding focus areas for achieving inclusive agricultural growth: increased public investment of up to 5 per cent of GDP into the sector, diversification of agricultural growth to poorer regions and a wider range of crops on which the poor depend, a focus on small and marginal farmers, a separate focus on agricultural labourers as a distinct group requiring livelihoods support, and a recognition of the increasing role played by non-farm livelihoods in the livelihoods portfolio of farmer households.[1]

From the lens of poverty reduction, a review of more current data sources shows that many of the same sets of gaps continue to dominate, with little structural change having been achieved in the intervening period. The main positive changes observed during the past five years were a significantly higher average annual growth rate of agricultural GDP and increasing wage rates for agricultural labourers. In addition, horticulture is emerging as a major driver of growth for agricultural livelihoods, growing much more rapidly than cereal crops.

3.1 Income and employment from agriculture

As per Census 2011 data, at the national level, 263 million people were dependent on agriculture for employment. Of this, farmers constituted 45 per cent and agricultural workers 55 per cent of total employment. Twenty two per cent of total employment in the agricultural sector—and 72 per cent of agricultural workers—derived less than six months of employment from agriculture.

Women constitute 30 per cent of farmers and 43 per cent of agricultural workers nationally. Wide variations by state are prevalent with Rajasthan having a significantly higher proportion of women farmers and agricultural workers; and Uttar Pradesh and Bihar having a significantly lower proportion of women farmers and agricultural workers.

2004–05 IHDS data, excerpted in Table 4.1, reveals the extent of diversification of rural households away from agriculture. Although farming and agricultural labour are common sources of income for households, with a high proportion of households reporting income from both sources, the income returns for both sources are low, accounting for only 19 per cent and 7 per cent of total household income respectively.[2] Farming and agricultural wages make up only 55 per cent of total rural income with a variety of other sources including

Table 4.1: Structure of rural income

	Mean (₹)	% HH with income from source	% of total rural income	Median income from source
Total Income	36,755	100	100	22,500
Total Wage and Salary	16,944	70	46	15,900
Salaries	7,632	18	21	24,100
Agricultural Wages	4,507	39	12	900
Non-Agricultural Wages	4,805	29	13	12,700
Total Self-Employment	16,672	73	45	9,389
Business	4,807	17	13	18,000
Farming/Animal Care/Agr. Propo	12,285	69	33	5,944
Family Remittances	1,042	6	3	10,000
Properties and Pensions	1,473	8	4	9,500
Government Benefits	204	16	1	650

Source: IHDS, 2004–05.

---

[1]SOIL Report, 2010, pp. 28–29.

[2]The India Human Development Survey (IHDS), p. 15.

non-agricultural wages, self-employment in small businesses, remittances and government benefits accounting for 45 per cent of rural household income. Median incomes from agricultural employment are also significantly lower than corresponding figures from other livelihood sources, although it should be noted that agricultural wages have increased significantly since this data was collected.

3.2 Growth in agricultural GDP

Growth rates in the agricultural sector were higher in the Eleventh-Plan period from 2007–08 to 2011–12 relative to the previous five years (see Figure 4.1). The average annual growth rate for the sector for this period was 3.6 per cent, significantly higher than the 2.4 per cent achieved during the Tenth Plan period from 2000–01 to 2006–07. An important driver of this increased growth has been the higher GCF—a measure of investments in the sector—which almost doubled in the last 10 years and registered a compound average annual growth rate of 8.1 per cent.[3] Growth in GCF, in turn, was driven by the private sector, with private investments such as the purchase of tractors, for example, comprising 82 per cent of GCF in the sector in 2009–10.

The Working Group on Agriculture for the Twelfth Plan attributes increased growth

Figure 4.1: Growth rates of agricultural GDP (%)

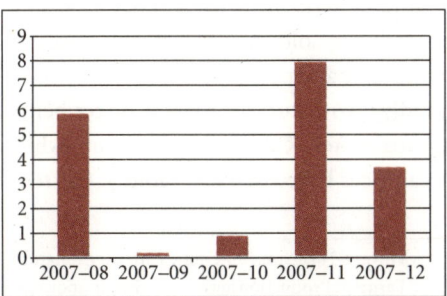

Source: Figure computed from Planning Commission (Government of India). 2013. *Twelfth Five Year Plan (2012–2017) Economic Sectors*, Volume II (Delhi: SAGE Publications India Pvt. Ltd.), p. 1, Table 12.1.

---

[3]Economic Survey of India (2012–13). New Delhi: Government of India, p. 174.

rates in the sector primarily to five factors:[4] better terms of trade for agricultural commodities, increased production of better quality seeds, increased public and private investment in the sector, adoption of better technology, and institutional factors such as the RKVY scheme that gave more flexibility to states to allocate public scheme funding according to the local context.

Increased public investments in the agricultural sector and related rural infrastructure, such as rural roads, are widely believed to have had significant impact in raising agricultural growth rates over the past five years. However, increased public spending has come mainly in the form of increased input subsidies. In 2008–09, the total fertilizer subsidy stood at ₹99,494.7 crore, which was more than 3.5 times the ₹28,035 crore total public investment in agriculture in areas such as irrigation and research and extension services.[5]

The trend of increased prices for agricultural commodities in international markets, transmitted to Indian markets through increased MSPs for a range of crops (illustrated in Figure 4.2) has been one of the main drivers of agricultural GDP growth. MSPs for common paddy increased by 32 per cent between 2010–11 and 2012–13, and those for coarse cereals and wheat increased by 79 per cent and 17 per cent respectively over the same period (figures not adjusted for inflation).

3.3 Increase in input usage

Corresponding to higher agricultural growth rates, the usage of two inputs, credit

---

[4]Report of the Working Group on Crop Husbandry, Agricultural Inputs, Demand and Supply Projections and Agricultural Statistics for the Twelfth Five-Year Plan (2012–17). 2011. Planning Commission, Government of India, October 2011. Available at: http://planningcommission.nic.in/aboutus/committee/wrkgrp12/agri/crop_husbandry.pdf, accessed in October 2013.

[5]Sharma, Vijay Paul. 2012. 'Dismantling Fertilizer Subsidies in India: Some Issues and Concerns for Farm Sector Growth', September. Indian Institute of Management, Ahmedabad, p. 3.

Figure 4.2: MSP for selected crops (₹ per quintal)

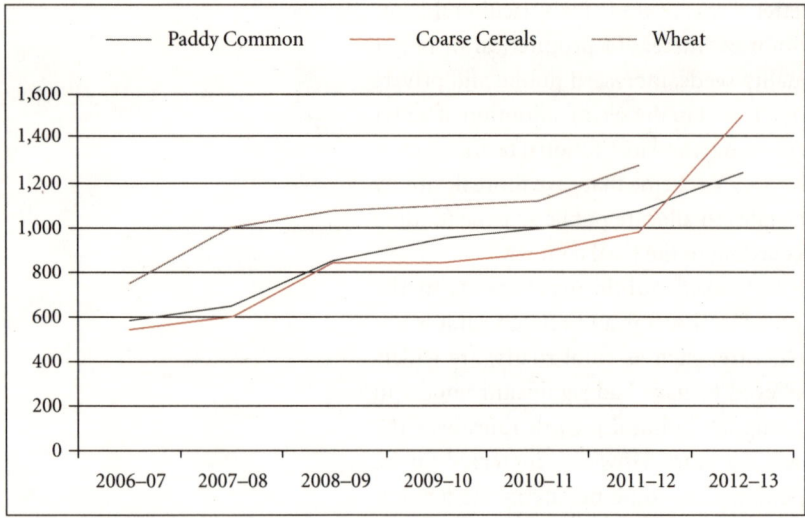

Source: RBI data.

and fertilizers, have shown a significant increase. Overall credit flows to the agricultural sector increased from ₹125,309 crore in 2004–05 to ₹511,029 crore in 2011–12, an increase of over four times. However, available evidence suggests that small and marginal farmers are being left out of increased credit flows to the sector in general and this is a major area requiring intervention. As illustrated in Figure 4.3, despite comprising an increased proportion

Figure 4.3: Share in landholdings, agricultural accounts, and disbursements by landholding size

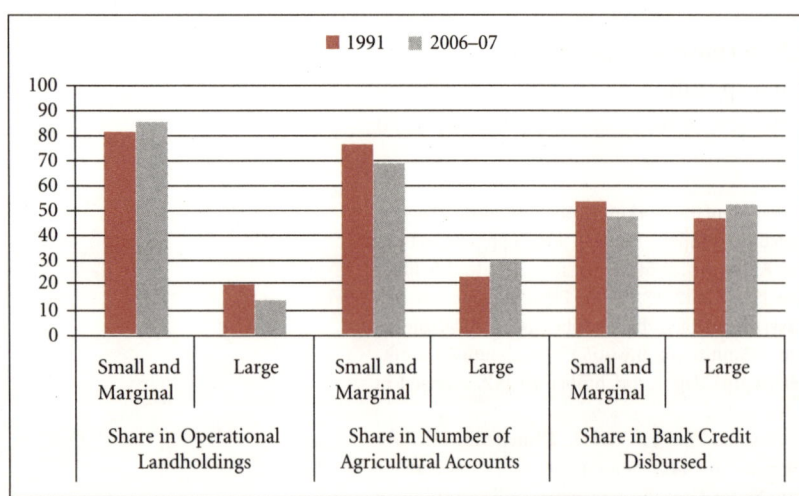

Source: RBI data.

of operational landholdings and total operated area, their share in credit disbursed declined from 53.66 per cent in 1991–92 to 47.61 per cent in 2006–07, and their share in the number of bank accounts fell from 78.85 per cent to 53.66 per cent during the same period.[6]

Total fertilizer use as well as fertilizer use per hectare has also shown an increase over the previous five years. Fertilizer usage shows marked increase even for small and marginal farmers with usage increasing from 104 kilograms per hectare in 1996–97 to 140 kilograms per hectare in 2006–07 for marginal farmers, and from 83 to 128 kilograms per hectare for small farmers during the same period.[7] Fertilizer subsidies have, therefore, resulted in increased fertilizer usage even by small and marginal farmers, but the appropriateness and efficiency of fertilizer usage, especially by marginal farmers remains a major area of concern.

Fertilizer prices were partially decontrolled in April and May 2010 when the government implemented the Nutrient-Based Subsidy (NBS) Policy for phosphatic, potassic, and complex fertilizers. Under the NBS, the government pays a fixed subsidy and the maximum retail price (MRP) is left open to be decided based on market supply and demand. However, one of the main fertilizers, urea, has been left out of the price decontrol exercise and the government continues to fix the MRP and pay a subsidy on each bag sold. As a result, the prices of phosphatic and pottasic fertilizers have risen rapidly—with current market prices being approximately ₹20–28,000 per ton—while urea prices have risen less rapidly. Current

[6]Mehrotra, Nirupam. 'Emerging Patterns in Share of Small Farms in Production and Credit: Implications for Policy Formulation', Paper submitted for 12th Annual Conference on Money and Finance in the Indian Economy, Indira Gandhi Institute of Development Research (IGIDR), Mumbai, 15 January 2010, p. 6.

[7]Sharma, Vijay Paul. 2012. 'Dismantling Fertilizer Subsidies in India: Some Issues and Concerns for Farm Sector Growth', September. Indian Institute of Management, Ahmedabad, p. 8.

urea prices in the market are approximately ₹5,500 per ton.

As a result of this large price difference, there has been a steep fall in the consumption of non-urea fertilizers in almost all states over the last two years. While urea usage rose by about 1 million ton, demand for non-urea fertilizers fell by more than 6 million tons, leading to poor soil nutrient balance.[8] The ideal use of fertilizers, expressed as a ratio of the percentage of Nitrogen, Phosphorous, and Potassium, or the NPK ratio, is 4:2:1. In 2012, a number of states had highly skewed NPK ratios, with fertilizer usage in Rajasthan having an NPK ratio of 35:16:1.[9]

Data on fertilizer use (see Table 4.2) shows that marginal farmers used twice as much fertilizer per hectare than large farmers, and small farmers used 90 per cent more fertilizer per hectare than large farmers. Overuse and inefficient use of fertilizers pose a number of challenges for sustainable farming livelihoods, including declining soil nutrient balance leading to lower yields, and increased costs of cultivation due to higher amounts being spent on fertilizers. Soil testing and knowledge dissemination to farmers is a key area for intervention to help correct imbalances in fertilizer use.

Table 4.2: Fertilizer usage by landholding size

	1996–97	2006–07	Percentage increase
Marginal (<1.0 ha)	104	140	35
Small (1.00–1.99 ha)	83	128	54
Semi-medium (2.00–3.99 ha)	75	108	44
Medium (3.00–9.99 ha)	68	95	40
Large (>10.0 ha)	51	68	33
All groups	77	113	47

Source: Government of India.

---

[8] http://www.livemint.com/Politics/deY7aSKol9AVNEdi6zPToM/EY-to-study-nutrientbased-subsidy-impact-on-fertilizer-pric.html, accessed in October 2013.

[9] Ibid.

A centrally sponsored scheme, the National Project on Management of Soil Health and Fertility (NPMSHF) was introduced in 2009 to expand the network of soil testing laboratories (STLs), to test soil samples, and to issue soil cards to farmers. The soil cards sought to clearly communicate soil analyses to farmers so as to encourage optimal use of fertilizers. However, as of 2012 there were only 1,087 STLs nationally. Although, according to the Ministry of Agriculture, 5.05 crore provisional soil cards have been handed out to farmers, there is limited evidence of impact from the field. One thrust of livelihood interventions in the sector should be to increase awareness of the importance of soil testing, to link farmers to the NPMSHF scheme, and to ensure that the quality of testing and soil cards given are satisfactory.

3.4 Rise in agricultural wages

Agricultural labourers have seen an improvement in their livelihoods over the period from 2002 to 2010. Agricultural wage rates—across a range of activities—of both men and women increased by more than 200 per cent during this period, as listed in Table 4.3. Wage rates of women, however, continued to lag significantly behind those of men. As of 2010–11, average wage rates of women across all agricultural activities were only 79 per cent of those of men.

Between 2010–11 and 2013, wage rates have risen even faster. According to Ministry of Labour data, as of February 2013, average wage rates across agricultural labour activities for men was ₹180.3, a 47 per cent increase over just a two-year period. However, as shown in Table 4.4, there were significant variations in wage rates between states, with wage rates in Bihar and Uttar Pradesh lagging significantly behind the national average. Agricultural wage rates also lagged significantly behind wage rates in the non-farm sector. For example, the highest wage rate for men in agricultural labour, for ploughing, lagged 28 per cent behind wage rates for carpenters in rural areas at the all India level.

Table 4.3: Agricultural wage rates (2002–11)

Year	Ploughing	Sowing	Weeding	Transplanting	Harvesting	Winnowing	Threshing	Average across activities	Percentage increase
2002–03									
Men	71.53	62.62	53.9	57.33	58.03	52.88	57.22	59.07	
Women	40.46	44.2	44.9	48.24	47.86	44.11	46.84	45.23	
2004–05									
Men	72.28	66.09	57.79	62.06	61.95	54.93	59.15	62.04	5
Women	41.58	46.17	46.73	50.98	50.99	42.69	46.63	46.54	3
2006–07									
Men	81.79	73.29	64.97	69.47	68.45	66.18	67.4	70.22	13
Women	42.37	51.41	52.82	56.44	55.69	51.04	54.41	52.03	12
2007–08									
Men	91.38	79.28	70.07	73.79	75.24	71.06	73.5	76.33	9
Women	49.96	57.18	58.27	61.93	62.31	56.09	59.41	57.88	11
2008–09									
Men	102.9	90	80.15	83.28	87.05	81.23	85.06	87.10	14
Women	55.43	65	68.02	71.43	71.58	65.08	67.66	66.31	15
2009–10									
Men	120.85	104.52	92.78	98.29	102.82	96.32	100.23	102.26	17
Women	70.43	79.47	78.94	86.71	84.95	79.02	82.12	80.23	21
2010–11									
Men	145.51	125.75	111.22	120.19	122.53	112.82	117.78	122.26	20
Women	87.23	98.17	95.79	104.17	102.36	94.83	97.08	97.09	21

Source: Ministry of Labour.

Table 4.4: Wage rates for selected farm and non-farm activities for selected states (February 2013)

	Male		Female		Male carpenter
	Ploughing	Sowing	Ploughing	Sowing	
All India	209.96	118.93	182.61	147.65	268.68
Bihar	185.28		172.41	145.78	239.62
Madhya Pradesh	128.68		126.53	112.59	163.73
Rajasthan	216.82		197.78	159.38	347.22
Uttar Pradesh	167.97		165.48	134.11	276.69
Odisha	145		138.89		245.76

Source: Ministry of Labour.

There is an ongoing debate over the cause of agricultural wage increases, with one view crediting Mahatma Gandhi National Rural Employment Guarantee Act (MGNREGA) with creating a minimum floor wage and subsequent shortages of farm labour and higher negotiating power among the poorest. The counter view points to the relatively low uptake—in terms of average days of employment generated, especially in the poorest states—and the relatively minuscule percentage of total rural wages represented by MGNREGA outlays to argue that overall economic growth, urban migration, and increased global market price trends for agricultural commodities are the key drivers of rural agricultural wage increases.[10]

3.5 Rapid growth of horticulture

Increasing per capita income and urbanization are driving demand for more fruits and vegetables, leading to significantly higher growth rates in horticultural production. Growth rates of horticultural output over

[10]For example, Bhalla, Surjit. 2013. 'The Unimportance of MNREGA'. *Indian Express*. 24 July. Available at: http://www.indianexpress.com/news/the-unimportance-of-nrega/1145676/, accessed in October 2013.

Figure 4.4: Production of fruits and vegetables (million tons)

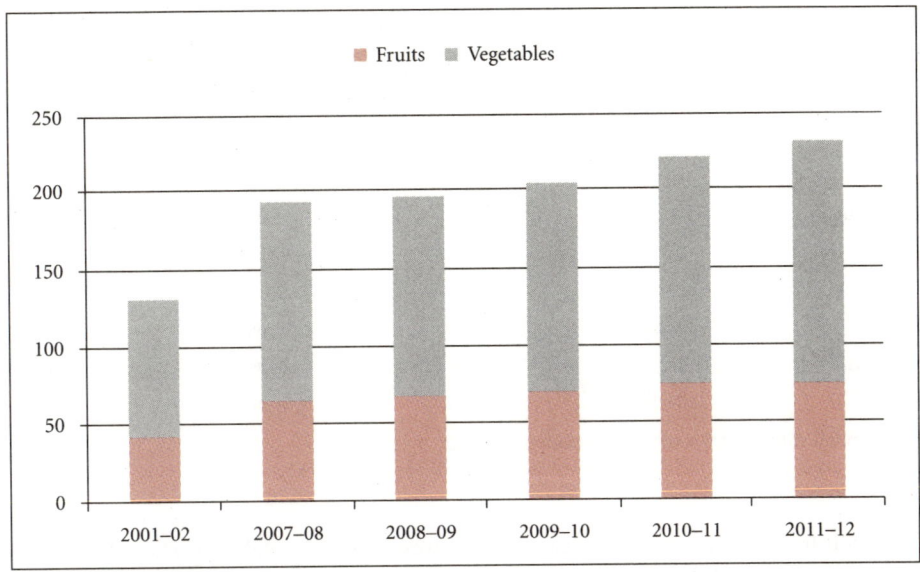

Source: Economic Survey of India, 2012.

the previous five years was 4.7 per cent relative to a 2.7 per cent growth rate for non-horticultural crops comprising foodgrains, oilseeds, and fibres.[11] Over the past decade, the growth rates for horticulture have been even higher, with production increasing by 47 per cent between 2001 and 2007 (see Figure 4.4). Cropping area and total production of fruits and vegetables have been growing at approximately 6 per cent over the past decade while foodgrains and pulses grew at less than 2 per cent over the same period.[12]

According to an assessment of supply-demand scenario by the Working Group on Foodgrains for the Twelfth Five-Year Plan, domestic supplies of cereal crops are likely to exceed demand for the plan period ending in 2016–17.[13] It is unclear how the proposed NFSA will influence demand and supply of cereal crops as the level of increased procurement under the Act is still unclear. The main crops for which demand is slated to exceed domestic supply in this period are pulses and oilseeds, and fruits and vegetables.[14] These projected supply-demand gaps provide an opportunity for livelihood interventions targeting horticultural livelihoods that assist small and marginal farmers to diversify and improve their incomes through shifting a part of their cropping to higher value fruits and vegetables.

3.6 Key areas of concern

In spite of the relatively positive trends in output, wages, and diversification towards higher value non-cereal crops, there are key weaknesses in the sector. These include: the higher proportion of the poor—concentrated geographically in a few states in central and north India—dependent on agricultural livelihoods; increasing distress faced by small and marginal farmers, fueled by declining landholding sizes, rising costs of cultivation, and inefficient supply chains; and skewed public investments primarily in the form of input subsidies that disproportionately benefit large farmers. In addition, two significant additional gaps require increased focus: the historical lack of focus on the large number of women farmers

---

[11]Twelfth Five-Year Plan. Volume II. Planning Commission of India. New Delhi: SAGE Publications, p. 7.

[12]Ministry of Agriculture, Government of India.

[13]NCAER—Agricultural Outlook and Situation Analysis Reports. February 2013. p. x.

---

[14]Ibid.

Table 4.5:   Profile of agriculture for selected states

	Rural poverty* – number of person (lakhs)	Proportion of total workforce employed in agriculture[+]	Agricultural GDP growth rates over the Eleventh Plan period	Share of agriculture and allied sector in state GDP
All India	2,166.58	55.2%*	3.6%	14.1%
Bihar	320.40	74%	3.3%	23.57%
Madhya Pradesh	234.06	70%	4.4%	23.76%
Rajasthan	84.19	62%	5.5%	20.89%
Uttar Pradesh	479.35	59%	2.8%	22.53%
Odisha	126.14	62%	3.1%	17.33%
Chhattisgarh	88.90	75%	7.3%	19.17%
Jharkhand	104.09	63%	8.0%	14.77%

Source: *Tendulkar Method, Planning Commission, 2011–12.
+*Based* on Census 2011 data, including both marginal and main workers, urban and rural.

and agricultural labourers; and increasing adverse environmental impact in terms of declining water tables and soil fertility.

As illustrated in Table 4.5, a few states where the highest number of the rural poor reside—Bihar, Madhya Pradesh, Rajasthan, Uttar Pradesh, Chhattisgarh, and Jharkhand—have a higher proportion of the population employed in agriculture compared to the national average; and a higher than average contribution of agriculture to state GDP. Although these states have been showing a positive trend in growth rates in agricultural GDP over the Eleventh Plan period, more initiatives are needed to improve agricultural livelihoods in these states.

Cost of cultivation increasing for farmers

According to data from the Directorate of Economics and Statistics, there has been a significant increase in the total cost of cultivation between 2007–08 and 2010–11. For example, looking at the data on cost of cultivation of paddy in five selected states—Bihar, Madhya Pradesh, Uttar Pradesh, Odisha, and Chhattisgarh—there have been cost increases ranging from a 38 per cent increase in Bihar to a 76 per cent increase in Madhya Pradesh, driven by cost increases in labour, seeds, fertilizers, and interest on working capital. The single largest cost component was the cost of labour, accounting on average for 36 per cent of total costs

across the five selected states. Increased cultivation costs are putting pressure on the sustainability of small and marginal farmers and interventions that provide livelihood support through optimal use of inputs and collective procurement and diversification of households' income sources will be critical in sustaining their livelihoods.

Landholding sizes are declining

According to the World Bank's annual World Development Report in 2008,

> . . .average landholding fell from 2.6 hectares in 1960 to 1.4 hectares in 2000, and it is still declining. Average farm holding size is getting smaller with overall average farm size in 2010–11 estimated at 1.16 hectares compared to 1.23 hectares in 2005–06, and 2.26 hectares in 1970–71.

Figure 4.5, reproduced from NCAER's AOSAR, illustrates the trend of declining average landholding sizes, the increasing proportion of small landholdings in the country, and how current trends will result in average landholding size of only 1 hectare within the next five years.

Sixty-three per cent of landholdings in India now stand at less than 1 hectare (see Figure 4.6). According to data from the Ministry of Agriculture, average landholding size for this segment is 0.4 hectares (see Figure 4.7).

Figure 4.5: Number of landholdings and average landholding sizes

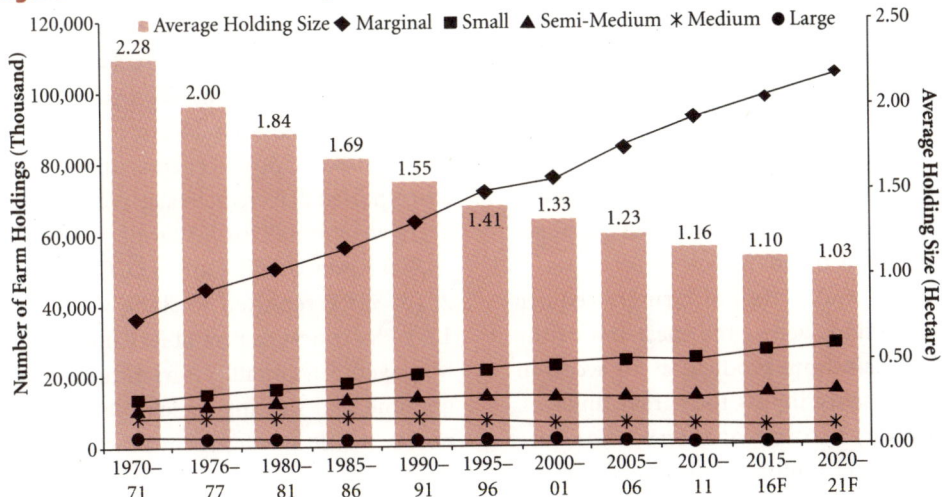

Source: Data from Directorate of Economics and Statistics, Ministry of Agriculture.
Note: Extrapolations beyond 2010–11 are based on trend growth in each variable between 1970–71 and 2010–11.

Figure 4.6: Distribution of operational landholdings

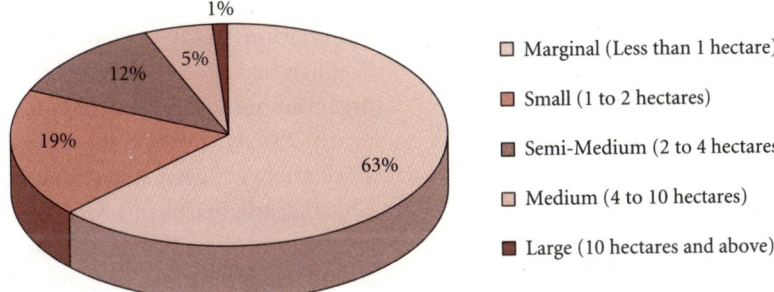

- Marginal (Less than 1 hectare)
- Small (1 to 2 hectares)
- Semi-Medium (2 to 4 hectares)
- Medium (4 to 10 hectares)
- Large (10 hectares and above)

Source: Ministry of Agriculture, 2001 data.

4. Areas for intervention and overview of existing interventions

This section highlights key areas for livelihood interventions based on the current trends in the agricultural sector described above and gives an overview of selected livelihood interventions in each area. A review of available evidence presented above highlights areas—both gaps and opportunities—that livelihood interventions need to focus on. They include the following:

4.1 Small landholdings

Smallholder farmers are beset by a range of problems related to the small size of farms, their consequent small revenue streams, and

Figure 4.7: Average size of operational holdings

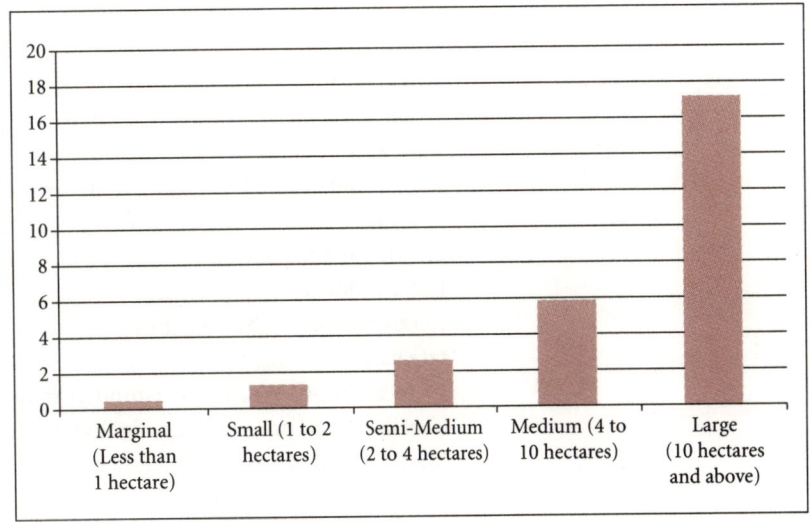

Source: Ministry of Agriculture, 2001 data.

lack of resources. They often lack sufficient marketable surplus; their relative cost of accessing technology, information, credit, and markets are high; they are disadvantaged in their ability to access irrigation networks; and they are more vulnerable to various risks such as price fluctuations, changes in weather patterns, and changes in market demand.

Small and marginal farmers require interventions across the spectrum of the value chain from production, to access to better quality inputs to market linkages. However, two sets of interventions are particularly important to overcome the diseconomies of scale faced by such farmers: aggregation of farmers and produce through collectives; and access to legal titles through tenancy reforms.

Aggregation

Civil society initiatives in this area typically seek to organize farmers into self-managed collective structures; and, thereby, address problems associated with small landholdings through opening up economies of scale in procurement, storage, and transportation to markets. Often, such initiatives also seek to empower farmers through training and provision of technical services to better manage existing local resources so as to improve productivity and incomes.

The most common institutional form for these collectives are Producer Companies. Some well-known examples flagged in previous SOIL reports include the Indian Organic Farmers Produce Company Ltd, Kerala, producing certified organic products; Vanilla India Producer Company Ltd (Vanilco), also in Kerala with members growing and marketing Vanilla; and Banana India Producer Company Ltd (BIPCL), in Kerala, formed by banana growers to facilitate value addition.

In addition, World Bank-funded state-level livelihood programmes—including the Madhya Pradesh District Poverty Initiatives Project (MPDPIP) and the Society for Eradication of Rural Poverty (SERP) in Andhra Pradesh—are a major driver of aggregation efforts. MPDPIP between 2001 and 2008 reported that they had organized 17 district-based produced companies with 42,000 shareholder producers, of which 15 were agri-based producer companies. They also reported that credit linkages of over ₹45 crore were mobilized for farmers through 26,000 Kisan Credit Cards (KCCs). As of 2013, SERP reported working with over 1.6 lakh farmers as part of its Community Managed Sustainable Agricultural programme and shifting 11 lakh farmers to non-pesticide management practices and farming.[15]

Key civil society initiatives that aggregate a large number of farmers into collective structures include those by Pradhan, Dhan Foundation, Action for Social Advancement (ASA), and Bharatiya Agro Industries Foundation Development Research Foundation (BAIF). As of March 2012, Pradhan had promoted 1,190 cluster-level organizations and 43 federations covering nearly 25 lakh households spread across 42 districts in seven states: Assam, Bihar, Chhattisgarh, Jharkhand, Madhya Pradesh, Odisha, and West Bengal. The main crops covered under the interventions are paddy, maize, minor millets, wheat, fruits, and vegetables.

As of March 2011, Dhan reached a total of just under 10 lakh households organized into 283 producer federations in 12 states through initiatives covering agriculture, microfinance, and water conservation. So far, Dhan and the farmer federations have mobilized ₹805 million towards conservation and development of over 1,300 irrigation tanks and ponds. ASA is working with soybean farmers in Madhya Pradesh and spurring the adoption of best practices such as seed treatment, line sowing, use of recommended doses of inputs, equal wages to women labourers, safe usage of pesticides, and other environmental safeguards. As of

---

[15]https://www.serp.ap.gov.in/SHG/index.jsp, accessed in October 2013.

2011–12, ASA had trained 14,306 soybean farmers who have been certified by an independent third-party certifier, aggregated produce from certified farmers, and created supplier relationships with European buyers that resulted in higher revenue and income for the farmers. Across all its activities, ASA has organized farmers into 40 producer companies having a total turnover of over ₹230 million.

Under its Wadi programme, BAIF has worked with 200,000 tribal families in the states of Maharashtra, Gujarat, Karnataka, Rajasthan, Madhya Pradesh, Uttar Pradesh, Bihar, Jharkhand, and Chhattisgarh to plant fruit orchards in 62,500 hectares of degraded lands. The Wadi programme seeks to improve biodiversity while providing additional income to poor tribal families. BAIF promoted 49 tribal cooperatives and an apex marketing federation—Vasundhara Agri-Horti Producer Company Ltd (VAPCOL)—to market fresh produce generated by the Wadi programme under the brand name 'Vrindavan'. VAPCOL had a total turnover of ₹5.6 crore in 2010–11.

Despite significant donor funding for aggregation efforts, there is still little independently verified data and information available on the performance and commercial sustainability of producer companies post-grant funding, which is hampering the development of standard models of aggregation that can be scaled up. A key area for donor intervention is to commission independent reviews and studies of the shareholdings, operations, and audited financial statements of a sample of producer companies, so as to create sector-wide benchmarks for the cost of promotion, best practices in operations, and commercial viability.

Tenancy reforms

Although there are a number of initiatives that look at aggregating producers into collective structures and many of them work with tenant farmers, the agenda for tenancy reforms at the state and national level is languishing. Currently, most states either prohibit leasing of land completely or place severe restrictions on such leasing, leading to informal tenancy arrangements that serve as a barrier for small farmers to access credit and subsidized inputs (see Box 4.1).

The Annual Economic Outlook 2012–13 of the Prime Ministers Economic Advisory Council (PMEAC) estimates (based on field studies in different parts of the country) that the area under informal tenancy varies between 15 and 35 per cent of total cultivated area and that more than 90 per cent of tenant farmers were either landless labourers

---

Box 4.1: *Tenancy laws*

Tenancy laws are a state subject and vary from state to state. But they broadly fall under four categories:

- **Virtual ban** on agricultural tenancies: Kerala, Jammu & Kashmir
- **General prohibition** on agricultural tenancies, but exemptions for certain categories such as widows and minors: Karnataka, Himachal Pradesh, Madhya Pradesh, Uttar Pradesh, Odisha, and Telangana area of Andhra Pradesh
- **No explicit prohibition, but discourage tenancies** by empowering tenants with protected rights on the tenanted land, either as perpetual tenants or through rights to purchase within a specified period: West Bengal, Punjab, Haryana, Gujarat, Maharashtra, Bihar, and Assam
- **Few restrictions on tenancies**, although there are minimum lengths of tenancies and/or maximum rent levels: Rajasthan, Tamil Nadu, and non-Telangana areas of Andhra Pradesh

Source: Flow of Credit to Agriculture Sector with Special Reference to Tenant Farmers, Oral Lessees and Agricultural Labourers, IBA Sub-Committee on Flow of Credit to Agriculture, Indian Banks Association.

or marginal farmers.[16] Legalizing tenancy arrangements and registering them formally would lead to better functioning of land leasing markets, which would benefit farmers across different sizes of landholdings. Small and marginal farmers would benefit from being able to augment their landholdings and increase their labour efficiency through leasing in, and labour-scarce and/or large farmers benefit by being able to lease their land and pursue occupational diversification without risk of losing their ownership rights. Formal tenancy rights would also play a key role in increasing access to credit for small and marginal farmers by enabling them to seek membership in Primary Agricultural Cooperatives and to access formal bank financing.

4.2 Yield gaps

For the primary cereal crops grown, there is not only lower yields compared to international standards but also large variability in yield within and between states. In rice, for example, the poorest states all have a lower yield than the national average, ranging from 29 to 54 per cent of the yield achieved in Punjab, the highest yielding state.

The gaps are not only based on differences between resource endowments, such as landholding sizes, and the difference between irrigated and rain-fed agriculture. They also reflect a lack of adequate focus on strategies to increase yields for low resource-endowed farmers. There is room for a number of measures targeting such farmers, including research and experimentation on new strains of seeds, and improving their growing practices through the provision of soil testing, training, and extension services.

Improving extension services

A key intervention to improve yields is improved extension services to transmit better growing practices and technology to farmers. In 2005–06, a central government scheme—the Agricultural Technology Management Agency (ATMA)—was launched to improve the quality of public extension services across the country and to specifically target small, marginal, and women farmers. ATMA is a registered society of farmers and key stakeholders at the district level, which facilitates planning for local extension needs. Local plans are aggregated upwards to the district and state level, with the central government funding up to 90 per cent of planned expenditures. ATMA mandates that women farmers and women extension functionaries utilize 30 per cent of its resources and activities.

Currently, ATMAs are operating in 614 districts across 28 states. Since its inception, the Ministry of Agriculture reports that it has benefited 2.19 crore farmers, 25 per cent of them women, through extension activities and that 6,919 'farmer schools', which are model farms run by local farmers, have been set up. An impact assessment study based on a sample survey of farmers in Uttar Pradesh and Haryana[17] found that there has been an increase in extension activities such as trainings, demonstrations, and exposure visits after the launch of the ATMA programme and that 52 per cent of farmers surveyed felt that they had gained knowledge of new practices and technologies. However, only 31 per cent of farmers found the training programmes 'fully useful' and 26 per cent did not find them useful at all while the remaining termed them as partially useful.

Another intervention that has achieved significant scale and has the potential to transform the model of extension service provision is the work by Digital Green on developing and disseminating videos of farmers explaining and demonstrating a range of best practices. The recordings are

---

[16]Economic Outlook. 2012/13. Economic Advisory Council to the Prime Minister. Government of India. August, 2012, p. 59.

[17]Evaluation and Impact Assessment of ATMA. AFC India Limited.

made by experts at the grassroots level—scientists from government institutions, NGO experts, field staff, and progressive farmers—but the videos are recorded in local languages and dialects, and local farmers, individually or in groups, usually feature in the videos. As of January 2011, 2,021 videos had been developed and disseminated to nearly 123,000 farmer households across seven states—Andhra Pradesh, Bihar, Jharkhand, Karnataka, Madhya Pradesh, Uttar Pradesh, and Odisha. Digital Green also partners with other organizations with field presence—including PRADAN and SERP—to display the videos in target villages, interact with farmers to promote adoption of best practices, and conduct follow-up studies to measure adoption rates of improved growing practices.

More interventions such as these are needed to further improve the quality of extension services, especially in terms of developing content modules comprising a package of practices for different crops covering the entire agricultural value chain. An International Food Policy Research Institute review of extension services in December 2010 found that '. . .despite a wide range of reform initiatives in agricultural extension in India in the past decades, the coverage of, access to, and quality of information provided to marginalized and poor farmers is uneven'.[18]

The International Food Policy Research Institute (IFPRI) review also flags that the scope of agricultural extension services need to be expanded from simply the transmission of new technology to improve productivity to a wider role of '. . .developing human and social capital, enhancing skills and knowledge for production and processing, facilitating access to markets and trade, organizing farmers and producer groups, and working with farmers toward sustainable natural resource management practices'.[19]

Technology interventions: Hybrid seeds and drip irrigation

Technology interventions looking at higher yields have occurred primarily in two sets of areas: higher quality seeds and more efficient irrigation systems.

Major yield increases during the last decade—primarily relating to cotton, maize, and basmati rice—were driven by the use of new, better quality seeds. The private sector has played an increasing role in the development of new seed varieties that currently accounts for 39 per cent of total seed production. According to the Planning Commission, production of quality seeds—from both the private and public sector—doubled from 140 lakh quintals in 2004–05 to 280 lakh quintals in 2009–10, contributing significantly to increased yield performance during the Eleventh Plan period.

However, use of quality seeds varies by region and crop and is still low relative to total seed use by farmers. Further interventions are needed both for development of new seed varieties specifically suited to small and marginal farmers in rain-fed areas; and for distribution of better varieties to small and marginal farmers as part of agricultural extension systems. With increasing private sector involvement, there is also the need for a better regulatory system to protect farmers against non-performance of seeds in relation to explicit and implicit claims of seed germination rates. The Seeds Bill, which sought to improve the regulatory infrastructure on seeds, was introduced in Parliament in 2004 but is still under consideration of the Parliamentary Standing Committee on Agriculture.

In irrigation, studies have confirmed higher yields in a number of crops through

[18]Glendenning, Claire J., Suresh Babu, and Kwadwo Asenso-Okyere. 2010. 'Review of Agricultural Extension in India: Are Farmers' Information Needs Being Met?' International Food Policy Research Institute (IFPRI), Discussion Paper 01048.

[19]Ibid.

the adoption of drip irrigation technologies.[20] Adoption of drip irrigation is spreading rapidly, although from a very low base, due to the development of low-cost technologies and a number of new providers selling drip irrigation systems to farmers. These providers include major private companies such as Jain Irrigation and Netafim as well as social enterprises such as International Development Enterprises (IDE). Jain Irrigation alone reports that it has sold 30 lakh micro-irrigation systems as of 2012 and that its sale of such systems has been increasing at a compound annual growth rate of 24 per cent between 2008 and 2012. Products offered by providers include drip and sprinkle irrigation systems, rope and treadle pumps, and water storage systems that enable small farmers to irrigate their land cost-effectively without the need for electricity.

However, a 2013 intervention by International Water Management Institute (IWMI)-Tata Water Policy Research Programme in Coimbatore District of Tamil Nadu found that over 90 per cent of farmers who invested in drip irrigation systems did not know how to use them properly and that increases in crop productivity were disappointing.[21] They found that intensive training and instructions in the use of the drip irrigation systems were required to achieve yield increases.

System of Rice Intensification (SRI)

One of the key initiatives targeting yields that has achieved scale is the SRI—a package of better growing practices to improve rice yields. Although household-level adoption data is not available, SRI is now being more widely adopted—especially in the rice-growing states of Tamil Nadu, Himachal Pradesh, Uttarakhand, Andhra Pradesh, and Tripura—due to concerted efforts by a range of donors, NGOs, agricultural universities, and government agencies. A 2011 study covering 2,234 rice farmers in 13 major rice-growing states to analyze the adoption level and impact of various SRI practices found that SRI adopters displayed comparatively higher yield, higher gross margin, and lower production costs.[22] However, the study also found that only 20 per cent of farmers adopted the full package of practices and most farmers did not adopt the full package due to several constraints including the scarcity of water, labour shortages, and lack of knowledge of the full set of practices.

4.3 Underdeveloped supply chains and linkages to markets

Lack of supply chain infrastructure and multiple intermediaries between farm and consumer lead to a number of problems including high wastage of fresh produce and poor price realization for farmers.

Studies by the World Bank and McKinsey & Company estimate that 20–40 per cent of India's total production is lost to wastage.[23]

The high level of wastage in the system is due to poor and multiple handling, improper

[20] See, for example, Kumar, Dinesh, Madar Samad, U.A. Amarasinghe, and O.P. Singh. 2006. 'Water Savings and Yield Enhancing Technologies: How Far Can They Contribute to Water Productivity Enhancements in India Agriculture?' Draft, IWMI-CPWF Project on Strategic Analyses of India's National River-Linking Project, International Water Management Institute (IWMI), Colombo, Sri Lanka. Available at: http://nrlp.iwmi.org/PDocs/DReports/Phase_01/13.%20Water%20Saving%20Technologies%20-%20Kumar%20et%20al.pdf, accessed in October 2013.

[21] See 'Making a Difference Drop by Drop'. 2013. IWMI. Available at: http://www.iwmi.cgiar.org/Publications/Success_Stories/PDF/2013/Issue_18-Making_a_difference_drop_by_drop.pdf, accessed in October 2013.

[22] Palanisami, K., K.R. Karunakaran, and Upali Amarasinghe. 2012. 'Impact of the System of Rice Intensification (SRI): Analysis of SRI Practices in 13 States of India'. IWMI-Tata Water Policy Programme.

[23] CII-McKinsey & Company. 1997. *Modernizing the Indian Food Chain, Food & Agriculture Integrated Development Action Plan (FAIDA)*. New Delhi: CII and McKinsey & Company; Mattoo, Aaditya, Deepak Mishra, and Ashish Narayan. 2007. *From Competition at Home to Competing Abroad: A Case Study of India's Horticulture*. Washington, DC: World Bank; New Delhi: Oxford University Press.

Figure 4.8:   Wastage in the supply chain for selected commodities

Source: World Bank, 2007.

bagging without crating, lack of temperature-controlled vehicles and storage facilities and poor infrastructure (roads, warehouses and market yards).[24]

Figure 4.8, taken from the same World Bank report, shows data on wastage for specific commodities at various stages of the supply chain.[25]

Other studies point to the poor infrastructure at the local *mandi*s, which is the first stop for agricultural commodities after they leave the farm. The majority of

wholesale markets in the country are not paved, do not have grading or cold storage facilities, and lack basic sanitation and pest control facilities.[26]

There is evidence that fractured supply chains with multiple intermediaries result in arbitrary pricing for consumers and poor revenue realization for farmers. Figure 4.9 shows large price variations in selected commodities across major Indian cities that cannot be explained by factoring in transportation costs between

Figure 4.9:   Regional price variations for fruits and vegetables

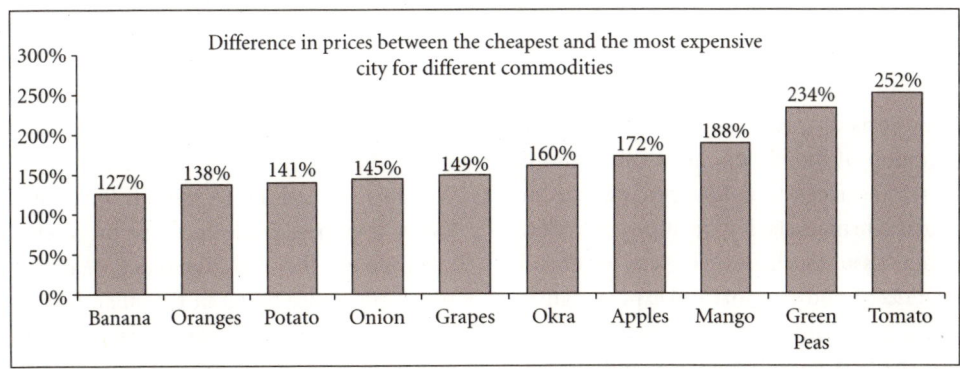

Source: World Bank, 2007.

[24] Mattoo, Aaditya, Deepak Mishra, and Ashish Narayan. 2007. *From Competition at Home to Competing Abroad: A Case Study of India's Horticulture.* Washington, DC: World Bank; New Delhi: Oxford University Press.
    [25] Ibid.

[26] Fafchamps, M., R.V. Vargas-Hill, and B. Minten. 2008. 'Quality Control in Non-staple Food Markets: Evidence from India', *Agricultural Economics*, 38(3): 251–66.

these cities.[27] Large price fluctuations in the prices of key staples such as tomatoes and onions over the past year reiterate the extent of supply chain gaps, as the price differentials are not strongly correlated with lower production volumes; and the higher wholesale and retail prices are not being transmitted back to farmers.

The complexity of interventions required to address the multiple gaps in existing supply chains has meant that there are few examples of successful interventions at scale. Creating and strengthening end-to-end supply chains requires interventions across a spectrum of activities covering aggregation, procurement, storage and delivery of produce to buyers, processing and packaging of produce, and connecting to or setting up of a distribution and retail network. The logistical challenges of undertaking such interventions coupled with infrastructural gaps have led to even private sector efforts by large business conglomerates such as Reliance and Tata—who recently closed Khet Se, its fresh produce procurement and distribution joint venture set up in 2008—failing to become commercially viable despite significant investments.

Supply chain interventions need to address gaps across a range of areas including:

Information access

Farmers have limited access to supply chain-related information that would help them in making optimal production and sales decisions. Although the widespread adoption of mobile phone technologies is increasing access to market pricing data for proximate markets, information on a range of other issues such as end buyers, buyer and producer trends, import and export regulations, grade and standards specifications, post-harvest handling advice, and storage and transport recommendations are not being generated and widely disseminated to farmers.

A number of interventions are seeking to leverage the widespread adoption of mobile technologies to lower costs of collecting and disseminating information on prices and growing practices to farmers. Reuters Market Lite, a commercial provider, transmits agricultural information—such as crop advisory, block-level weather forecasts, commodity news and information, and spot market prices—over mobile phones to farmers. Reuters reports that it has achieved 1 million unique subscribers so far in an estimated 50,000 villages across 13 states and is providing information for 300 crops and about 1,300 markets.

Procurement, logistics, and distribution

The chain of activities between procurement and sale of agricultural produce involve a number of discrete points of intervention, but require integrated end-to-end solutions coordinating between farmers, intermediaries, logistics providers, distributors, and retailers; and developing infrastructure, processes, and technologies so as to deliver produce to buyers in a timely and cost-effective manner. Large infrastructural gaps in storage capacity, especially cold storage capacity, poor transportation infrastructure, and information asymmetries along the supply chain make the logistical exercise involved daunting and costly.

In addition to the large aggregator models—such as Pradhan, Dhan and ASA—described above, a few small interventions are seeking to build information technology-based solutions for more efficient supply chain management. eFarm, a social enterprise based in Chennai, has set up a network of collection centres close to villages and a network of distribution centres in urban areas. Key parts of their business model include training transporters in handling fresh produce to minimize wastage, forecasting demand and supply to guide procurement volumes and on-time delivery, and developing a back-end information

---

[27]Mattoo, Aaditya, Deepak Mishra, and Ashish Narayan. 2007. *From Competition at Home to Competing Abroad: A Case Study of India's Horticulture.* Washington, DC: World Bank; New Delhi: Oxford University Press.

technology system that enables it to track operations in real time. Another start-up, Logistimo, has developed mobile applications for basic, low-cost mobile phones that enable semi-literate users to generate real-time data on orders, inventory levels, and transaction history from collection and distribution centres.

Agricultural Produce Marketing Centre (APMC) act reforms

One of the key bottlenecks to the lack of large private investments into supply chain gaps has been policy uncertainty and the continued grip of APMCs on local procurement. APMCs regulate who the farmers sell to, who can participate in the market, and where markets can be established. Although they were set up to benefit farmers, the wide powers enjoyed by APMCs have resulted in collusive behaviour and cartelization by local traders, obscuring the price discovery process at the first stage of the supply chain. The distance of APMCs from village also disadvantage small and marginal farmers, who mostly sell to brokers who are able to aggregate produce at the farm gate and incur transportation costs to the APMCs.

Seventeen states—Andhra Pradesh, Arunachal Pradesh, Assam, Chhattisgarh, Goa, Gujarat, Himachal Pradesh, Jharkhand, Karnataka, Maharashtra, Mizoram, Nagaland, Odisha, Rajasthan, Sikkim, Uttarakhand, and Tripura—have undertaken APMC reforms allowing direct marketing, contract farming, and private markets. An additional four states—Delhi, Madhya Pradesh, Punjab, and Haryana —have undertaken partial reforms involving either direct marketing or contract farming; and three states—Bihar, Kerala, and Manipur—have no APMC Act at all, with Bihar having repealed the existing Act.

However, in practice, poor infrastructure and the continued power of APMCs— trading licences are given according to norms set by the APMC governing councils—and political lobbying by traders has resulted in very few private market yards being set up even in states that have undertaken reforms. Licences are given in a non-transparent manner, for a fixed time period, and often with arbitrary conditions, for example, preventing trade within 25–50 kilometres of an existing *mandi*, which discourages private investments in market yards. The case of Metro Cash and Carry, that was granted a licence in 2011 under the reformed APMC Act in Karnataka to set up private market yards, which was then subsequently cancelled due to protests by traders in the state[28] exemplifies the weak political resolve towards reform in practice and the continued disincentives for private investments into market yards. Given the existing dynamics and the inability of established Indian corporates to build supply chains, it is unlikely that FDI in retail, promoted as a solution to supply chain gaps in the sector, will have any meaningful impact in the short run.

The Twelfth Plan Working Group on Horticulture and Plantations concluded that

> …that the present model of Market Sector Reforms which is trying to create space for a new set of modern markets in coexistence with much less transparent procedures in APMC regulated markets is unlikely to result in any major private investment in modern marketing infrastructure.[29]

It recommended that both APMCs and private markets be regulated by the same set of rules, which would involve redefining the role of APMC management and removing their powers for arbitrary decision-making on registering buyers and setting up of private markets in APMC areas.

The experience of Bihar, which completely repealed the APMC Act, suggests that further APMC reforms need to be carried

---

[28]http://www.business-standard.com/article/companies/k-taka-govt-cancels-private-market-yard-licence-of-metro-cash-carry-111022800255_1.html, accessed in October 2013.

[29]Twelfth Five-Year Plan. Volume II. Planning Commission of India. SAGE Publications, p. 24.

out with caution and in conjunction with a host of other reforms and incentives such as tax holidays that promote private market yards. Bihar repealed the Act in 2006 and all the APMCs across the state were abolished. However, a study of the impact of the repeal found that it had actually created a large vacuum in terms of institutional mechanisms for the sale of agricultural produce, and small-scale farmers have become even more dependent on traders that were earlier functioning though the *mandis*.[30] Anecdotal evidence from practitioners also suggests that small farmers are now facing even more coercion and exploitation in local agricultural markets.

In addition to APMCs, inter-state barriers and differing taxation regimes in each state are also a major bottleneck to creating efficient supply chains and policy reforms are needed to create a unified national market through removal of such inter-state barriers and a single point taxation at the first point of sale.

4.4 Policy and regulatory issues

The overall policy framework for agriculture lags behind mounting problems as well as new opportunities opened up by the growing economy. For example, 60 per cent of net sown area in India is still rain-fed, but government efforts in research and extension services still largely focus on green revolution type efforts that are applicable only to irrigated areas.

The growing emphasis on input subsidies is also a mismatch with declining size of landholdings. Such subsidies disproportionately benefit large farmers:

Although marginal farmers constituted the majority of agricultural households in the country that use surface irrigation, they receive roughly 27% of surface irrigation subsidies (i.e. they operate 27% of the canal irrigated area). Approximately 32% of the subsidies accrue to large farmers, who represent 7% of households with access to irrigation, and less than 1% of all agricultural households in the country.[31]

Government subsidies and unclear regulations also continue to impede and crowd out private investment in the agricultural sector. High MSPs and the consequent role of the government as the single largest buyer of foodgrains act as a disincentive for private investment in grain storage, handling, and distribution.[32] The government has introduced a series of reforms in the last decade, including removal of plant-size restrictions and licensing requirements in food processing activities, and amendments in the APMC Act enabling commercial buyers to purchase directly from farmers. But, as described in the case of APMC reforms above, actual implementation varies widely from state to state and agriculture continues to be one of the most regulated sectors of the economy.

A number of CSOs and research institutions have come together in nationwide networks to draw attention to agrarian distress and to affect policy change in various areas. The Revitalizing Rain-fed Agriculture (RRA) Network is a national consortium of academics, bureaucrats, and representatives of CSOs working to promote policies and public investments focusing on rain-fed agriculture. The Alliance for Sustainable & Holistic Agriculture (ASHA) is another nationwide informal network of more than 400 organizations—including farmers' organizations, consumer groups, women's organizations, environmental organizations,

[30]Intodia, Vijay. 2011–12. *Investment in Agricultural Marketing and Market Infrastructure—A Case Study of Bihar*. National Institute of Agricultural Marketing (NIAM), Jaipur, Rajasthan. Available at: http://www.ccs-niam.gov.in/report/Final%20report%20of%20Bihar%20research%20study.pdf, accessed in October 2013.

[31] Sur, Mona and Dina Umali-Deininger. 2003. *The Equity Consequences of Public Irrigation Investments: The Case of Surface Irrigation Subsidies in India*. Annual Meeting, 16–22 August, Durban, South Africa 25853, International Association of Agricultural Economists, World Bank.

[32]Gulati, Ashok and Rip Landes. 2004. 'Farm Sector Performance and Reform Agenda', *Economic and Political Weekly*, 39(32, August 7): 3611–19.

organic farmers' cooperatives, individual scientists, social activists, doctors, health activists, journalists, and artists—spread across 20 states. The network's advocacy efforts focus on

> . . .securing an assured income for all farm households in the country; promoting and scaling up ecological farming around the country through appropriate policies, legal/regulatory frameworks and programs; ensuring that rights of farming communities over their productive resources like land, water and seed are not denied or violated; and through the above, assuring that all Indians have access to adequate, safe, nutritious and diverse foods.

4.5 Adverse environmental impact

Agriculture in India is increasingly plagued by a host of environmental problems including declining water tables and degradation of soil and water-quality. Partly due to power subsidies for farmers that encourage use of water pumps, India is amongst the top two countries in the world in terms of cropping area under groundwater irrigation. As illustrated in Figure 4.10, a significant percentage of underground aquifers in the biggest agricultural production states are being overexploited.[33]

According to the World Bank's World Development Report 2008:

> . . .intensive and continuous monoculture of rice (summer season) and wheat (winter season) has led to serious soil and water degradation that has negated many of the productivity gains from the green revolution. Soil salinization, soil-nutrient mining, and declining organic matter are compounded by depletion of groundwater aquifers and buildup of pest and weed populations and resistance to pesticides. In India's Punjab, extensive use of nitrogen fertilizer and pesticides has also increased concentration of nitrates and pesticide residues in water, food, and feed, often above tolerance limits.

[33]World Bank. 2008. World Development Report 2008: *Agriculture's Performance, Diversity, and Uncertainties*. Washington, DC: World Bank.

Figure 4.10: Development and overexploitation of groundwater reserves in selected states (percentage)

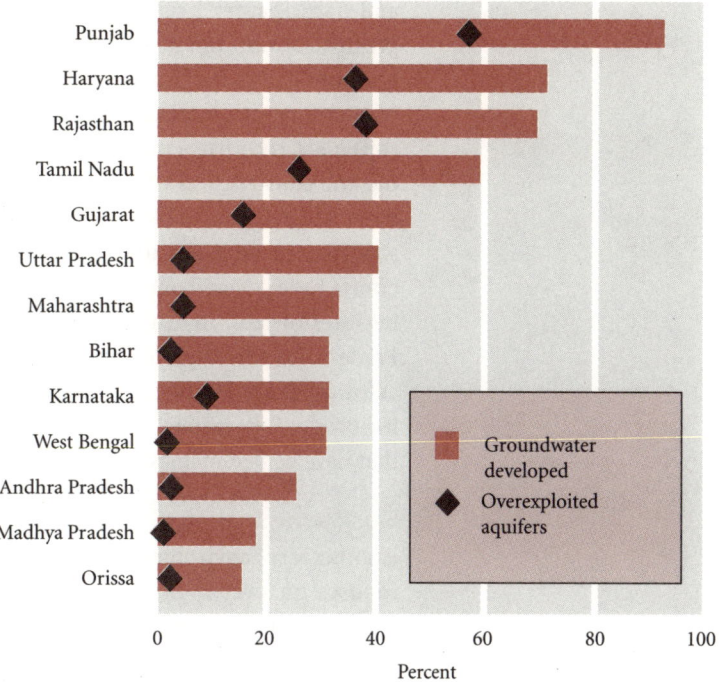

Source: World Bank, 2003.

Note: 'Groundwater developed' is a percentage of all available groundwater in a state. 'Overexploited aquifers' is a percent of administrative blocks in which groundwater extraction exceeds recharge.

Water conservation

A number of existing interventions work on water conservation and the more efficient use of water. Dhan Foundation works towards reviving traditional irrigation tanks prevalent in South India and organizes farmer households around the tanks. The BAIF Development Research Foundation undertakes a range of activities around water conservation, rehabilitation of degraded land, and preservation of forest ecosystems. Its Watershed Development Programme reaches 663 villages, covers 3.5 lakh hectares, and reaches approximately 120,000 families in Gujarat, Maharashtra, Karnataka, Rajasthan, Madhya Pradesh, Uttar Pradesh, Andhra Pradesh, and Bihar. In these areas, BAIF undertakes a range of conservation efforts including contour-bunding, gully-plugging, developing farm ponds, and revival of open wells, bore wells, and rivulets.

The Aga Khan Rural Support Programme (AKRSP) operates a number of projects that promote soil and water conservation including the formation of watershed and participatory irrigation management groups, development of irrigation and groundwater recharge systems, promotion of micro-irrigation devices such as drips and sprinklers, river basin management including the construction of over 1,000 check dams and irrigation tanks, and other watershed management measures. Together, such efforts have covered approximately 40,000 hectares of land in Gujarat and Madhya Pradesh. In areas impacted by drought, agricultural pests or salinity, AKRSP has worked to introduce alternative, more resilient crops that have helped increase farmer incomes.

Biodiversity

Another set of environmental interventions focuses on preserving biodiversity and indigenous crops through documentation of traditional crops, preservation of seeds, and training on conservation practices. Navdanya is one of the leading actors in this space, having set up 65 community seed banks in 16 states and training over 500,000 farmers in sustainable agricultural practices.

4.6 Access to credit and other financial products

One of the key factors that has an adverse impact on agricultural productivity and incomes of poor farmers is inadequate access to credit. Since Independence, the government has taken a variety of measures aimed at increasing credit flows to the agricultural sector including setting up of cooperatives, nationalization of commercial banks, setting up Regional Rural Banks (RRBs), setting up the NABARD, and launching of the KCC scheme.

Currently, the Government of India has stipulated a target of 18 per cent of net bank credit of scheduled commercial banks (SCBs) to the agricultural sector under priority sector lending rules. However, despite these efforts, 40 per cent of cultivators did not have access to formal sources of credit as of 2002 (see Table 4.6).

The RBI estimated that this figure had actually increased to 50 per cent of farm households in 2009.[34] The Task Force on Credit Related Issues of Farmers estimates that the segments of farmers who do not have access to credit are '. . .particularly small and marginal farmers, tenant farmers, share croppers and oral lessees'.[35]

Agriculture-specific loan products

Surprisingly, despite the role played by civil society initiatives in growing the microfinance sector in India, there is comparatively little work on developing agriculture-specific loan products, perhaps because of the anti-cultivator bias which many MFIs have inherited from the Grameen model, as also the large role played by government institutions in agricultural finance. Microfinance loans themselves rarely reach farmers as they are targeted at livestock and petty trading activities. The weekly and monthly repayments schedules, which are an integral part of the microfinance model, are not suited to agricultural lending, where there is a three

Table 4.6: Relative share of borrowing of cultivator households from different sources

(Per cent)

Sources credit	1951	1961	1971	1981	1991	2002
1	2	3	4	5	6	7
Non-Institutional	**92.7**	**81.3**	**68.3**	**36.8**	**30.6**	**38.9**
of which						
Money Lenders	69.7	49.2	36.1	16.1	17.5	26.8
Institutional	**7.3**	**18.7**	**31.7**	**63.2**	**66.3**	**61.1**
of which						
Cooperatives Societies/Banks	3.3	2.6	22.0	29.8	23.6	30.2
Commercial Banks	0.9	0.6	2.4	28.8	35.2	26.3
Unspecified	–	–	–	–	3.1	–
Total	**100.0**	**100.0**	**100.0**	**100.0**	**100.0**	**100.0**

Source: All India Debt and Investment Survey and NSSO.

---

[34] Chakrabarty, K.C. 2009. 'Banking—key driver for inclusive growth', Address by Dr K.C. Chakrabarty, Deputy Governor of the Reserve Bank of India, at the Mint's *Clarity through Debate* series, Chennai, 10 August 2009. Available at: http://www.bis.org/review/r090826e.pdf, accessed in July 2013.

[35] Report of the Task Force on Credit Related Issues of Farmers. 2010. Government of India. Available at: http://indiamicrofinance.com/wp-content/uploads/2010/12/nabard-taskfore-report-farmers-credit.pdf, accessed in October 2013.

to four month gap between investment in inputs and revenue from harvests. Average loan sizes of under ₹10,000 are also too small even for small and marginal farmers.

On of the largest recent credit access interventions in the agricultural sector is KCC scheme, a government initiative to provide hassle-free credit to farmers. Under the scheme, commercial banks, cooperative banks, and RRBs offer farm loans at 7 per cent to borrowers and they get a 2 per cent interest rate subvention from the government for loans up to ₹3 lakh, i.e. the actual interest rate is 9 per cent, but a government subsidy is given directly to the bank to cover a 2 per cent reduction in interest rates to the borrower. According to RBI data, ₹1.6 trillion has been disbursed through 20.3 million KCCs as of March 2012.

Under civil society initiatives, BASIX's work on developing models of financing through commission agents and input suppliers at various points of the agricultural value chains has been covered in previous SOIL reports. As of 2012, BASIX Krishi, has initiated a pilot project where it acts as a business facilitator responsible for origination, monitoring, and collection of agricultural loans for 16 IDBI branch locations in Maharashtra, Odisha, and Karnataka.

One of the key areas of growth in agricultural financing is Warehouse Receipt Financing (WRF), which provides up to 75 per cent of the value of agricultural commodities stored in accredited warehouses. The Warehousing Development and Regulation Authority (WDRA) was put in place through an eponymous Bill in 2007 and seeks to provide a framework to promote and regulate warehousing and negotiable warehouse receipts. The WDRA has appointed eight agencies tasked with accreditation of warehouses and reported receiving 318 applications comprising warehousing capacity of over 11 lakh metric tons from 19 states as of 2012.

ASA has assisted 40 producer companies that it promoted to access working capital through WRF and reports three issues with such financing. First, central accreditation either does not exist or banks do not trust the accreditation by WDRA, and each bank carries out its own due diligence and monitoring on each warehouse that originates receipts for financing. This slows down and complicates the process of accessing WRF. Second, since banks are giving anywhere between 60 and 75 per cent of the value of commodities stored, gap financing is required for the rest of the amount. Thirdly, although WRF works well for working capital finance, it does not fulfil the requirement for term loans to cover investments in farm infrastructure and productivity enhancements.

Insurance

Crop and weather-linked insurance is a rapidly growing area for interventions. The Ministry of Agriculture manages four Central Sector Crop Insurance Schemes— the National Agricultural Insurance Scheme (NAIS), the Pilot Modified National Agricultural Insurance Scheme (MNAIS), the Pilot Weather Based Crop Insurance Scheme (WBCIS), and the Pilot Coconut Palm Insurance Scheme (CPIS)—to provide financial protection to farmers against crop damages due to natural calamities, pests and diseases, and adverse weather conditions. According to the Ministry, 29.5 million farmers are insured through these schemes as of 2012.

A number of CSOs including Basix and the Dhan Foundation are also piloting weather-based insurance products to reduce risks faced by farmers. Basix, in collaboration with private insurance company ICICI Lombard, provided weather index-based crop insurance to more than 10,000 farmers. This microinsurance scheme is based on a rainfall index where payments are based on whether rainfall measured at a local weather station reaches a specified threshold or not.

Another social enterprise that is playing a key role in developing the agricultural insurance market in India is Weather Risk Management Services Limited (WRMS). They work on various aspects of creating an ecosystem around agricultural insurance and providing support to implementing organizations including developing model weather insurance contracts, getting regulatory approval, building institutional capacities of insurance providers, linking insurance providers with international reinsurance markets, and advising the government on insurance subsidies.

4.7 Inadequate focus on women farmers and agricultural workers

Despite the large number of women farmers and agricultural labourers (see Figure 4.11), there has historically been a lack of focus on interventions specific to improving their incomes and working conditions. Due to increasing distress faced by smallholder farmers and the range of gaps in the agricultural sector, interventions have mainly proceeded from the starting point of enhancing viability of smallholder farming and increasing incomes of small and marginal farmers. Such interventions, as described earlier, have spanned the spectrum from aggregation to yield improvements to supply chain logistics to developing market linkages. However, ascertaining the role of women and enhancing their participation and decision-making power in each of these

different spheres is a major gap area that livelihoods interventions need to address moving forward.

Interventions need to look more closely at the role of women in agricultural production and value chains as a whole and shift the focus towards promoting a greater share of household income and control over assets and decision-making to women within the household, a large number of whom currently work as unpaid family labour. Interventions targeting women engaged in agricultural livelihoods need to work on a spectrum of gaps including land titles being predominantly held by men; the lack of agricultural extension and credit services targeted specifically at women and developed keeping their needs in mind; and the low number of women's collectives in farming.

A major new intervention targeting women in agriculture is the Mahila Kisan Shashaktikaran Pariyojana (MKSP), a sub-component of the NRLM. Launched in 2011, MKSP seeks to empower women in agriculture by promoting community institutions of women farmers and making investments to enhance their participation and productivity. However, the scheme is still in a nascent stage.

Figure 4.11: Distribution of female employment in agricultural sector in selected states

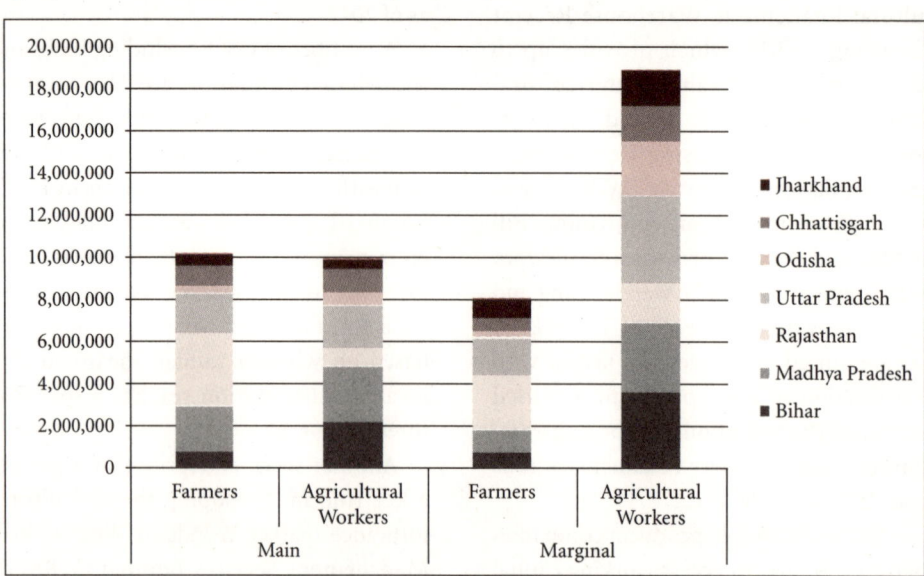

Source: Compiled from Census 2011 Data on Main and Marginal Workers.

5. Conclusion

There have been a number of positive developments over the Eleventh plan period from 2007–08 to 2011–12 including relatively higher agricultural GDP growth rates compared to the previous plan period, growth in wage rates for agricultural labourers, and a relatively rapid increase in horticultural output.

However, there continue to be a number of structural gaps that are impediments to sustainable agricultural livelihoods, particularly for small and marginal farmers. These gaps include increasing distress faced by small and marginal farmers, fueled by declining landholding sizes and lack of access to credit; rising costs of cultivation and inefficient supply chains; significant yield gaps between different states for the same crops; skewed public investments, primarily in the form of input subsidies; increasing adverse environmental impact in terms of declining water tables and soil fertility; and the relative lack of information and focus on solutions that enhance the decision-making power of women in different spheres within agricultural livelihoods.

Livelihood interventions need to focus on both developing scalable models of addressing these structural gaps and on research and advocacy to influence policy bottlenecks, particularly in the five states— Bihar, Madhya Pradesh, Rajasthan, Uttar Pradesh, and Odisha—where the bulk of the poor in India live, and where agriculture continues to employ a significantly higher proportion of the workforce relative to the national average. Projected supply-demand gaps also provide opportunity for livelihood interventions to focus on horticultural livelihoods that assist small and marginal farmers to diversify and improve their incomes through shifting a part of their cropping to higher value fruits and vegetables.

Although a wide range of interventions by government and by civil society— described above—are underway, one of the key gaps in such interventions is systematic data collection and impact assessment that helps to develop and fine-tune scalable models of interventions. For example, despite a number of interventions working on aggregation of small and marginal farmers into producer companies, there is still little independently verified data and information available on the performance and commercial sustainability of such producer companies post-grant funding, which is hampering the development of standard models of aggregation that can be scaled up. A key area for donor intervention is to commission independent reviews and studies of the shareholdings, operations, and audited financial statements of a sample of producer companies, so as to create sector-wide benchmarks for the cost of promotion, best practices in operations, and commercial viability.

Other areas for increased focus identified in this chapter include those relating to promoting more efficient use of inputs, improving content and delivery of extension services, lowering cultivation costs, and developing intervention models that focus on women farmers and agricultural labourers. Increased cultivation costs are putting pressure on the sustainability of small and marginal farmers and interventions that provide livelihood support through optimal use of inputs and collective procurement; and diversification of households' income sources will be critical in sustaining their livelihoods.

Given the increasingly skewed fertilizer usage, a major thrust of livelihood interventions in the sector should be to increase awareness of the importance of soil testing, to link farmers to the NPMSHF scheme, and to ensure that the quality of testing and soil cards given are satisfactory. There is also the need for experimentation and development of financial products, including credit and insurance products, more suited to the needs of small and marginal farmers. Interventions are also needed to further improve the quality of extension services, especially in terms of developing content modules comprising a package of practices for different crops covering the entire agricultural value chain.

Research and advocacy is a major area for further intervention as there continues to be a number of information gaps including current data on access to and usage of credit, potential impact of specific APMC reforms, and the role of women in agricultural production and value chains. There is a need to build advocacy efforts through generating data and engaging with governments on a number of needed policy reforms including tenancy reforms; increased research and development on the needs of small and marginal farmers, including new strains of seeds; and on promoting public and private investments into a range of supply chain gaps.

Addressing existing supply chain gaps require complex interventions across a range of issues including farmers lacking access to information, lack of appropriate infrastructure, developing transportation and storage logistics, and creating linkages to commercial markets and buyers. Given the complex nature of undertaking end-to-end interventions, even large business conglomerates have failed to develop sustainable supply chain models that address all these gaps. Therefore, in undertaking supply chain

interventions, both donors and livelihood practitioners need to be realistic in bringing together coalitions of organizations that have expertise in different aspects of the supply chain. Interventions in this area also need to take a longer-term ecosystem-building approach.

A good analogy for effective agricultural supply chain interventions is the prolonged and multiple grant-funded interventions that were needed to address specific issues in microfinance—such as technology, new product development, and impact assessment, for example. These interventions developed iterative solutions to discrete problems and demonstrated it over a period of time before the solutions coalesced into commercially viable end-to-end models for the delivery of credit and private sector investments helped scale them up. This iterative approach to finding solutions and the growth of microfinance sector globally over the last decade offers a key lesson for interventions in the agricultural sector: donors and practitioners need to build in more rigorous measurement of results, and dissemination and advocacy based on such results, into the design and implementation of interventions across the spectrum of structural gaps covered in this chapter.

Social Protection and Livelihoods*

SAVITHA SURESH BABU AND KIRTI VARDHANA

Chapter 5

1. Introduction

This chapter explores the links between livelihood outcomes and behaviour and social protection. The focus is specifically on informal or unorganized workers—workers in informal enterprises and workers hired informally in the formal sector.

Drawing from National Commission for Enterprises in the Unorganized Sector (NCEUS), 'Unorganized workers consist of those working in the unorganized enterprises or households, excluding regular workers with social security benefits, and the workers in the formal sector without any employment/social security benefits provided by the employers'.

In India, these workers comprise about 93 per cent of the working population. There is also a high congruence between these workers and 77 per cent of the Indian population with a daily per capita consumption under ₹20.[1] The need for a social protection floor, beneath which workers should not be allowed to fall, is clear when we consider the nature of livelihoods and the extent of vulnerability.

Over the last decades, the Government of India has sought through various schemes to promote the livelihoods of this population,

and protect them from such vulnerabilities. Support has encompassed both that required to access incomes or resources to secure basic necessities for a dignified living, as well as protection from sudden shocks that lead to severe losses in income. More recently, the Government has flagged the idea of a social protection floor. This is significant at a time when the role the Government with respect to social protection spending has come under great scrutiny and there is a larger debate on Government actions with relation to economic uncertainty, especially in the context of low economic growth and large current account deficits.

The social protection measures with respect to livelihoods will need to encompass both these aspects but could also vary for different target segments. The nature of protection a farmer would require in a drought prone region would vary from that of an urban migrant, seeking to enter formal enterprises as a contract worker, or that of a slum dweller starting a small entrepreneurial venture. Women workers in both urban and rural areas have other specific requirements. Thus, social protection measures with respect to livelihoods are structured on a scale ranging from the securing of assets, the increased ability to take livelihood-related risks, and insurance of income and livelihood against possible sudden shocks.

Livelihood concerns can be articulated at three levels: increasing income and assets, enhancing capabilities, and ensuring access to entitlements and claims. Increasing

---

* With contribution from Gayathri Vasudevan, CEO, LabourNet.

[1] National Commission for Enterprises in the Unorganized Sector (NCEUS). 2007. 'Report on Conditions of Work and Promotion of Livelihoods in the Unorganized Sector'.

incomes and assets requires not only the creation of jobs, but also equipping people with the skills to access these jobs and access opportunity to invest safely in assets, leverage and protect these assets. Enhancing capabilities refers to increasing what people can do, through investments in education, health, etc. Accessing entitlements include ways in which the poor and marginalized are supported in acquiring work, land, and transfers. MGNREGA, for instance, has made work an entitlement.

A long-term view on securing livelihoods, as the concluding part of this chapter argues, requires substantial investments in skill development. This is particularly important with respect to the youth and urban migrants, whose capabilities translate most directly into earning power and ability to take some risks and protect themselves from others.

We begin the chapter by spelling out what social protection means, and what a social protection floor must include. We'll then consider the role of the government with respect to provision of social protection. This will be done through an analysis of specific schemes and entitlements and their links to livelihood behaviour and outcomes. We first cover those schemes and entitlements associated most with the rural population, securing income, on the one hand, and, protecting from shocks, on the other. Then we cover those more relevant to urban (migrant) populations, again straddling income security and protection from shocks. We then move on to a discussion on food security and its relevance to livelihoods, and the somewhat related agenda of streamlining transfers from government to its poor citizens through direct cash payments. We conclude with our view on the way forward.

2. Understanding social protection

Historically, our understanding of social protection has emerged from the experience of poor and vulnerable workers in developing countries. The need for protection emerged from the understanding that merely extending the social security available to formal sector workers to those in the informal sector (such as insurance and Provident Fund) would not be appropriate. This was because the minimum social and economic standard of living taken for granted in the formal sector (particularly of the developed world) could not be assumed in the context of informal workers. Most workers needed not only *basic* social security but also *contingent* social security.[2]

Basic social security is understood as access to minimum resources to lead an economically dignified life in society. Contingent social security refers to provisioning for adversities that may result from human life and work such as injuries, sudden unemployment, and ill health, as well as eventualities such as old age and death. Another useful framework to understand social protection is to look at the levels suggested by Sandhya V. Iyer and Sita Prabhu:[3]

Level 1: Nutrition and Education
Level 2: Asset and Employment
Level 3: Social Assistance

While the three levels are related, they assume particular significance in different life periods. Level 1 is the domain of children and adolescence. Level 2 the working population, while Level 3 seeks provision for old age or any form of destitution. This corresponds with United Nations Chief Executive Board's outline of elements and dimensions of social protection floor. They

[2]Kannan, K.P. 2010. 'The Long Road to Social Security', Hivos Knowledge Programme.

[3]Iyer, Sandhya and Sita Prabhu. 2001. 'Financing Social Security; A Human Development Perspective', in Mahendra Dev, Piush Antony, V. Gayathri, and R.P. Mamgain (eds), *Social and Economic Security in India*, pp. 83–99. New Delhi: Institute of Human Development.

consist of dimensions of income security over the entire life cycle (childhood, working age, and old age) and adequate access to health and other essential services such as water, sanitation, food, and shelter.[4]

In a recent document, UNDP defines social protection more broadly as, 'the set of policies and programmes designed to reduce poverty and vulnerability by promoting efficient labour markets, diminishing people's exposure to risks and enhancing their capacity to protect themselves against hazards and interruption/loss of income'. In sum, social protection comprises those measures which aim at preventing, reducing, and eliminating economic and social vulnerabilities to poverty and deprivation.

The term 'social floor' or 'social protection floor' has been used to mean a minimum set of basic social rights, services, and facilities that a global citizen should enjoy. ILO defines social protection floor as 'nationally defined sets of basic social security guarantees which secure protection aimed at preventing or alleviating poverty, vulnerability and social exclusion'.[5]

A social protection floor should comprise at least the following four basic social security guarantees:

1. Access to a nationally defined set of goods and services, constituting essential health care, including maternity care, that meets the criteria of availability, accessibility, acceptability, and quality
2. Basic income security for children, providing access to nutrition, education, care, and any other necessary goods and services
3. Basic income security, for persons in active age who are unable to earn sufficient income, in particular in cases of

sickness, unemployment, maternity, and disability
4. Basic income security for older persons

Of these, basic income security, particularly for those in active age but unable to earn sufficient income, is of primary concern in this chapter.

3. Government as provider of social protection

Figure 5.1 represents some of the government schemes targeted at different sections of the population, based on differing life cycle needs. For children, where the primary concern is to ensure adequate nutrition and a right to education, the ICDS, *Sarva Shiksha Abhiyan*, and Mid Day Meal schemes in schools are significant. ICDS seeks to provide nutrition to pregnant and lactating women, adolescent girls as well as early childhood care and education. *Sarva Shiksha Abhiyan* focuses on improving enrolments and quality of school education. Mid Day Meals are provided for government school children, to encourage school attendance. For the elderly as well as the disabled, pensions are provided through the NSAP. Our focus in this chapter will be on the working population—adults and their families—and schemes meant to provide income and nutritional security and risk protection.

---

[4] Srivastava, Ravi S. 2013. 'Social Protection floor for India', Executive Summary, International Labour Organisation, New Delhi.

[5] Ibid.

Figure 5.1: Schemes that provide social protection at different stages of life cycle

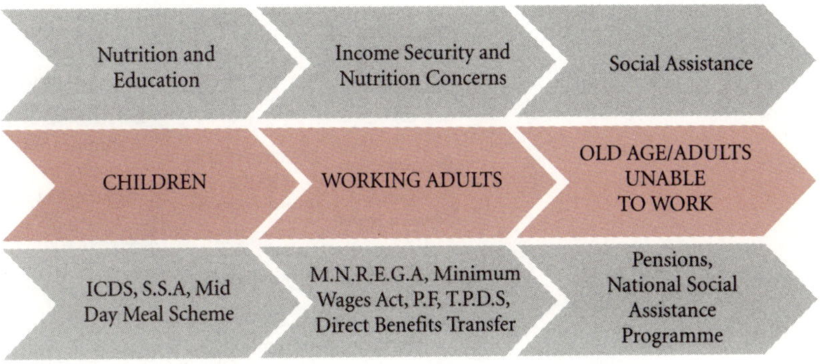

Source: Compiled by authors.

Table 5.1:   Percentage of GDP spent on social protection

Time period	Expenditure on social protection (as % of GDP)
1995–96	1.06
2005–06	1.35
2010–11	1.75

Source: Tabulation of information presented in Ravi Srivatsava. 2013. 'Social Protection floor for India', Executive Summary, International Labour Organisation, New Delhi.

Both in terms of the number of schemes for social protection, and the extent of coverage, the government's role has been expanding in recent years.

Table 5.1 presents the increase in government spending on social protection related sectors. It includes expenditure on elementary education, health and family welfare, labour and labour welfare, social security, welfare, and rural development. There has been a substantial increase in the percentage of GDP spent on social protection from 1.06 per cent in 1995–96 to 1.75 per cent in 2010–11, mostly led by the centre.[6] Together, the central and state government expenditure on these sectors has increased by about 0.83 per cent of GDP between 1995–96 and 2011–12.[7]

Government-led interventions with respect to protection of livelihoods and incomes, protection against risk and nutritional security, operate at multiple levels.

Figure 5.2 represents various schemes and legislations which seek to provide *income security* and *risk protection* to informal sector workers. The figure has been made for ease of representation and is not exhaustive. Certain schemes can fall into more than one category, as in the case of Rashtriya Swasthya Bhima Yojana (RSBY) which provides an insurance cover up to ₹30,000 for households, in both rural and urban areas. While RSBY has been placed under the broad category of income security (since it acts as a shock absorber and, therefore, protects from sudden depletion in incomes, it could equally be placed in the 'support for families'.

A broad distinction has been made between rural and urban workers in discussing income security and risk protection. While this is a crude distinction, since most urban workers have a rural base, we discuss

Figure 5.2:   Social protection for workers in rural and urban India

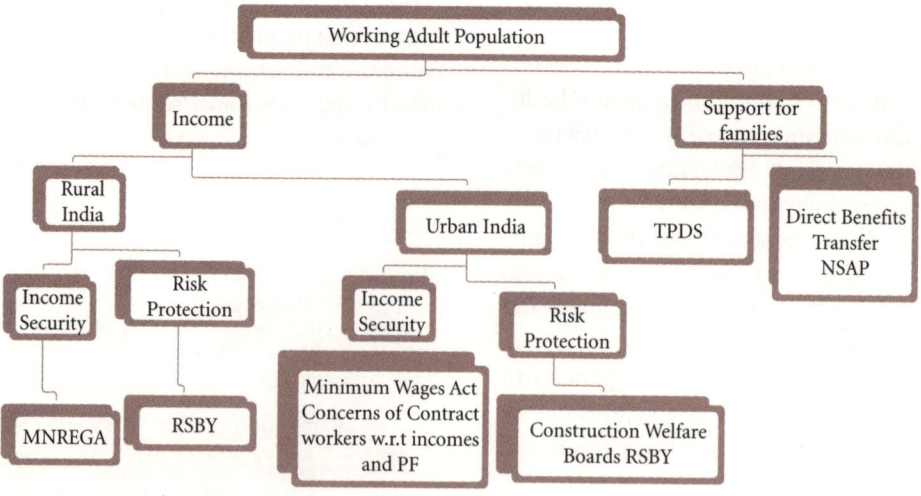

Source: Compiled by authors.

---

[6]The states spend almost twice as much as the central government does on these sectors but their expenditure (as % of GDP) has not changed much in the last decade.

---

[7] Srivastava, Ravi S. 2013. 'Social Protection floor for India', Executive Summary, International Labour Organisation, New Delhi.

both NREGA and RSBY as predominantly rural schemes.

In the urban context, we will discuss the protection offered to construction workers in the informal sector and contract workers in the formal sector. Most workers in the construction sector are migrants from rural areas and have specific livelihood concerns. To consider the concerns of these workers, we will explore the Minimum Wages Act and provisions made by Construction Welfare Boards for registered workers. In urban areas, we have the presence of a large number of informal workers within the formal sector—these contract workers have specific livelihood concerns. To explore their concerns, we will explore challenges with respect to implementing the Contract Workers (Regulation and Abolition) Act, 1970.

Finally, we consider social protection targeted at families—either to improve nutrition or secure income and assets. The NSAP is included in this category as for many poor families pensions are a significant source of income. In our consideration of the various schemes, we seek to understand the intent of the scheme, its reach as well as impact and challenges related to implementation.

4. National Rural Employment Guarantee Act and Scheme

In rural India, the most substantial intervention with respect to livelihoods and social protection is the NREGA and the scheme (NREGS) which has stemmed from it. Since its inception, NREGA has generated 1,348 crore person days of employment and has involved an expenditure of around ₹2 lakh crore.[8]

By making access to work a right, NREGA has contributed substantially to social protection by securing income. Government

allocation to provisions of this Act is to the tune of ₹33,000 crore for 2012–13.

NREGA is the most widely studied central government scheme today. While it has been hailed a success in making work an 'entitlement', it has also been subject to severe criticism, on grounds of design and implementation. Even opinion on the impact of the scheme is polarized: while proponents argue on the evidence of increases in MPCE of families who have accessed work through the scheme, opponents believe increased wages and MPCE can be explained by other factors such as increased economic growth. Critics also say that it is a temporary distress solution, not a long-term solution, to the challenge of ensuring livelihood protection or promotion. The financial feasibility of the scheme for a country as large as India has also been questioned. Additionally, large-scale misappropriation of funds during implementation, without regard for budgetary allocations, is a serious concern that has been raised. An audit by the Comptroller and Auditor General (CAG) and recommendations by a recent Parliament Committee has brought to light many concern, discussed below.

The MGNREGA project aspires to be both 'a safety net' and 'create assets' (see Figure 5.3). Let us consider the achievements

Figure 5.3: Current features of the NREGS

Structure
- Through the Act, every person above 18 years of age is entitled to work within 5 km of her or his place of residence.
- If employment is not provided within 15 days, she or he is entitled to unemployment wage allowance.
- This allowance is not to be less than one-fourth of the wage rate for the first 30 days and not less than one-half of the wage rate for the remaining period of the financial year.

Wages & Livelihoods Perspective
- Nearly 5 crore households across India have accessed employment through the Act.
- While the minimum wages paid under the scheme vary in different states, they average to about ₹120 a day.

Focus
- The Act targets semi-skilled or unskilled workers and social protection is one of its primary objectives, as it seeks to ensure any person willing to work is provided work.
- Additionally, there is explicit focus on marginalized groups such as women, SCs and STs.
- The nature of works to be taken up is to be decided through consultative processes at the village level, so that community assets are created.

Source: MNREGA Guidelines, 2013.

[8] Mahatma Gandhi National Rural Employment Guarantee Programme. 2013. *Report to the People*, Ministry of Rural Development, Department of Rural Development, Government of India, New Delhi, 2 February 2013. Available at: http://nrega.nic.in/netnrega/WriteReaddata/circulars/Report_to_the_people_English2013.pdf (last accessed on 8 November 2013).

Table 5.2: NREGA as safety net and asset creator

Safety net	Asset creation
• Guaranteed employment for 100 days per household, within 15 days of applying for work • Work is to be provided within a 5 km radius of the village • Explicit focus on marginalized groups such as women, SCs, and STs • Unemployment allowance entitlement if work is not provided • Facilities such as drinking water, crèches to be made available at worksites	• Works that can be undertaken under the scheme relate to water conservation, drought proofing, irrigation, flood control, land development, and rural connectivity • Land development work can be undertaken on lands of small and marginalized farmers

Source: Tabulation by authors based on MNREGA Guidelines, 2013.

and challenges on both these fronts (see Table 5.2).

The criticism raised by policy analysts against NREGA's design refer to the Act's promise of 100 days of guaranteed employment to unskilled workers. The argument is that this interferes with the labour market, preventing it from making its natural adjustments, and leads to a stunting of skills. Guaranteed unskilled employment would mean that there is little motivation to acquire skills. The criticism raised around implementation relates critiques relate to the non-compliance with the provisions of the Act: large scale financial irregularities and low quality of assets generated through MGNREGA work are the two large issues raised (see Table 5.3).

4.1 NREGA as a safety net

Nearly 50 per cent of workers accessing work through the Act have been women. It has been noted through field studies that this work has helped women achieve economic independence, as the money is not given away to husbands or other male members, but retained by them. Further, the scheme has covered households belonging to the most marginalized communities. One survey found that 81 per cent of the sampled workers live in a *kaccha* house, 61 per cent are illiterate, and 72 per cent have no electricity at home. As per the survey, SC and ST families constitute 73 per cent of the sample (this is higher than government figures, which indicate 56 per cent). Thus it is argued that 'it is hard to think of any other development programme that involves SC/ST communities to this extent, without any reservation or quota'.[9]

In an analysis of the effect of NREGA in Jharkhand and Chhattisgarh (states affected by LWE), it was demonstrated that had MGNREGA not been implemented, many households would not have had the purchasing power to buy sufficient foodgrains at a time when prices were increasing.[10] Studies compiled under MGNREGA Sameeksha suggest an increase in both household incomes and MPCE as a result of the scheme. While sceptics argue that increased agricultural productivity over the same time period has contributed to this increase, some correlation between NREGA and higher household income seems to exist. Apart from increase in income and expenditure, it is asserted that the scheme has increased the bargaining power of labour in several districts, pushing up the market wages and reducing exploitation of agricultural labour.

It is difficult to make conclusive statements as the experiences of NREGA have been different in different states. However, anecdotal evidence and social audits strongly indicate at least some impact of NREGA on the increase in wages. On the other hand, NREGA by itself may not be able to account for wage increase in total. In an analysis of

Table 5.3: Summary of the main critiques raised against NREGA

Faulty design	Faulty implementation

• Provision of guaranteed wage employment interferes with the labour market
• Availability of work reduces motivation to acquire 'skills' preventing any possible 'move up' for informal workers
	• Lack of awareness among workers about all provisions
	• Large scale financial irregularities
	  • Corruption
	  • Non-utilization of funds
	• Low quality of assets generated
	• Non-completion of works taken up

Source: Compilation by authors.

[9]Dreze, Jean and Reetika Khera. 2009. 'The Battle for Employment', *Frontline*, 3–16 January.

[10] Bannerjee, Kaustav, and Partha Shaha. 2010. 'The NREGA, the Maoists and the Developmental Woes of the Indian State', *Economic and Political Weekly*, XLV (28, 10 July).

increased agricultural wages, it is suggested that wider choice of work and the depth of off-farm opportunity generally has contributed to the increase.

Across the world, increase in urban migration and construction-related activity has been seen to push up agricultural wages, as fewer labourers are left behind for the farm. Labour markets contract as demand grows relative to supply, increasing the wages of labour. Indian data shows that workforce engaged in agriculture declined from almost 65 per cent in 1993–94 to 53 per cent in 2009, and that of construction increased from 3.1 per cent to 9.6 per cent over the same period.[11]

4.2 Challenges in providing a safety net

In a recent audit by the CAG on the functioning of NREGA, several indicators of ineffective implementation have been raised:

- The average employment per rural household per year has declined from 54 days in 2009–10 to 43 days in 2011–12. This could indicate implementation or delivery problems, or declining interest.
- Only about 72 per cent of beneficiaries were aware of the number of days of employment to which they were entitled. Around 70 per cent of respondents were aware of the time period within which wages were to be paid.
- Sixty five per cent of beneficiaries reported that they received wages within 15 days, 16 per cent within one month, 11 per cent between one to two months, 4 per cent within two to three months, and 2 per cent reported delays of more than two months—a clear indication calling for tightening of payment-related procedures.

- Only half of the interviewed beneficiaries were aware of the prescribed quantum of work which entitled them to full wage payment. Similarly, only around 56 per cent were aware of the manner of wage calculations.

The most positive finding of the CAG audit was that employment was provided, in most cases, within nine days of the registration with the scheme. However, low levels of awareness, delays in wage payment, and faulty wage calculation have been pointed out as serious lapses.

The relatively low levels of awareness about the scheme affect its success substantially, since higher awareness levels among workers is directly connected to better implementation. Although awareness has increased, there are weak spots in the messaging. For instance, creation of worksite facilities or payment of unemployment wages. In a survey undertaken in 2008 across several states, it was found that even in 'high awareness' states, such as Rajasthan, clarity on minimum wages and provision for payment within 15 days was low.[12]

Lack of awareness also affects maintenance of job cards and muster rolls. Job cards are meant to record the number of hours individual workers put in at work; it is their personal record. Muster roles at worksites are to be maintained to account for hours of work and payments due to individual workers. In several social audits, it has been found that muster roles are not maintained at worksites and workers don't have entries on their job cards. This clearly has direct implications for timely and full wage payments.

NREGA payments are increasingly made through bank/post office accounts of workers. We explore the reasons for this shift from worksite payments to account payments, and discuss the challenges posed to the scheme by the banking system.

---

[11]Gulati, Ashok, Surbhi Jain, and Nidhi Satija. 2013. 'Rising Farm Wages in Rural India—The Push and Pull Factors', Discussion Paper 5, Commission for Agricultural Costs and Prices, Department of Agriculture, Government of India, New Delhi.

[12]Dreze, Jean and Reetika Khera. 2009. 'The Battle for Employment', *Frontline*, 3–16 January.

Initially, payments were made through cash at worksites. With this system, it was relatively easy for contractors and gram sarpanchs to embezzle funds, by inflating the number of hours on muster rolls. It was to prevent this that payments through bank accounts or post office accounts were initiated based on the belief that separating the implementing agency from the payment agency would decrease corruption substantially and aid financial inclusion since bank accounts were opened for workers.

However, a detailed study of the change from worksite payments to bank account/post office payments indicates how banks do not always serve the intended purpose of increasing transparency and reducing leakages in NREGA.[13] The intent to separate implementing agency from payment agency proved hard to achieve in context of social networks and feudal realities of rural India. Relations of patronage and dependence may have impeded this separation effectively. Through a survey of wage payments through banks and post offices in two states, the researchers demonstrate various ways in which embezzlement occurs. Considering these at some length is useful to understand how leakages continue even as measures specifically introduced to prevent them are put in place. The three ways are deception, collusion, and exploitation (see Figure 5.4).

It is interesting to note that despite these challenges, most workers preferred payments to be made through banks rather than at the worksite. Many of them felt that after being accompanied a few times, they would be able to handle bank transactions on their own. So, the point is not to dismiss bank transfers completely, but to fine-tune procedures to ensure greater access, a point that can be made for NREGA in general. Availability of work records with workers through job cards could be a significant move in this respect, as could mechanisms to make public announcements that money had been credited into workers accounts.

4.3 NREGA as creator of assets

There are ground reports of how NREGA works have benefitted villages. For example, Jarugumalai, a village in Salem District, Tamil Nadu, which once could be reached only by trekking through slippery rocks, can now be accessed easily with a mud road laid for 3.5 km under the scheme. Apart from new roads and drought prevention works, the expansion of works permitted under NREGA has major implications for livelihoods. Land development works taken up under the scheme on the farms of small and marginal farmers is said to have increased productivity of lands. In fact, some of these farmers are said to have voluntarily opted out of the scheme because of the improvement (MNREGA Sameeksha). This kind of evidence has led to discussions on the potential to further expand the types of work that can be done under MGNREGA. One recent report said the Textile Ministry is considering a scheme in which workers work with companies (struggling to find labour) and have payments made by NREGA. This would 'guarantee employment', provide

Figure 5.4: Three routes by which leakages are sustained in NREGA

Deception

- Instances where a worker was not even aware that a bank account existed in his name. This becomes possible due to informal networks between contractors, bank managers, and gram sarpanchs/*abikartas*.

Collusion

- With real or imaginary workers, instances where bank accounts had been opened in the names of family members of *abikartas* or other upper caste persons of the village who had never worked at NREGA worksites. The 'wages' paid to these accounts were being embezzled by abikartas and bank managers.

Exploitation

- Instances where workers had to give parts of their wages to 'sarpanchs' or '*abikartas*' for accompanying them to the bank to withdraw wages. While these were sometimes to return advance payments, this was not always the case.

Source: Tabular representation of the findings of a study by Adhikari and Bhatia. 2010. 'NREGA Wage Payments—Can We Bank on the Banks?', *Economic and Political Weekly*, XLV (1, January 2). Tabular representation is by the authors of this article.

---

[13]Andhikari, A. and Kartika Bhatia. 2010. 'NREGA Wage Payments: Can We Bank on the Banks?' *Economic and Political Weekly*, XLV (1), 2 January.

labour for industry as well as help workers acquire new skills. Similar suggestions have been put forth for agricultural labour as well. For example, large farmers in need of workers could register with Panchayats and have the payments made for agricultural work through NREGS.[14]

Some of the most severe criticism of NREGA relates to non-completion and poor quality of the infrastructure created under the scheme. There are anecdotal reports of roads constructed under the scheme not lasting for a single monsoon. Some of the observations from the CAG audit are pertinent:

- Works amounting to around ₹4,070 crore were incomplete even after one to five years of launching.
- There are impermissible works undertaken to the tune of about ₹2,252 crore.
- Although Bihar, Maharashtra, and Uttar Pradesh constituted 46 per cent of the rural poor, the states have utilized only 20 per cent of the total funds released under the Act.

Based on these points, the refrain from the urban middle class has been that NREGA, in effect, amounts to a 'rural cash transfer scheme'. This contrasts sharply with the perception of rural workers, who in a survey, indicated that NREGA had led to the creation of useful assets in the villages (83 per cent). Seventy per cent of the sampled workers felt that the work being done at the worksite was 'very useful' and another 22 per cent felt that it was 'quite useful'. Only 3 per cent considered it 'useless'.

4.4 Design—A critique of the intent behind the scheme

By guaranteeing work for unskilled workers, MGNREGA may provide a 'safety net'. But it also interferes with labour markets. Increasing costs of agricultural labour, it has been suggested, pushes up the cost of agricultural production more than we can afford.[15] Providing cash rather than employment, argue Panagariya and Bhagwati in their new book, would work as a 'safety net', and yet not interfere with the functioning of the labour market.[16]

Another major critique is the low technology base of NREGA-related work. This means low productivity and stagnation with respect to increase in skills of workers. By engaging a large section of our rural population in largely unproductive and low skill-based jobs, the scheme is choking labour supply to higher productivity and higher skill sectors where it is required the most. The deep concern is that without an increase in skill development, workers will get accustomed to income security and allowances as an entitlement and will be unable to move out of 'protection-based' livelihood base for several years to come.

This chapter argues that the future lies in expanding the works permissible under NREGA, and in finding ways to provide skill-based training within the scheme itself. A recent statement by the Union Textile Minister where he suggests a tie-up with garment manufacturing companies may be a step in this direction. Companies would provide workers jobs as well as skill training, while the wages would be paid by the MGNREGA scheme under the proposal. Similar options could be explored with respect to agriculture: large farmers could register with Panchayats for workforce requirements and the wages could be paid through NREGA.

The challenge, from a livelihoods perspective, would be to ensure these tie-ups offer decent jobs to labour—who are clearly

---

[14] Gulati, Ashok. 2013. 'Growth Pull not MNREGA push', *Financial Express*, 7 May 2013.

[15] Gulati, Ashok, Surbhi Jain, and Nidhi Satija. 2013. 'Rising Farm Wages in Rural India—The Push and Pull Factors', Discussion Paper 5, Commission for Agricultural Costs and Prices, Department of Agriculture, Government of India, New Delhi.

[16] Bhagwati, Jagdish, and Arvind Panagariya. 2013. *Why Growth Matters: How Economic Growth in India Reduced Poverty and the Lessons for Other Developing Countries*. A Council on Foreign Relations Book. United States: PublicAffairs™.

vulnerable—and at the same time, improve their capability to move out of the 'safety net', over a course of time.

Rural India, risk protection

Daily expenditure is a necessity for ensuring basic nutrition and essential services for the poor. Informal workers often have highly uneven incomes and must work hard to smoothen consumption in spite of these peaks and troughs. In this milieu, sudden dips in income due to deterioration of health or disasters can push a worker or his or her family rapidly into deeper or more prolonged poverty.

Access to health care services is part of the stated social protection objectives in India. The NRHM, launched in 2005, aims to revitalize public health care through central government funding for a range of programmes including employment of female ASHAs in villages, provision of funds to health facilities, and financial incentives to encourage women to give birth in government health facilities or accredited private facilities. In 2007, the RSBY was launched to provide free in-patient treatment for families below the poverty line.

5. Rashtriya Swasthya Bima Yojana (RSBY)

The scheme provides BPL households an in-hospital insurance cover of up to ₹30,000 per annum with coverage available for all pre-existing illnesses. Public and private hospitals are covered by the scheme. A family of five can insure itself through a one-time payment of ₹30. The premium is paid by the government—75 per cent by the central government and 25 per cent by the state governments. With government covering the full cost of the premium, it was expected that insurance agencies would be fully motivated to enrol households.

Since 2007, the scheme has expanded to include specific groups of workers. All NREGA workers (both above poverty line [APL] and BPL) are now eligible under the scheme, as are construction workers registered with the various Construction Welfare Boards.

Currently, nearly 3.6 crore BPL families are enrolled for the scheme, as per the RSBY site. The total number of families cumulatively enrolled since inception is 7.1 crore (as at end August 2013).

The linkages to livelihoods have been reinforced by various studies—the argument has been that the 'effective implementation of the scheme will not only reduce morbidity and encourage greater labour force participation by reducing and managing current disease burden, but it will also limit entry into poverty'.[17]

5.1 Challenges

A detailed study of its roll-out in Amaravati District in Maharashtra found that satisfaction levels with RSBY were fairly high. However, it does face many challenges, particularly with respect to enrolments and access.[18] Rajashekar et al. (2011) document that within six months of roll-out in Karnataka, over 85 per cent of the BPL was aware of the programme and 68 per cent had enrolled, but this experience is unique. Enrolment rates tend to vary widely across states with rates as low as 39 per cent in Maharashtra.[19] In the study in Amaravati, awareness was low, with most respondents aware of the facility through informal networks rather than institutional mechanisms.

Apart from enrolment, use of the product to access health care has been low. Rajasekhar et al. record extremely poor

---

[17] Rathi, Prateek, Arnab Mukherji, Gita Sen. 2012. 'Rashtriya Swasthya Bima Yojana—Evaluating Utilisation, Roll-out and Perceptions in Amaravati District, Maharashtra', *Economic and Political Weekly*, XLVII (39, 29 September).

[18] Rajasekhar, D., Erlend Berg, Maitreesh Ghatak, R. Manjula, and Sanchari Roy. 2011. 'Implementing Health Insurance: The Roll Out of Rashtriya Swasthya Bhima Yojana in Karnataka', *Economic and Political Weekly*, XLVI (20, 14 May).

[19] Narayana, D. 2010. 'Review of the Rashtriya Swasthya Bima Yojana', *Economic and Political Weekly*, XLV (29, 17 July).

utilization in Karnataka, also reported in the study in Amaravati District.[20] Studies on patterns of utilization show better uptake in urban areas and district headquarters, compared to smaller and more remote villages. Even after being enrolled, RSBY enrollees from remote areas faced greater transport costs—a deterrent to programme utilization.

The nature of deterrents is also made clear through an analysis of hospital insurance claims over two years, available to the network of Self-Employed Women's Association (SEWA) members.[21] Four major concerns have been identified in the provision of insurance for workers of VimoSEWA. These are

1. Over 40 per cent of claims are for readily preventable conditions or conditions that can be treated without hospitalization, therefore, inefficient
2. Drug expenditures—even in public hospitals—comprise the bulk of expenditure
3. Hysterectomy is amongst the top reasons for using insurance for women
4. Claims patterns are inequitable
5. There is no outpatient department (OPD) provision, creating false incentives to get admitted (links back to point 1)

The author of the analysis argues it is necessary that preventive health be given sufficient attention in order to avoid hospitalization. Also, since it was found that urban women are more effective in accessing their claims, greater attention needs to be paid to the entitlements of rural women and families. It is also necessary to investigate closely the reasons why hospitalization is sought across the states. In the study of claims in VimoSEWA, hysterectomies were performed for women in the age group of 22–45. Whether the medical procedure was actually necessary in all cases, was not clear.

While the need for RSBY is not questioned, making insurance available to families across states requires concerted action, to raise awareness, and provide active support to implementation, particularly to those located in geographically remote regions.

Urban areas

In 1951, the urban population in India was around 62 million people accounting for about 17 per cent of the total population. By 2011, the urban population was 377 million, or 31 per cent of the population. While the percentage of population may still be higher in rural India, flows of migration to urban areas continue to grow, notwithstanding schemes such as NREGA which had hoped to slow the tide.

Migrants to urban areas become casual workers in informal occupations such as domestic house-help, for temping agencies such as security, or as casual or contract labour in factories, within the formal sector. A large proportion joins the construction sector. In considering income security and risk protection of urban informal workers, we look at two major groups:

- Construction workers
- Contract and other informal workers in the formal sector

Construction and casual work in the formal sector are not the only means of livelihood for urban migrants. We take these as a focus to understand social protection concerns of urban workers. This is because they account for the livelihoods of a large proportion of urban migrants. Neither is it always possible to classify workers into sectors, since they may have more than one source of workers. For instance, women construction workers might also be accessing parallel employment as domestic workers.

[20] Rajasekhar, D., Erlend Berg, Maitreesh Ghatak, R. Manjula, and Sanchari Roy. 2011. 'Implementing Health Insurance: The Roll Out of Rashtriya Swasthya Bhima Yojana in Karnataka', *Economic and Political Weekly*, XLVI (20, 14 May).

[21] Desai, Sapna. 2009. 'Keeping the "Health" in Health Insurance', *Economic and Political Weekly*, XLIV (38), 19 September.

6. Construction workers' welfare

At the national level, there are more than 3.2 crore construction workers in India today. 'To put this in perspective, the industry's workforce approximates the population size of Kerala or Jharkhand and is larger than small states such as Uttarakhand or Delhi.'[22] Employing 11 per cent of India's workforce, it is the second largest employer after agriculture.

The nature of employment in this industry is primarily casual. In 2009–10, more than 95 per cent of the workers did not have a job contract on paper and around 80 per cent received wage payment on a weekly or a daily basis, without any provision for paid leave or social security such as provident fund, pension, or maternity health care.

A notable proportion of construction workers are migrants, which makes it hard for workers to access state welfare benefits, whether in a different state or a district. In 2007–08, the proportion of migrants among construction workers was 33 per cent in urban areas and 19 per cent in rural areas.

Construction sector

- 3.2 crore workers
- Second largest employer after agriculture
- Employs 11 per cent of India's workforce
- More than 95 per cent workers don't have job contracts
- Thirty-three per cent of construction workers are migrants in urban areas

---

Clearly, the rapid real estate expansion and growth of the construction sector has led to an increase in the jobs. But social protection for workers here is negligible. While the Building and Other Construction Workers Act (BOCWA) was enacted in 1996 to provide workers safety and dignified working conditions on paper, implementation of its provisions are dismal. To avail benefits under the Act, workers need to be registered with Construction Welfare Boards of various states. Such registration has reached only 12 per cent of all construction workers nationally. Since the social protection measures offered by BOWCA are only available to registered workers, a large section of workers have no access to them.

6.1 Building and Other Construction Workers Act, 1996

Passed in 1996, the Act applies to any establishment[23] employing more than 10 people and has to comply with the provisions of the Act.

As per Section 18 of the Act, every state government is required to constitute a State Building & Other Construction Workers Welfare Board. The Board is mandated to carry out the following functions:[24]

1. Provide immediate assistance to a beneficiary in case of accident
2. Make payment of pension to the beneficiaries who have completed the age of 60 years
3. Sanction loans and advances to the beneficiary for construction of houses
4. Pay premia for Group Insurance Scheme of the beneficiaries
5. Give financial assistance for the education of children
6. Meet medical expenses for treatment of major ailments
7. Make payment of maternity benefit to the female beneficiaries
8. Make provisions and improvement of such other welfare measures and facilities as may be prescribed

---

[22] Soundarajan, Vidya. 2013. 'Construction Workers – Amending the Law for more Safety', *Economic and Political Weekly*, XLVIII (23, 8 June).

[23]Establishment, in this case, refers to the construction site, but it is the owner or controller of the site (i.e. the developer or 'client') rather than the builder, who is liable to comply with the law. This is because it is this owner/controller who is identified as the 'principle employer'. Legal compliance is contracted from principle employer to builder as part of his contract, but the principle employer remains ultimately responsible.

[24]As per the Ministry of Labour and Employment.

The Act also requires state governments to frame policies to ensure regular working hours, adequate rest, and fair wages for workers (including overtime wages). It requires that safe drinking water, sanitation facilities, accommodation, crèches, first aid, and other provisions for safety of workers are made.

Any construction worker who has worked in construction for at least 90 days in the preceding 12 months, and is in the age group of 18 to 60 can register with a Construction Welfare Board (CWB). The exact process of registration varies from state to state. Usually, age proof, a certificate from the employer, and a fee not exceeding ₹50 are required. Some states have relaxed the process in parts. Odisha does not require age proof. Rajasthan, Punjab, and Haryana allow for labour contractors to give certificates of employment while other states don't.[25]

The resources of the CWBs are augmented by a 1 to 2 per cent cess on total construction cost, collected from the principle employer (the owner or controller of the construction site) under the Building and Construction Workers Cess Act (BCWCA), 1996. Unlike for other welfare boards, the BCWCA has made board establishment and cess levy compulsory for all state governments. The high rate of cess potentially creates substantial funds with which to finance workers' welfare.

6.2 Challenges to BOCWA implementation

While social protection measures mandated under BOCWA are laudable, few workers have access to these protective mechanisms. With only 12 per cent of workers registered with CWBs at an all-India level, clearly the Act is failing in its reach to workers. A vast section of workers are in fact unaware of the existence of the CWBs, according to ground-level reports.

A study on women construction workers in Gurgaon and Dwarka, National Capital Region (NCR), revealed no awareness at all about the welfare boards. Crèches, when provided, were the interventions of NGOs. With no separate bathing facilities for men and women, stagnation of water, and no functioning toilets, the living conditions specified by BOCWA were a distant pipedream.[26] These findings correlate with reports of 'labour camps' across the major cities of India.

The physical safety of workers and their protection from occupational safety risks and hazards are serious concerns in the construction sector. While the BOWCA specifies first aid and various other safety precautions to be made available at site, few sites follow procedures. Reports of casualties in the press are extremely common. Labour department officials, meant to undertake periodic checks of construction sites, frequently fall short, for reasons ranging from understaffing to collusion.

To be eligible for any benefit in the case of accident or death of a family member, workers must be registered with the CWBs.

Figure 5.5: Coverage by construction welfare boards

No coverage
- Thirteen states including Assam, Goa, Uttarakhand, Dadra and Nagar Haveli, Daman and Diu

Low coverage
- Around 10 per cent of workers in Bihar, Chhattisgarh, Goa, Gujarat, Jharkhand, Karnataka, Odisha, Punjab, Tripura, Andaman and Nicobar, and Chandigarh

High coverage
- Kerala (99%), Tamil Nadu (75%), and Madhya Pradesh (68%)

Source: Compiled by the authors.

[25] Soundarajan, Vidya. 2013. 'Construction Workers – Amending the Law for more Safety', *Economic and Political Weekly*, XLVIII (23, 8 June).

[26] Dalmia, Aaradhana J. 2012. 'Strong Women, Weak Bodies, Muted Voices', *Economic and Political Weekly*, XLVII (26–27, 30 June).

The process of registration is a challenge. In a city like Bangalore with high levels of construction activity, only 85,000 workers are registered with the Karntataka Construction Workers Welfare Board, while the estimated number of construction workers is 12 times this.[27]

Even if awareness exists, challenges with the registration process prove a hindrance. Workers who have worked for at least 90 days in the preceding 12 months are eligible. But registration requires documents of age proof, a certificate of employment, and photographs. Additionally, it involves interacting with labour department officials. As a large number of construction workers are migrants, and may not be familiar with the local language, administrative procedures can themselves prove a major roadblock.

In March 2013, a bill was introduced in the Rajya Sabha to amend the BOCWA. The proposed amendments will remove the upper age limit for registration (60 years) and cancel the requirement of prior work in the sector for 90 days. It is also hoped that the Amendment will help to simplify the process, to increase registration of workers.

6.3 Women construction workers

Women migrant workers are particularly hard to enumerate because it is difficult to separate those migrating for marriage from those migrating for labour (and of course many women are migrating for both purposes simultaneously). One estimate puts the number of women in construction workers at 33 per cent of total. Apart from various forms of physical insecurity women face at work, upward mobility is found to be more limited for women. A study in Tamil Nadu found that women are restricted to playing the role of helpers at construction sites and struggle to move up to the more skilled work (such as masonry or plastering). Most men workers learn this on the job through informal training, not usually available to women. Formal courses in masonry targeted at women have emerged in Kerala and Ahmedabad, and have had strong impact on the incomes of women. In Kerala, the increase was almost 300 per cent.[28]

7. Contract and casual worker welfare in the formal sector

In India, contract workers are protected by the Contract Labour Regulation and Abolition Act, 1970. A contract labourer is defined in the Act as one who is hired in connection with the work of an establishment by a principal employer through a contractor. While the contractor supplies labour for the establishment, a principal employer controls and/or owns the establishment. Prior registration with the government is required for employing contract workers. Theoretically, contract labour is authorized only for non-core, non-perennial tasks. But in recent years, many state governments have waived this restriction and taken a permissive approach to use of contract labour in core processes year-round.

Contract workers need to be paid as per Minimum Wage Act prevalent in the state. For their health and welfare, certain provisions are mandated such as safe drinking water, canteen facilities, first aid facilities, etc. Social security cover—in terms of provident fund benefits and medical insurance—must also be provided to contract workers.

In actual practice, there are a lot of concerns and deviations observed within the contract labour system in India. These concerns stem from multiple sources:

- The use of contract labour to replace regular workforce in core and perennial operations means unequal pay for equal work

---

[27] Kurup, Deepa. 2013. 'Working Sans Safety Net', *The Hindu*, 31 July.

[28] Annette, B. 2008. 'A Study on Gender Discrimination among Construction Workers and the Means of Empowering Women Construction Workers with Special Reference to Tiruchirappalli'. Available at: http://shodhganga.inflibnet.ac.in/handle/10603/5120?mode=full

- Non-timely/non-payment of wages and other dues such as the Provident Fund, Employees' State Insurance (ESI), and bonus to the contract workers, by the contractor
- Low adherence to minimum wage requirements, health insurance, and maternity benefits access, by the principle employers
- Non-regularization of contract workers on employer roles in spite of long-serving and plant expansion, primarily to avoid increased wage and benefits costs. This means such workers have no bargaining power (since they enjoy no status with which to make demands) and no accumulated seniority or progression path

In a globalized world of fast changing and competitive markets, there is no option but to install a flexible framework for labour, capital and business and industry. Such a framework has a direct bearing on FDI, economic growth, and employment. Various countries have liberalized their labour laws, with differing levels of effectiveness, to make these more investor and employer-friendly. Critics argue that the same liberalization has weakened job security, collective bargaining, and, sometimes, even the skill requirements of the workforce. In India, this trend is evident in the rising level of contract workers, despite shrinkage and stagnation in regular employment over the last few financial quarters. In short, India's labour force for the formal sector, is rapidly becoming informalized.

8. The National Food Security Act and the public distribution system

Food security includes the availability, access, and absorption of food. In this chapter, our focus is on access; making sure poor households have sufficient food to meet their nutritional requirements. The passage of the NFSA in July 2013 has led to a renewed interest in food security. We will explore NFSA along with the PDS, as the new Act will be based on the PDS as it has existed in its targeted form since 1997.

As per the provisions of the Act, up to 75 per cent of the rural population and up to 50 per cent of the urban population will have uniform entitlement of 5 kg of foodgrains per month at highly subsidized prices of ₹3, ₹2, ₹1 per kg for rice, wheat, coarse grains, respectively. This amounts to entitling about two-thirds of the 1.2 billion population to subsidized foodgrains under the PDS. Other features are—children aged six months to 14 years will receive take-home rations or hot cooked food, maternity benefit will be provided to pregnant and lactating mothers, and a food security allowance will be given in case of non-supply of foodgrains or meals (see Box 5.1).

The benefits assured by the Act are mostly already in place through the PDS, the Supplementary Nutrition Programme and the Mid Day Meal Schemes. What is new in the Act is the extension of outreach of the PDS to cover nearly 75 per cent of the rural and 50 per cent of the urban population, be it with a reduced subsidized ration of 25 kg per household per month, in lieu of the ear-

---

Box 5.1: *Main features of NFSA (Ordinance)*

1. PDS to cover 75 per cent of rural and 50 per cent of urban population
2. Each individual to get 5 kg of foodgrains per month @ ₹3 per kg for rice, ₹2 per kg for wheat, and ₹1 per kg for coarse grains
3. *Antyodoy* households to get 35 kg per month
4. Pregnant and lactating mothers to get nutritious meals as per continuing norm plus 6,000/- onetime benefit
5. Cooked meals to children up to 14 years in school as per continuing norms
6. Supplementary nutrition to children under six as per continuing norms
7. End-to-End computerization and Aadhaar linked delivery
8. Eldest woman of the family to be treated as family head

Source: Compiled by the authors.

lier 35 kg. Further, the eldest woman in the family is now taken as the head of the family, a departure from an age-old practice of taking the eldest man. Commensurate with this change, the subsidy element of the PDS will soon be transferred in cash to the bank accounts of these women. Based on evidence that cash in the hand of woman will be used for the family and not wasted, the shift also ensures that, should a woman be deserted by her husband, her entitlement will hold good, and the husband cannot cancel her card.

A three-tier independent grievance redressal system will further ensure transparency and reduce leakages. Beneficiary identification will be left to the states, which may frame their own criteria or use social, economic, and caste census data.

The manner in which the Act was passed—first by ordinance and then recently pushed through by a sitting Lok Sabha—has come under criticism, leading to comments that this is more electoral gimmick than a sustainable and well-conceived programme.[29] There has been a furore by some media commentators over the additional fiscal burden the government will bear as a result of the Act. They argue that the Bill will add the subsidy woe of the government, taking it to new levels (expected to be 2 per cent of GDP by 2017). Besides, to strengthen the procurement chain, it is argued, a huge investment in human resources and infrastructure will be required. At present, the government procures only 30 per cent of India's total grain and pulse production. To meet the increased demands of the Act, procurement must increase, pushing India into even greater imports, with commensurate widening of the CAD.

Other commentators have dismissed the argument that the subsidy bill will increase, and have instead, criticized the Act for not going far enough in its provisions. Dipa Sinha argues that the Act's provisions are not as expensive as they are claimed. She writes,

> The current food subsidy is around ₹90,000 crores. With an average subsidy of ₹20 per kg; the food bill will cost about ₹1,24,000 crores (for 62 mn tonnes). This is around 1.2% of the GDP and not 3% as projected by media reports. The other figure that is repeatedly quoted by the media is that food subsidy was only ₹25,000 crores 10 years back and it has been constantly increasing at a rapid rate. The reality is that as seen in the figure below from the Economic Survey of 2013 over the last 10 years the food subsidy has hovered around 1% of GDP. Interestingly, the percentage of households accessing foodgrains from the PDS has gone up from 28% in 2004–05 to 39% in 2009–10 and 44% by 2011–12 despite the expenditure remaining constant at less than 1% of GDP. This has also been accompanied by steep reduction in leakages in the PDS.[30]

Proponents of food security critique the Act for the undue haste in its passage and for not addressing the issue with sufficient depth. They critique the reduction in entitlement from 35 kg to 25 kg, bringing it below the calorie requirements specified by Indian Council of Medical Research. Neither, it is argued, does the Act sufficiently address malnutrition among children. While it converts Mid Day Meal and take-home rations in schools to legal entitlements, this is not accompanied by specific interventions for the malnourished.[31]

Critiques notwithstanding the NFSA present an opportunity to move away from the partiality and exclusion that has plagued the PDS since 1997.

The PDS was introduced in 1965 as a universal system integrating food procurement and distribution. The government procured grains from farmers and distributed them across the country. The scheme was based

---

[29] Rajalakshmi, T.K. 2013. 'Half Baked Scheme', *Frontline*, 9 August.

[30] Sinha, Dipa. 2013. 'National Food Security Ordinance: Anything But Expensive', *Economic and Political Weekly*, XLVIII (30), 27 July.

[31] Such specific interventions would require the provision of calorie-dense foods, growth monitoring, nutrition, health education as well as access to basic health care, sanitation, and drinking water.

on the understanding that the market could not ensure access to sufficient foodgrains by the poor. Performance of the scheme varied across states. In 1997, the government abolished the universal, in favour of the targeted PDS. Targeting meant families classified as APL could no longer access food through the system. Several studies showed that APL cardholders were often extremely poor.[32] Thus in effect, the scheme was excluding a large proportion of India's poor. In a report on the extent of exclusion through Targeted Public Distribution System (TPDS), a *Down To Earth* Report claims that 76 million of India's poor have been excluded from the scheme over the last decade, as data about beneficiaries has not been updated since the 1991 census. Quoting from the report,

> The country's population was 840 million in 1991, significantly less than 1,210 million as per 2011 census. But the government recognizes only those beneficiaries whose names appear in the 2000 population projections, which, too, were based on the 1991 census. Population projections were not made in 2010. In 1993–94, the Planning Commission decided that at least 36 per cent of the country's population should be given the benefits of PDS. The decision was taken on a recommendation made by an expert group on estimation of proportion and number of poor. The expert group was chaired by D.T. Lakdawala. Following this, the government calculated the number of beneficiaries as 359.2 million. Ever since, no change has been made in the number despite two censuses.[33]

Quoting activist Kavita Srivastava, the report ends, 'Had the government given PDS privileges to 36 per cent people based on 2011 census, there would have been 76 million more beneficiaries. But the government stuck to the population projections of 2000.'[34]

There is potential within NFSA to move the PDS away from the current APL-BPL system which excludes a large section of the poor. This could be done by identifying only the rich, and covering everyone else.

> The NFSO proposes to do this by covering 67% of the population at uniform prices of ₹3 for rice, ₹2 for wheat and ₹1 for millets, while excluding the rest. The 67% is to be divided across the states based on their level of development. So states like Bihar, Uttar Pradesh and Rajasthan can expect to cover 80% or more of their rural population under the PDS.[35]

Also, the Act, for the first time, recognizes maternity entitlements for all pregnant women. This is seen as recognition of rights of children less than six months for the first time. Maternity benefits are intended to help women rest and focus on breastfeeding. However, there are concerns that limiting maternity entitlements to only two pregnancies penalizes women for subsequent pregnancies.

Two other critiques of NFSA deserve mention. First, that it is based on the TPDS which is itself subject to heavy leakages, and second, that it is anti-farmer.

In response to the first, recent studies indicate that leakages in PDS are being effectively addressed in states such as Tamil Nadu, where the system has been overhauled substantially. 'The PDS is functioning better in states where the BPL coverage has been expanded, where issues prices have been decreased and reforms in PDS have been initiated which is precisely what the NFSO aims to do'.[36]

---

[32] Ramakumar, R. 2011. 'PDS in Peril', *Frontline*, 19 November–2 December.

[33] Jitendra. 2013. 'Public Deprived System, *Down To Earth*, 31 July.

[34] Ibid.

[35] Sinha, Dipa. 2013. 'National Food Security Ordinance: Anything But Expensive', *Economic and Political Weekly*, –XLVIII (30), 27 July.

[36] This is from Sinha, Dipa. 2013. 'National Food Security Ordinance- Anything But Expensive', *Economic and Political Weekly*, XLVIII (30, 27 July). She references the following in her piece to make this particular assertion: Drèze, Jean and Reetika Khera. 2011. 'PDS leakages: the plot thickens', *The Hindu*, 12 August; Himanshu. 2011. 'A revived PDS is visible now', Livemint, 16 August; Khera, Reetika. 2011. 'Revival of the Public Distribution System: Evidence and Explanations', *Economic and Political Weekly*, 46 (44, November 5); Sen, Abhijit and Himanshu. 2011. 'Why Not a Universal Food Security Legislation?', *Economic and Political Weekly*, 46 (12, 19 March).

The popularity of PDS in preference to cash, reported in a detailed survey conducted in 2011 in nine states, is a direct endorsement of the system.[37] It was found in this study that people preferred to receive food instead of cash in all states except Bihar. At the time of the survey, it is likely that many of the technical fixes since introduced in Bihar, had not yet been implemented.

Since 2011, however, Bihar has made significant headway, as Himanshu writes:

> A former laggard in this respect, Bihar was the state with the highest leakage and lowest percentage of population accessing PDS has shown a surprising turnaround. Per person consumption of PDS cereals in Bihar was 0.66 kg in 2009–10 as against the national average of 1.8 kg per person. By 2011–12, per capita consumption of rice and wheat from PDS increased to 2.2 kg per person, marginally higher than 2.1 kg per person nationally. What about leakages? As against 65 per cent leakage in PDS in 2009–10, Bihar has managed to reduce leakage in 2011–12 to only 12 per cent.[38]

The anti-farmer criticism is countered with data from a recent editorial in *Economic and Political Weekly*.

> In 2011–12, total cereal procurement was 63 million tonnes (mt), in 2012–13 it was 71 mt. Total distribution was 55 mt and 56 mt in the two years, respectively. The new PDS is expected to see distribution go up to 62 mt. So how is the demand of the new PDS going to take procurement to impossible levels and turn agriculture upside down by pushing aside all non-cereal crops?[39]

Further, it can be argued that the Act provides a fresh opportunity to promote investment in agriculture, in land and water management and cold storage and warehouse facilities. The impact of investment could bring multifold improvement in the employment and returns to farmers and, hence, reduce poverty in the country.[40]

The real concern with the Act—and with which both proponents and opponents concur—is the undue haste with which it was passed, without the process of consultation with subject matter experts and other political parties. The critical issues in need of consultation include: the means of identification of the beneficiaries, method of implementation, and the benchmarking of population within various states eligible for the scheme.

9. Delivering social protection: Direct benefit transfers

The government has been pushing towards streamlining of delivery of cash and in-kind scheme benefits through direct payments, in cash, to beneficiary bank accounts. Among the advantages are: the scope for combining payments against multiple welfare schemes, the reduced transaction cost by reliance on technology and bank clearing systems rather than clerical manpower, and—in transforming some in-kind benefits into cash, such as cooking fuel, PDS, and school vouchers—the poor are 'empowered' as customers in the market, rather than treated as dependent beneficiaries.

The government has already commenced pilots of direct benefit transfers (DBTs),

---

[37] Jose, Jijo. 2011. 'The PDS Learning Curve, Down to Earth', 18 August.

[38] In the same article, Himanshu goes on to discuss the poorly performing states and homes in on Gujarat. He writes,

> Not only has the percentage of population purchasing from PDS declined from 26% in 2009–10 to 22% in 2011–12, the average consumption from PDS per person has also declined from 0.8 kg per person to 0.6 kg per person. But the worst aspect of PDS performance in Gujarat is the fact that it is now the state with the highest leakage in PDS in 2011–12: The figure rising from 45% in 2009–10 to 69% in 2011–12. Among big states, Gujarat had the highest leakage in 2011–12.

See http://www.livemint.com/Opinion/TTLqU0Cg2iF4hYtJSHtMRI/PDS-a-story-of-changing-states.html, accessed in October 2013.

[39] Editorial. 2013. 'Case for a Food Security Programme', *Economic and Political Weekly*, XLVIII (30, 27 July).

[40] Ibid.

notably for the NSAP which incorporates five pension and disability benefits. In a study of the scheme in two states (Rajasthan and Karnataka), such DBTs were found to be 'small but effective'. The study found that the extent of leakages were negligible. The argument made is that while in in-kind systems such as the traditional PDS, leakages and corruption can occur not only at the time of enrolment but also in subsequent visits to the fair price shop, DBTs offer little scope for leakage once beneficiaries are enrolled as pensioners.[41]

Opposition to cash transfers stems from perceptions of what the poor themselves would prefer, as well as an understanding of intra-household dynamics[42] and the possible greater inconvenience of reliance on bank and post office branches which can be some distance from the village or hamlet. There is also concern that some supply-side markets are not sufficiently developed in India to provide any real choice to the new beneficiaries-turned-consumers.

In the same survey quoted above, most people preferred to receive food rather than cash. While this may be understood simply in terms of comfort zone, the reasons articulated for this preference were clearly well thought out. As one of the surveyors writes,

> These reasons ranged from remoteness of banks and markets to the fear of misuse of money on goods such as clothes, medicines or children's material wants. An old woman told us how difficult it would be for her to first travel miles to withdraw money from the bank and then take the money to a market which would

be equally far away. A young woman doubted the government's intention and ability to deposit money in her family account every month and index the amount transferred to inflation as and when the prices increase.[43]

A further doubt about rendering in-kind benefits in cash is that the new influx of cash could have an inflationary effect and increase the prices of commodities.

Based on the NASP and other pilots, the government is currently upscaling its trials which are now underway in 20 districts of 16 states, covering seven schemes including scholarships, cash benefits for pregnant and lactating mothers, conditional cash transfers for girls and stipends for trainees and job seekers through coaching-cum-guidance, and vocational training. During the first phase of implementation (1 January to 31 March 2013), the DBT is intended to cover 26 such schemes in 43 districts.

Table 5.4 gives the detail.

The NREGA programme has also shifted its entire payment system to direct transfers to banks and post offices.

Clearly, the benefits of DBTs can be substantial but there are certain conditions which must be in place to secure success. Latin American countries such as Brazil and Nicaragua have used cash transfers to reduce poverty as well as increase access to educational and health services. A report on these experiences is careful to emphasize the conditions of success. 'Conditional Cash Transfers have been successful in reducing poverty and show promise in promoting education and health outcomes where reforms are backed by efforts to step up service provision and quality.' In terms of improving targeting and delivery, it was found that the creation of a national registry and means of identification helped the process substantially—perhaps making a case for Unique Identification Number (UID)

---

[41]Dutta, Puja, Stephen Howes, and Rinku Murgai. 2010. 'Small but Effective: India's Targeted Unconditional Cash Transfers', *Economic and Political Weekly*, XLV (52), 25 December.

[42]While food is generally seen as a woman's domain, cash is more a man's, and even if benefits are transferred to women's accounts, male members can make legitimate claims on it. Thus rendering benefits in cash may lead to a dip in the nutritional consumption (in the case of PDS). Rao, Nitya. 2013. 'Cash Transfers', Letter in *Economic and Political Weekly*, XLVILL (4, 26 January).

[43]Dutta, Puja, Stephen Howes, and Rinku Murgai. 2010. 'Small but Effective: India's Targeted Unconditional Cash Transfers', *Economic and Political Weekly*, XLV (52), 25 December.

Table 5.4: List of 25 schemes implemented for direct benefit transfer (as on 10 April 2013)

Sl. no.	Ministry/department	No. of schemes		CS/CSS	Name of the scheme	Share of centre	Funds flow
1	M/o Social Justice & Empowerment	6	1	CSS	Post Matric Scholarship for SC Students.	100%	MSJE to State Govt to District to Beneficiaries.
			2	CSS	Pre-Matric Scholarship for SC Students.	100%	MSJE to State Govt to District to Beneficiaries.
			3	CSS	Pre-Matric Scholarship for Children of those engaged in unclean occupations.	100%	MSJE to State Govt to District to Beneficiaries.
			4	CS	Upgradation of merit of SC Students.	100%	MSJE to State Govt to District to Beneficiaries.
			5	CSS	Post Matric Scholarship for OBCs.	100%	MSJE to State Govt to District to Beneficiaries.
			6	CS	Top Class Education Scheme.		
2	M/o Human Resource Development, D/o Higher Education	3	1	CS	Scholarship to Universities/College Students.	100%	MHRD–Beneficiary through Canara Bank Account
			2	CS	Fellowship Schemes of UGC.		MHRD–UGC Beneficiary through Canara Bank Account.
			3	CS	Fellowship Schemes of AICTE.		MHRD–AICTE–Institution-Beneficiary
3.	M/o Human Resources Development, D/o School Education & Literacy	2	1	CS	National Means cum Merit Scholarship.	100%	SBI to Beneficiary Accounts
			2	CS	National Scheme for Incentive for the girl child for secondary education.	100%	Canara Bank to Beneficiary Accounts
4	M/o Tribal Affairs	3	1	CSS	Post-Matric Scholarship Scheme for ST Students.	100%	MOTA to State Govt. to District to Beneficiaries.
			2	CS	Top Class Education System.	100%	MOTA to Institutes to Beneficiaries
			3	CS	Rajiv Gandhi National Fellowship.	100%	MOTA to UGC. to Beneficiaries
5.	M/o Minority Affairs	3	1	CSS	Matric Scholarship Scheme.	100%	Through State Govt to District to Bank to Beneficiary
			2	CS	Maulana Azad National Fellowship.	100%	Through UGC to beneficiary
			3	CSS	Merit cum Means Scholarship Scheme.	100%	Through State Govt to Institutions to Beneficiary
6	M/o Women and Child Development	2	1	CSS	Indira Gandhi Matriva Sahyog Yojana (IGMSY).		
			2	CS	Dhanalakshmi Scheme.		
7	M/o Health & Family Welfare	1	1	CSS	Janani Suraksha Yojana.		
8	M/o Labour and Employment	5	1	CS	Scholarship to the Children of beedi-workers.	Cees on sale of beedi to finance Beedi Welfare Fund	Money flows to beneficiaries from Beedi Welfare Fund
			2	CS	Housing subsidy to beedi-workers.		
			3	CSS	Stipend to children in the special schools under the Child Labour Projcet.	100%	Fund Released to District Societies
			4	CS	Stipend to trainees under the Scheme of Welfare of SC/ST job seekers through Coaching, Guidance and Vocational Training.	100%	Field Institutes of DGET
			5	CSS	Payment of stipend to trainees under the Scheme of Skill Development in 34 Districts affected by Left Wing Extremism (LWE).	100%	State Treasury, Directorate of Employment and Training institutes
	Total No. of Schemes	25					

Source: Planning Commission of India, http://planningcommission.nic.in/sectors/dbt/25_schemes.pdf (last accessed on 8 November 2013).

> **Box 5.2:** *Tying up DBTs with Aadhaar*
>
> 'Aadhaar' is a 12-digit individual identification number issued by the Unique Identification Authority of India on behalf of the Government of India. This number will serve as a proof of identity and address, anywhere in India and will consequently form the basic, universal identity infrastructure over which Registrars and Agencies across the country can build their identity-based applications.
>
> By providing a clear proof of identity, Aadhaar is expected to empower poor and underprivileged residents in accessing services such as the banking system and streamline the channelling of the various services provided by the government and the private sector, under the DBT process. From a social protection perspective, Aadhaar has been proclaimed a game-changer. It is expected to 'clean up' the targeting of beneficiaries and ensure smoother delivery of cash or food to the poor. However, several challenges have been pointed to in this direction, including the changing nature of biometrics.
>
> A pilot in East Godavari District of Andhra Pradesh linking PDS to UID has revealed some of the challenges. 'When cardholders go to buy their PDS rations, their ration card number and UID number are punched into an "e-Point of Sale" (ePOS) machine. If the two match, they have to authenticate their fingerprint. If a successful authentication does not occur in five attempts, a mobile number can be entered, and a "one time password" (OTP) is sent to that number. After successful fingerprint authentication or use of the OTP, the sale can proceed.' This outline of the process highlights the multiple points at which it can go wrong. Even with an OTP specifically in place to help in cases where biometric identification does not work, Khera found instances of elderly widows who couldn't access their rations or had to make repeated trips to the ration shop. PDS outlets were found closed because a machine was not working (not because there was no grain inside!). Cases where ration card numbers were not recognized by the machine also meant many couldn't access their rations.
>
> These are serious concerns for families that depend on PDS to meet nutritional requirements. While UID potentially has a powerful streamlining effect, the challenges that come with sophisticated technology and the linkages required between multiple data systems and technology platforms are considerable.
>
> *Source:* Reetika Khera. 2013. 'Lessons from the East Godavari Pilot', *The Hindu*, 11 April.

in India.[44] See Box 5.2 on the DBT-Aadhar link in India.

K.S. Suryanarayana has commented that DBTs can succeed if the following conditions are met: (i) Aadhaar-based identification and targeting for poverty alleviation programmes must be valid and efficient; (ii) poor households must have sufficient liquidity to buy foodgrains or LPG at subsidized prices; (iii) subsidies are price-indexed to insulate poor people from periodic price inflation; and (iii) there is no constraint on physical access.[45]

Much of what is envisaged under DBTs depends on management of the delivery system. While technology in the form of biometric verification, core banking, Automated Teller Machines (ATMs), smart cards, SMS alerts can significantly enhance the capacity of the system, success depends on the robustness of each of these and its fit for purpose, as well as on smoothening the interoperability between them. All these are questions of institutional design, informed by the ultimate goal of making it work for the poor.

10. Conclusion: Social protection and beyond

The government's role in social protection has recently become the focus of public debate, in a context where growth has slowed

---

[44]Bastalgi. 2011. 'Conditional Cash Transfers as a Tool of Social Policy', *Economic and Political Weekly*, XLVI (21), 21 May.

[45]Suryanarayana, M.H. 2013. One Pager-200, International Policy Centre for Inclusive Growth, Brazil, May.

and social protection pay-outs have increased. The issues are nicely summed up in what has come to be termed, the 'Bhagwati–Sen debate'. While Amartya Sen and Jean Dreze emphasize that economic growth is not possible without enhancing initial capabilities of people (especially investment in nutrition and education), Bhagwati and Panagariya[46] argue that economic growth must precede social protection-related investments. In letters exchanged in *The Economist*, Amartya Sen has asserted that he is not against growth. In fact, he just believes economic growth in itself is insufficient. 'To go much farther and faster', he argues, 'far greater investment is needed in critical areas like nutrition and education'.

Framing the debate between Sen and Bhagwati as one of 'growth' verses 'redistribution' would be simplistic, since both sides incorporate the various core theories of modern economics:

1. Human capital's and public investment's contribution to growth (Keynes)
2. Poverty shifts due to growth, depending on initial distribution and inequality levels (the poverty elasticity of growth)

Going by its recent pronouncements and budgetary outlays in social sector-related programmes, the government is surely emphasizing enhancing 'initial capabilities'. However, whether this is pure political posturing prior to elections or a genuine commitment to 'inclusive growth', time will tell.

While the role of the state in creating 'initial capabilities' and a social protection floor is unquestioned, a consensus is emerging that an umbrella of social protection measures, continuing till perpetuity, cannot be the solution to India's development and inclusive growth agenda. The need to curb perpetual costs has been further highlighted in the context of continuing economic

uncertainty and the challenges faced by India in recent times. The passage of the recent Food Security Act by the Parliament has brought to the fore the divisions among academics, economists, and policymakers concerning the cost of social protection in periods of slow/no growth, and the growing need for firm resolve in policymaking.

Clearly, renewed focus on economic growth is a necessity for India to be able to afford the social protection cover required by its most needy citizens. The discussion has now turned towards the enablers that would make this growth happen, in particular, job-plenty (rather than jobless) growth and the development of skills required to avail these jobs. The skills agenda is discussed at length in Chapter 6. From a social protection perspective, the emerging view is that the government must enable an ecosystem in which the majority of citizens move to a market-based self-reliance, where they can secure their own incomes and protect themselves reasonably from risks and shocks. This ecosystem must incorporate clear policy and policy implementation, a job creation framework, a job quality framework, and skill development incentives. In withdrawing from mass-scale provision of social protection and becoming a facilitator of such an enabling ecosystem, the government will be better able to focus its limited resources on the most needy.

There have been many instances of market-based initiatives that aim to create effects similar to the social protection introduced by the government. These include: the creation of 'no frills' savings bank accounts by banks and supporting financial education programmes; women group-focused programmes such as Andhra Pradesh's SERP which use mutual structures and self-help to build social protection, and skills-led livelihood enablement models of private training providers such as LabourNet (Figure 5.6).

Many of these models will take root and be sustainable if they are backed by realistic business models that embrace the frugality

---

[46]Bhagwati and Panagariya. 2013. *Why Growth Matters: How Economic Growth in India Reduced Poverty and the Lessons for Other Developing Countries.*

Figure 5.6: *A model—'Protection through skilling'*

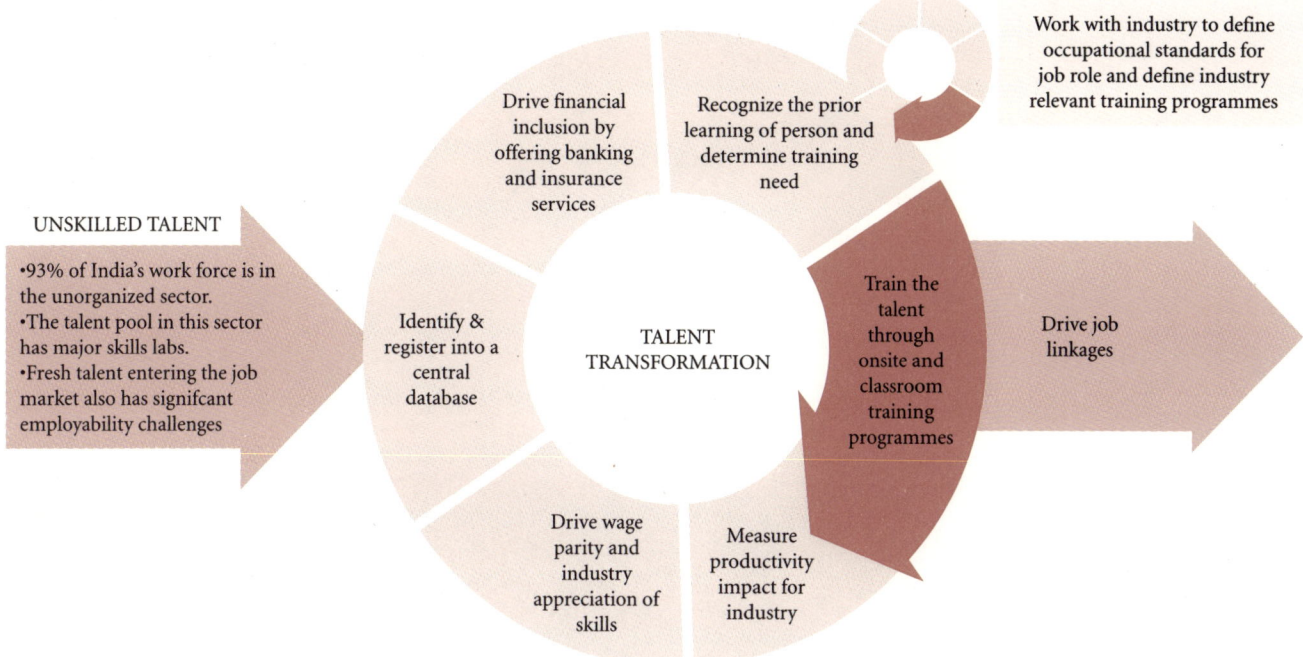

Source: LabourNet corporate presentation.

and scale demanded by the 'Bottom of the Pyramid' approach. The success of the government's policy should also perhaps be measured by the space that it vacates for these models to take root as well as the enabling ecosystem that is created to support these models.

We are in a defining period in the Indian context. The elections during the coming year will further enhance the clash of ideas, between social protection led by unsustainable state populism versus that led by models based on market and mutual or self-help forces which require a government which is, above all, a responsible enabler and enforcer.

Suggested reading

Ministry of Rural Development, Government of India. 2012. 'NREGS Sameeksha—An Anthology of Research Studies on MNREGA from 2006–2012', Orient Blakswan.

Skilling India

ORLANDA RUTHVEN

1. Introduction

The Government of India's policy on skills was reborn during the Eleventh Plan which ran from 2007 to 2012. The new policy was a major departure in several ways. First, the long-standing focus on self-employment schemes and the informal sector is at an end, replaced with a new focus on wage jobs. Second, schemes which had run largely through government institutions, local government, and elected bodies are now run by private agents implementing programmes according to government requirements and/or with its funds. Third, there is a powerful drive to scale, to extend the reach and capacity of the skills sector to absorb a much greater proportion of youth. This drive to scale now dominates over the more multifaceted role which the government played earlier, in provision and regulation of training and even in the maintenance of standards of employment.

This chapter explores the current state of skills policy in India and the evidence that we have so far, of its impact and effectiveness for poor people's livelihoods. The government's skills policy is at once supply-led and private sector-led. While the new world of PPPs is heralded as the way to create both scale and quality, the approach is associated with remarkably little engagement with industry employers. At the same time, the ultimate customer, the learner—young, poor, mostly rural Indians—is marginalized by the scale imperative.

For all its investment in a skills policy, the government and its partners have had little discussion about what skill *is*, what it's *for* and, above all, how it is best acquired. This chapter hopes to contribute by reviewing the government's policy, with reference to international experience and a livelihoods perspective.

Section 2 sets the economic scene and discusses the availability and quality of employment to less educated, mostly rural, youth, in 2013, two years after the topic was discussed in detail at a more upbeat moment. Section 3 discusses the government's skills and vocational training policy before and after the shift marked by the Eleventh Plan. Section 4 reflects—with the help of case illustrations and some aggregate figures—on the kinds of outcomes which are thus far emerging for learners and institutions. Section 5 takes a step back and discusses some of the areas which are neglected and unproblematized in the current government-led discourse: the weak school base and how to respond to this, the under-focus on the role of in-situ or on-the-job learning, partnerships with industry towards productivity and better wage share, and the challenge of life-long employability. Section 6 concludes.

2. What are the jobs out there?

In 2011, we reported how the informal sector employment growth of the early 2000s was replaced by a fall in all types of employment

Chapter 6

from the mid 2000s, explained mostly by rural people (especially women) removing themselves from the labour market. We also reported a growth in manufacturing since 2004; while this was higher in organized and capital intensive firms, there was nonetheless a sharp growth in employment as well as output. The same period recorded rising wages—even for casual workers—in contrast to the first half of the 2000s. Topping these encouraging figures were optimistic forecasts of hiring into regular jobs, apparently showing rapid recovery from (or immunity to) the recession which was raining down on the rest of the world.

This year's economic survey makes a sobering read. With an overall GDP growth of 5 per cent in 2012–13, industry's growth (which includes construction, mining and electricity, as well as manufacturing) has gone down from more than 9 per cent in 2010–11, to just over 3 per cent a year for the last two years, and hiring and expansion plans are increasingly being put on hold.

Even in 2011, the growth during the second half of the 2000s had failed to reflect in the NSSO's 66th employment round; we can now stop waiting, since that growth turned out to be a brief spike: the 66th Round report showed no indication of shifts in employment status nor in quality of jobs. A reduction in self-employment was reflected in an increase in casual employment (both of these being low quality compared to the third category of regular employment) which grew particularly sharply between 2008 and 2010. Regular employment, in spite of being liberally defined as those receiving a regular wage even if excluded from other statutory benefits, failed to increase as a proportion of all jobs, and in fact marginally shrunk.

The 66th Round also reported that men's employment in agriculture was on a slow but persistent decline (by 11 per cent in 22 years), while for rural women, the proportion was fluctuating but the trend was more-or-less constant. Rural men's participation in manufacture, on the other hand, declined much more sharply. In place of agriculture and manufacture,

rural men are now predominantly engaged in construction, trade and hospitality, and logistics. Rural women, on the other hand, have rapidly increased their involvement in construction, but no other off-farm trades. Sectoral shifts in urban areas are not nearly so sharp for men or women.

Higher productivity is a prerequisite for better jobs. But it is a necessary yet insufficient condition. There is no inevitable process of wage with productivity increase, and since higher productivity is a key way by which firm owners increase their income, its installation is generally accompanied by all kinds of management practices aimed at reducing the claims which workers have to the share of this gain. The challenge of delivering better wages from better productivity is discussed in Section 5.

The 2011 SOIL report flagged the concept of elasticity in employment *quality*: in what conditions and in which sectors does economic growth have the effect of raising the number, not just of jobs, but of *quality* jobs? Let us look briefly at updates and case job roles for some of the ascendant sectors which were listed among those supported by the National Skill Development Corporation (NSDC), reviewed in SOIL 2011.

2.1 Construction

The construction sector grew by 4.3 per cent in 2012–13, down from 9 per cent in 2010–11. Until 2010, construction wages increased rapidly with enormous growth combining with a rise in exploitative conditions. An increasing proportion of work is managed through output-based (or 'measurement') contracts, rather than daily waged casual work, and the demand for speed from the client and builder make for extremely long hours.[1]

It is the working conditions (hours, exposure, nomadism and travel, loneliness and alienation, poor status, tough work, etc.),

---

[1]Deshingkar, P. and S. Akter. 2009. 'Migration and Human Development in India'. Human Development Research Papers. UNDP. New York; Ruthven, O. 2012. Labour Migration and Business Responsibility in India: Research and Action Project. New Delhi: GIZ.

rather than low wages, which keep workers in short supply in construction jobs. Large builders such as L&T and HCC struggle to acquire labour for these reasons; and efforts to create their own training facilities and to offer good terms of service to workers have not fully addressed this problem.

2.2 Retail, hospitality

While tourism, hotels, and restaurants took a hit from the global downturn in 2009–10, they appear to be recovering, though growth is slow, hampered by high tax regimes and poor infrastructure. While trade also contracted between 2006 and 2008, it recovered in 2011 before taking another hit. But the forecasts are good, with growth of 15–20 per cent expected over the next five years. Trade has now reached a 16 per cent share in the country's GDP. Organized retail remains a very small part of this, continuing to be hindered by obstacles of poor infrastructure and regulation.

The growing up-market and organized portion of these sectors have contributed to a higher share of employment going to higher earners, an indicator that there is a growing number of better jobs to be had in this sector.[2] At the same time, retail and hospitality job roles epitomize 'soft skills' which are both harder to learn than motor or domain skills, and require less schooling. As such, these sectors have been one of the mainstays of the new private skills providers. With their client-facing content, such jobs offer huge scope for India's less schooled youth and for those with aptitudes for relationships and interpersonal warmth.

2.3 Automotive and other engineering sectors

Following its high of 11 per cent growth in 2009–10, manufacturing (machines and non-machines, such as automotive) is now down to a measly 1 per cent. Within this, the automotive sector contracted throughout 2012–13 (while holding out well before

that). The explanation is not only the fragile global recovery, but also the deceleration in credit flows and investment, as well as the decline in the capital goods sector which has been contracting since mid-2011, hampered by decline in foreign investment and imports (exacerbated by the rupee's decline) and the stalling of new projects.

Rapid automation in sectors such as automotive and machine tools means that the demand for old style skilled workers (those who used to work manually or in semi-automation, using judgement and uncodified practice) has reduced, while demand for graduate engineers (to perform oversight, manage workforce, and operate repair shops) has increased. Demand for less skilled machine operators (CNC, automated quality checks) is clearly increasing, with a proliferation of jobs narrowly fixed on feeding and supervising machines.

2.4 Apparel manufacture

After its brief recovery following the first impact of the global downturn in 2010, the heavily export-geared apparel sector faced a dramatic contraction throughout the second half of 2011 and all of 2012. It was not until the second quarter of 2013 that a turnaround took root, largely thanks to the falling rupee. Now the prospects are bright, with industry associations expecting growth of 8–10 per cent for 2014. The sector has also been assisted by stability in the cotton price and a scrapping of excise tax.

With more than six million workers employed across 13,000 units, apparel is a key pathway of entry into wage employment for the rural poor willing to migrate to its clusters in Coimbatore, Bangalore, and NCR. It is also a mainstay for the myriad of new private training providers since workers require exceptionally low levels of education to qualify.

3. Government of India policy: Before and after

India is currently experiencing an *embarrage* of funds flowing from the government, to organizations who promise to skill and place

---

[2]Economic Survey. 2013. 'Industrial Performance'. Ministry of Finance. New Delhi.

candidates, and even to candidates themselves. The urgency founded on the powerful idea of a limited window to turn demography to dividend, is now compounded by election frenzy and by latecomers (line ministries, foreign donors) who follow in the surf of the skills *yatra*.

In all this, industry takes a back seat. While the apex associations are core passengers in the *yatra*, the voice of employers has become relatively quiet in the noisy *melee*. 'Skilling' now comes overwhelmingly in the form of short, paid-for courses, in which neither the employer nor worker are considered key customers or stakeholders.

This section will do two things. First, it will discuss briefly how India arrived at its brave new world of skills. Second, it will evaluate this world, with reference to the feedback bubbling from within the system and from international experience.

3.1 Background to the Eleventh Plan

Prior to the Eleventh Plan and the Government of India's renewal of skills policy, the vocational training and skilling sector was divided between the two Ministries, of Labour and Employment (MoLE) under the Directorate General of Employment and Training (DGET), and of Human Resources Development (MoHRD).

While DGET finances and regulates vocational 'training' for those who have dropped out of school, MoHRD has the same role for vocational 'education' for those who are still in, or have successfully passed out of, school. The distinction between 'training' and 'education' (or 'skills' and 'knowledge') is, of course, arbitrary and murky and increasingly challenged in the literature. Nonetheless, the two Ministries have built their respective domains mostly by working through separate sets of institutions: MoHRD delivers its 'vocational education' (VE) courses through schools and polytechnics. Schools offer certificates which feed into core CBSE exams, while polytechnics offer three-year diplomas for 10th pass outs. DGET, on the other hand, offers certificates for one or two-year courses from Industrial Training Institutes (ITIs), requiring mostly 10th pass, and a small number of Advanced Training Institutes for post ITIs. It also offers short courses for lesser schooled drop outs, known as Modular Employability Skills (MES).

Each of the two Ministries has its affiliation and accreditation council. The DGET's National Council for Vocational Training (NCVT) is an elected tripartite body which regulates the delivery of all the Ministry's courses, affiliates institutes, defines standards, creates content and curriculum, conducts the assessment, and issues certificates. The representation of apex industry associations (along with government and unions) is meant to ensure employer representation in the development of job and manual-skills-geared qualifications. State-level SCVTs are 'helpers' to NCVT, rather than autonomous or devolved institutions.[3]

The MoHRD's All India Council for Technical Education (AICTE) has its roots in the need for coordinated planning rather than regulation. It assists central government to plan and improve the quality of technical (or professional) education in the country. Thus it is governed by appointed bureaucrats from centre and state, as well as by appointed industry representatives. While it acts as the implementation wing of the MoHRD's Vocational Education and Training (VET) policy, it does not assess or certify, but instead its courses are certified by the respective state boards of technical education.[4]

---

[3]World Bank. 2006. *Skill Development in India: The Vocational Education and Training System*. New Delhi: World Bank.

[4]In spite of its lesser regulatory role, the AICTE is a statutory body while the NCVT is not. This anomaly has been raised and debated with a plan floated to enact the NCVT in the Parliament, but in the current environment of uncertainty, regarding the respective roles of central government bodies and sector skills councils in different aspects of VET regulation, this is likely to be delayed or even shelved.

Until the Eleventh Plan overhaul of India's Technical Vocational Education and Training (TVET) policy, the sector had arrived at the following features:

- ITIs: ITIs had grown up as feeder institutions for public sector and blue chip engineering firms. Rather than supporting the vast majority of India's informal sector employers, ITI certification has generally been seen as an escape route from self and informal sector employment. The course choice of courses remains biased towards engineering. Prior to the Eleventh Plan, the DGET opened the sector to private providers (known as Industrial Training Centres [ITCs]).[5] An ILO 2003 study showed internal efficiency of ITCs as better.[6] Compared to ITIs, ITCs spend relatively less on salaries and more on infrastructure and learning materials.[7] The window offered to private parties to run ITIs, however, has not reduced the red-tape involved in setting them up.[8] In spite of being accounted for in the design, ITIs have traditionally lacked links with local industry.[9]

- Apprenticeships: The Apprenticeship Training Scheme is shared across DGET and MoHRD, but the vast majority (77 per cent) of apprentices are those without diplomas, covered by DGET. The scheme offers a combination of on-the-job and classroom training for ITI graduates. The poor number of apprentices—a little over 2 lakh in 2011—indicate that the bulk of employers steer clear of the scheme because of its heavy bureaucratic costs.[10] As reported by TeamLease, employers find that there are too many regulations and clearances required; non-compliers face tough punishments; the costs of training can be high; there is a lack of recognition for the employers' training and mentoring role; employers lack tax incentives; and the regulations provide for no flexibility during economic downturns.[11] Furthermore, while employers have no obligation to employ an apprentice at close of training, courts have been known to interpret that they should be given preference, creating an obligation on the employer.[12]

- Short modular schemes: The Modular Employability Scheme (MES) of the DGET emerged initially out of the work of NCEUS Commission in the early 2000s. Today, 1,386 modules exist for short courses focused on specific trade and job-geared skills. In an effort to dig down into the informal sector, there is a provision in the scheme that prior learning on-the-job be assessed and recognized, though this has not been taken up successfully.

- Polytechnics: While the diplomas offered by polytechnics or 'community colleges' are as 'vocational' as ITI courses, they have been more vulnerable to the academic drift towards classroom and non-manual skill. 'Over the years, the diploma programmes have deteriorated losing the skills components, which has resulted in their being just a diluted version of degree education.'[13]

---

[5]Odisha plus all the southern states have been particularly proactive at promoting these privately run and financed ITCs.

[6]ILO. 2013. *Global Wage Report 2012/13*. ILO. Geneva.

[7]World Bank. 2006. *Skill Development in India: The Vocational Education and Training System*. New Delhi: World Bank.

[8] Ibid.

[9]Since 1998, Institutional Management Committees (IMCs) have been put in place to ensure a role for local employers in overseeing ITI operations, but by the DGET's own admission, the vast majority of these are inactive.

[10]TeamLease. 2012. India Labour Report 2012: Massifying Indian Higher Education. Bangalore, TeamLease.

[11]Ibid., p. 92.

[12] World Bank. 2006. *Skill Development in India: The Vocational Education and Training System*. New Delhi: World Bank, p. 30.

[13]Goel, V. 2012. 'The TVET System in India for Sustainable Development', Ministry of Human Resources Development, Government of India.

- Vocational Education in schools: Schools sought to offer vocational courses as early as the 1970s but the scheme languished in low demand (less than 3 per cent of higher secondary students chose VE in less than 10,000 participating schools), as students aspired to compete in academic subjects which would provide more secure pathways to higher education. VE has further suffered from underfunding and weak industry links.[14]

- Government efforts for the informal sector: Affiliated to diploma-awarding polytechnics, 675 Community Polytechnics train 450,000 local learners a year with no restrictions of age or prerequisite. Digging even deeper is the Jan Shikshan Sansthan (JSS), a scheme offering short courses managed through NGOs, which covered 1.5 million in 2005, mostly women. The National Institute of Open Schooling (NIOS) facilitates those taking CBSE exams from home and offers 85 courses, while near all of these require eighth pass and 54 of them (i.e. nearly two-thirds) require 10th.

To summarize, the state of play before 2009 was one in which TVET had become concentrated on the one hand, towards heavy and public sector industry; on the other, it reflected the academic aspirations of learners: the relatively high status attached to classroom and theoretical learning, and the commensurate low status attached to manual skilling. The latter shows up in the academic drift of the MoHRD's diplomas, in the broad and heavy theoretical syllabus of manual trade skills, in the relative neglect of in-situ and on-the-job learning, and in the stigmatization of VE in schools.

Pavan Varma reminds us that, for school-going children who may waiver in their attendance, the prospect of manual work was frequently invoked as a threat. 'Education was valued because it could widen the distance from the laboring multitudes.'[15] Commensurate with education as a status marker, the situation was one in which very little of quality or credential was offered to the multitudes labouring in the informal economy.

3.2 TVET policy overhaul: 2009 onwards

Overview

In 2007, the UPA government signalled vocational training as part of its core agenda. The motivation was linked to an understanding of India's demography on the cusp of offering a 'unique 25-year window of opportunity'.[16] As the National Skills Development Policy (2009) stated,

> As the proportion of working age group of 15–59 years will increase steadily, India has the advantage of demographic dividend. Harnessing this dividend through appropriate skill development efforts provides an opportunity to achieve inclusion and productivity within the country and also a reduction in global skill shortages. Large scale skill development is thus an imminent imperative.

The new skills policy was devised at a time of high growth (averaging 8.5 per cent between 2007 and 2010). Not only did this create confidence that jobs would come easily to those 'skilled'; the government may also have felt it appropriate to assist firms in the industrial south and west who were experiencing a growing shortage of labour. Along with the demographic imperative, the government leapt into a supply-led approach in which the predominant driver was government policy and funds.

---

[14]World Bank. 2006. *Skill Development in India: The Vocational Education and Training System*. New Delhi: World Bank.

[15]Varma, P. 2004. *Being Indian*. New Delhi: Penguin, p. 114.

[16] King, K. 2012. 'The Geopolitics and Meanings of India's Massive Skills Development Ambitions', *International Journal of Educational Development*, 32: 665–73.

The result is an astonishing momentum of policy reform and schemes, from different parts of government, competing headily with each other. As remarkable is the scale of commitment from the private sector. On the one hand, this has come from the apex industry associations, who have contributed substantially to the investment arm of government, the NSDC.[17] On the other hand, there is a huge wave of commitment from new private training providers, many pump-primed by the NSDC but who have also invested their own funds.

The new training providers are overwhelmingly private and structured as profit-making entities (74 of NSDC's 87 partners are for profits).[18] The skills sector now demonstrates PPPs in all their splendour and diversity: joint investment in 'PPP ITIs', apex (NSDC) investment in private providers, government granting of training fees to private providers, and government and industry co-promoting standards bodies such as sector skills councils (SSCs). Each of these is discussed in more detail in the following paragraphs.

In spite of the professed market orientation of the new policy, the targets and indicators are unmistakably the work of a spending administration and not those of industry or employers. They are poorly linked to market reality, and are input rather than outcome-focused, with job outcomes only recently entering the discourse. The famous 500 million figure, for example, implies an increase in India's 'trained' manpower from 2 per cent to 50 per cent in just 14 years. What appears to have been originally a ballpark estimate, became a target and then a policy.[19] In contrast to the wave of involvement by private training providers, industry remains marginal. Rather than engaging directly with industry, the government has left this task almost completely to its training partners.

The key players

National skills development corporation

Providing soft debt and equity to skills providers since 2009, the NSDC—parented by the Ministry of Finance—now has 74 active partners. In 2012–13, NSDC partners trained and placed 200,000, bringing the cumulative figure to about 450,000. By 2022, it is claimed, 70 million will have been trained[20] and a training capacity of 15 million seats and 4,500 centres will have been created in the country. A large proportion of courses (77 per cent) is short term, the majority in the service sector and delivered in or close to urban centres.

Sector skills councils

Long in their gestation, the SSCs have finally arrived. These are NSDC-promoted bodies governed by industry and government representatives, who will henceforth lead in setting and maintaining occupational standards,[21] developing curriculum for sector courses, accrediting training providers

---

[17] Ten of the largest apex associations in India have each contributed 5.1 per cent to NSDC, giving them 51 per cent share (while running costs come from the Ministry of Finance).

[18] This is an interesting situation: while India does not permit the running of an educational, teaching institution in a for-profit framework, there is no such restriction on coaching or training institutions, even though the target group for the latter may be much poorer groups.

[19] Where did this figure come from? Rumour has it that it was spoken by the late C.K. Prahalad, as member of the new National Skills Council, derived from a rough estimation of all the new entrants onto the labour market to 2022. See King, K. 2012. 'The Geopolitics and Meanings of India's Massive Skills Development Ambitions', *International Journal of Educational Development*, 32: 665–73.

[20] …a wee bit short of the 150 million touted.

[21] DGET (Ministry of Labour) initially led on occupational standards and the curriculum built from it, with an EU-funded project (EU-India Skills). The team worked with the automotive sector to map job roles and install training against these roles and painstakingly consulted industry to create buy-in and credibility for the new National Occupational Standards (NOS). Sadly, the DGET-EU project has been somewhat eclipsed by the noise and political energy of the Skill Certification and Monetary Reward Scheme (STAR) scheme.

and managing (through outsourcing) student assessment and certification. SSCs now functioning include those for the sectors in the following table.

Sector skills councils operational	
Agriculture	Leather
Automotive	Logistics
Banking, financial services and insurance	Media
Electronics	Plumbing
Food processing	Retail and hospitality
Gems and jewellery	Rubber
Health care	Security
IT & ITeS	Telecoms

SSCs hit the ground running on 16th August when the Ministry of Finance announced the Skill Certification and Monetary Reward Scheme, branded as the STAR scheme. The scheme offers a 'reward' of ₹10,000 to any young Indian interested in getting certified for a specific skill. The courses eligible under the scheme must be SSC-approved and designed against the SSC-floated occupational standards. The scheme is cash based, i.e. while the young learner must successfully complete the assessment to win the reward (he or she is not paid if he or she fails), he can keep whatever balance is left after training is paid.

Ministry of rural development

The NRLM is hotwired into the government's framework of targets, responsible for 20 million of the famous 500 million. It has transformed itself from leading the IRDP's self-employment focus to current skill-cum-placement focus. First, SGSY was converted from a self-employment programme, then Aajeevika Skills, under the 'mission mode' of the NRLM replaced it. MoRD, like NSDC, is in the business of big numbers, which leads to high velocity (fast student turnaround) and short courses. Offering a standard two or three months' training support per trainee, it also pushes training providers into tight margins, making it difficult to fund course development and, until now, counselling and

post-placement follow-up.[22] In most cases, industry doesn't pay to get the new primed supply, it comes for free. Even when a kid drops out, a replacement will be sent.

The Roshni Scheme and new Aajeevika Guidelines

The Ministry's latest scheme is small but an important departure from the targets-before-quality ethos, bringing realism that a 'second chance' cannot realistically be provided in three months. Targeting the 27 most LWE-affected districts in the country, the scheme moves away from the short-term incentives of the past, provides better rates for training costs, costs separately for food and board and offers to cover courses of up to 12 months. It also provides ₹6,000 per head of post-placement funding to help partners address grievances and cover mentoring and next-step costs which evolve after placement. It incentivizes training providers to select good employers, by pinning courses to particular salary scales.[23] The new Aajeevika guidelines are now in line with Roshni.

Post 2009 responses of DGET

Spurred by new economic growth and reports of highly underused infrastructure and inefficiencies, DGET began a period of upgrading and expansion, supported by the World Bank at the same time that the Government of India was initiating its TVET overhaul in the Eleventh Plan. Between 2005 and 2010, the number of ITIs expanded from 5,100 to 8,600 with a corresponding expansion of seating capacity from just

---

[22]The SGSY standard is ₹16,000 all-in for three months of training, including ₹2,000 which must be passed directly to the trainee. Thus a per month per head fee of around ₹4,500. Project implementing agencies (PIAs) could improve on this by deferring part of the training after arrival at placement, during which trainees would be escorted, inducted, and mentored by a trainer from the PIA. NRLM's Aajeevika has improved on this slightly by offering an additional fee for post-placement follow-up (check) but its payment terms are much stricter, with 35 per cent of training and board costs paid only at delivery of payslips after six months.

[23]Notes from presentations at the Roshni launch at Vigyan Bhavan in New Delhi on 25 July 2013.

under 0.75 million to 1.2 million. To drive this expansion, the Ministry has not only opened up ITI certification to private party providers, but also invited the private sector into existing government ITIs in 'PPP mode'.[24] DGET is tasked with training 100 million of the 500 million.

The DGET is increasingly working on reform of curricular, building up materials for soft-skills taught alongside technical courses as a compulsory part of the course. A German TVET expert, working with two private ITCs in early 2013, highlighted the kinds of shortcomings in the NCVT-designed courses, which detract directly from their ability to deliver job-readiness.

> The major aim of [a training provider] is to build up skills. Topics like measuring, handling of tools and equipment must be constantly exercised. At the moment the practical work is based mostly on experiments and writing reports about these jobs. Work is done in groups but most students are not really busy learning the skills needed…
>
> In the short time of my stay I have observed that a big portion of the daily task of teachers is the filling in of lists and report forms. It should be considered how this time consuming duties can be reduced or streamlined… As a top priority, the work of the teachers must become easier, more efficient and teaching should be more interesting for students. Secondly more exercises must be made to improve the basic skills.[25]

The key points are too much focus on paperwork, not enough focus on building skills (by repeated and applied practice), and not enough efforts to make teaching interesting. These points are in addition to the enormous challenge of generic or 'soft' employability skills which ITI graduates have traditionally lacked.[26]

From 2010, DGET began to make the case for a national vocational qualifications framework (NVQF, now renamed the National Skills Qualification Framework [NSQF]). For this purpose, it is reorganizing the two-year courses into a semester system which will allow them to fit more easily into the NSQF. The NSQF is discussed more below.

Post 2009 responses of MoHRD

MoHRD is tasked with training 50 million of the 500 million. The MoHRD took longer than the Ministry of Labour to join the Government of India's rallying call. From 2010, however, it joined with huge energy to lead on what became the NSQF.

The Ministry then moved on to schools. As described above, TVET in India's schools had never been a successful programme. In spite of the evidence, the Ministry has moved intrepidly ahead with a plan to rehabilitate and improve vocational subjects for 9th to 12th class students. Once again, it's PPP mode, with the Ministry calling private providers to partner with schools to install and deliver vocational labs and courses, while the CBSE and NCERT develop the curricular and materials for a whole new batch of courses.

The intent is to cover government and private schools and offer more job-geared courses to kids who might otherwise struggle to get through the rigorous 10th and 12th exams. But it is unclear how the Ministry has guarded against the problems associated with the earlier VE scheme and with global experience of VE, now well documented.[27] Head teachers, at a recent awareness conference on the new courses' programme, were well aware of these issues.[28]

The 2006 World Bank report was vocal on the topic. 'Experience worldwide suggest that India would do well to not expand its

---

[24]Ernst & Young and FICCI. 2011. 'Strategic and Implementation Framework for Skill Development in India'. New Delhi, FICCI.

[25]Franz Neblich, Senior Experten Service, Final Report, April 2013.

[26]ILO. 2003. Industrial Training Institutes of India: The Efficiency Study Report. ILO SOSS, New Delhi.

[27]World Bank. 2006. *Skill Development in India: The Vocational Education and Training System*. New Delhi: World Bank.

[28]Global Conference on Skilling in Schools, PHD Chamber, New Delhi, 18 July 2013.

VE system but focus on strengthening its general education system',[29] and 'time spent on vocational skills training can detract from the teaching of basic academic skills, badly in need of improvement and equally essential for labour market purposes'.[30]

More encouraging is the Ministry's effort to realign its polytechnics and inter-colleges as 'community colleges' in the US model. India has 1.1 million seats in polytechnics and perhaps a further several lakhs in inter-colleges, the former offering vocational diplomas, the latter, regular and vocational courses at 11th and 12th. Can the North American model of local industry partnership and inclusion for regional growth, be put to use in the ailing Indian context?

Potentially, yes. The scheme offers the chance for polytechnics and inter-colleges to partner with North American colleges and invest anew in courses and capacity, for example: build local industry links and understand local skills demand, design courses to reflect these and harness industry as a trainer; accommodate not only pass outs but drop outs short of core and transferable skills, and help to provide a genuine 'second chance'; design courses to ensure that students with fewer academic credentials genuinely access decent jobs.[31]

A national skills qualifications framework

Put up first by the DGET, the framework promises to provide transferability, flexibility, and better progression for students with less schooling and those wishing to move between vocational and academic streams. It does this by pegging all qualifications to a series of agreed levels, defined as competency standards and elaborated with descriptors to show the outcomes (things which a person can do) expected for a particular competency at a particular level.

These objectives are all good. But the government has shown far less appetite for the building blocks of quality and standards which support an NSQF, than it has for the framework in the abstract. This is partly because the discourse around the meaning and significance of an NSQF in India has become hyped, and all sorts of benefits and gains have been claimed to result from it, with little evidence. The NSQF came to be seen as the policy through which the quality of training itself can be raised, through which industry links can be secured and through which the general competitiveness of the labour force can be improved.[32]

Activities of other line ministries

While the details will not be covered here, there are several other line ministries—notably Agriculture, Sports & Youth Affairs, Women & Child Development, Tourism and Textiles[33]—which have become extremely active in skilling for their own sectors. Tourism Ministry, for example, has directly established 30 institutes in hotel management and five in food craft. Likewise, the Textiles Ministry has established National Institute of Fashion Technology (NIFTs) in all major metros and Apparel Training & Design Centres (ATDCs) provide better outreach to regions, training 45,000 annually across 177 training centres.

Assessment of the new policy

The government launched an extremely ambitious skills policy in a time of high growth. While there may have been tentative indications of demand for skilled labour in some industries, on the whole, industry was

[29]World Bank. 2006. *Skill Development in India: The Vocational Education and Training System*. New Delhi: World Bank, p. iii.

[30]Ibid., p. 16.

[31] International Conference on Community Colleges at Ashoka Hotel, New Delhi on 6–7 February 2013.

[32] Ernsberger, L. 2012. Implementing National Qualification Framework(s) in India: Challenges of Policy Planning in the Context of Human Development, the Demographic Dividend and the Informal Sector. London, Institute of Education. MA, Educational Planning, Economics & International Development; King, K. 2012. 'The Geopolitics and Meanings of India's Massive Skills Development Ambitions', *International Journal of Educational Development*, 32: 665–73.

[33]Ernst & Young and FICCI. 2011. 'Strategic and Implementation Framework for Skill Development in India'. New Delhi, FICCI.

absorbing and continues to absorb unskilled labour on a large scale, and train informally, on the job, which is exactly how the impressive growth of the late 2000s was achieved. As Madhav Chavan has put it,

strangely, there seems to be little noise from the business corner…the industries that rely on contracted labour for relatively low skill jobs are hiring people informally or through contract systems and training them on the job. Although they murmur that they don't get skilled people, there does not seem to be a real worry that their businesses will hurt for lack of skilled workers. On the contrary, it appears that their businesses will stall if they wait for the youth to be trained and skilled.[34]

Even at the time of 7–9 per cent growth, post-training placement was an issue due to poor skills match and high attrition of the newly trained. With growth now down to 5 per cent, demand has tapered and the government's supply side and short-course approach is somewhat exposed. On the other hand, Roshni and the new Aajeevika guidelines are an encouraging departure from the 'second chance in three months' myth and there are signs that Aajeevika Skills is working up an appetite for impact tracking.

If we review TVET models around the world, industry involvement is deep and multifaceted. Industry is the co-author of skills policy. An effective skills development system, writes the ILO, 'connects education to technical training, technical training to labour market entry, and labour market entry to workplace and lifelong learning'. VET policy 'helps to pivot an economy towards higher value added activities and dynamic growth sectors', to handle 'the pains and gains of change'.[35]

The involvement of industry in other countries spans several functions, covering: researching and agreeing on occupational standards as a base for learning outcomes; contribution to curriculum and materials; co-creation of assessments and their administration; co-certification; engagement with trainees as part of courses; offering of placements and on-the-job training; and the management and hosting of apprenticeships. In many/most countries, these various roles are coordinated and centralized through industry councils dedicated to engagement with training providers to meet their skills needs (the SSCs).

While being supply-led, the government's policy also conceives of skills as a means to employability and ultimately, economic growth, what McGrath has called 'productivism'.[36] There has been little discussion on the need to equip young people for general living, all-round citizenship or a career in a difficult 'jungle' of jobs and self-employments. While 'soft skills' get widely discussed and offered in some form, they are mostly interpreted as skills and attributes instrumental for service-oriented jobs (language, hygiene, greeting customers, etc.) or otherwise, behaviours acceptable to the disciplines of the shop floor.

4. Policy outcomes: Learners and training institutions

4.1 Appetite for impact

Until early 2013, the parameters of assessment of the government's skills intervention were relatively relaxed. Focused on inputs (numbers trained, centres running) as much as outputs, partners were able to exclude the more probing questions and still the business flowed. NSDC, for example, requested partners to fill in the placement wage and compare this with pre-training wages, but not all partners filled these columns, we learned. The MoRD for its part, insisted on evidence of placement in the form of

[34] Chavan, M. 2013. Ideas for India. IGC Centre. New Delhi, DFID, London School of Economics, University of Oxford.

[35] ILO. 2008. 'Skills for Improved Productivity, Employment Growth and Development'. ILO. Geneva.

[36] McGrath, S. 2012. 'Vocational Education and Training for Development: A Policy in Need of a Theory?' *International Journal of Educational Development*, 32: 623–31.

appointment letters but didn't worry what happened after that, and was happy to cover most of the training cost even if placement did not result.

In early 2013, things started to change. The MoRD's support to skills shifted from SGSY to the 'mission mode' of the NRLM: faster and tougher on outputs. Training providers were told they wouldn't get paid AT ALL unless they could meet the standard of 70 per cent placement after six months on the job. If the standard was met, even then the partner would only get covered for that number trained and placed up to six months and would not be covered for the others. But this tough line is accompanied by growing understanding of what it takes to make impact: better training, for longer periods and more post-placement support.

As we have seen, the NSDC has never been so rigorous on placements and less so recently, with the new STAR scheme for which no placement is required at all. At the same time, the organization has established a more rigorous performance framework whereby information not entered will block the submission. Placement wages and durations are required, though NSDC stops short of imposing standards for either of these. For the moment, partners have 'placed' a trainee when they give the name and address of an employer which is verified by NSDC or its monitoring agents at a later date. NSDC's engagement with quality remains focused on a series of documents in place[37] (handbook, lead manual, assessment tests, etc.) rather than output-oriented indicators.

The World Bank-housed Social Observatory, set up to support the various Bank-funded projects of MoRD, is now turning its attention to NRLM's skills work. With the aim of developing stronger systems for monitoring and impact through a live Management Information System (MIS), the Social Observatory team 'will work closely with MIS team of NRLM to initiate small studies and methods to bring out cases studies for decision-making. Learning from monitoring mechanisms would help reach out and build capacities in SRLM and NRLM.'[38] The Roshni scheme design and the change of command of the skills programme appear to be signalling a new appetite for impact.

Even NSDC, after its step away from impact under the political compulsion of the STAR scheme, is currently sourcing an independent monitoring body to manage and improve its impact tracking, on the parameters of relevance (to industry and to learners), effectiveness (realization on the ground), efficiency (outputs against inputs invested), impact (creation of sustainable employment, livelihoods, enhanced industry competitiveness), and scalability, sustainability (growth potential of positive results).[39] The time is right for new research, better quality tracking, and more good sense in policy.

As the skills sector makes longer roots in India, more quality and impact-oriented agencies are joining the space: the British Council, J-PAL, DFID… The rest of this section will draw on aggregate data provided by the NSDC, case illustrations, and discussions with training providers, to reflect on what output evidence is already emerging.

4.2 Learners

A little over 700,000 individuals have been trained by the NDSC's 74 partners by June 2013. A further 800,000 or so have been covered by the largest of the line ministry programmes, the NRLM (ex SGSY) of the MoRD. They have used a similar number of partners to achieve this figure. While the placement ratio for the NSDC is 62 per cent, the ratio from the MoRD is significantly higher, at just under 80 per cent.

What does it mean that someone has been trained? A key parameter is the length of training. The following graph (Figure 6.1)

---

[37] These documents include: separate 'soft skills' modules, 'syllabus', trainer manual, participants' workbook, participants' assessment, participants' feedback mechanisms, training delivery plan, certification, etc.

[38] http://www.aajeevika.gov.in/knowledge-management.html, accessed on 8 November 2013 .

[39] http://www.nsdcindia.org/pdf/nsdc-monitoring.pdf, accessed in October 2013.

Figure 6.1: Distribution of total courses offered by NSDC partners by duration

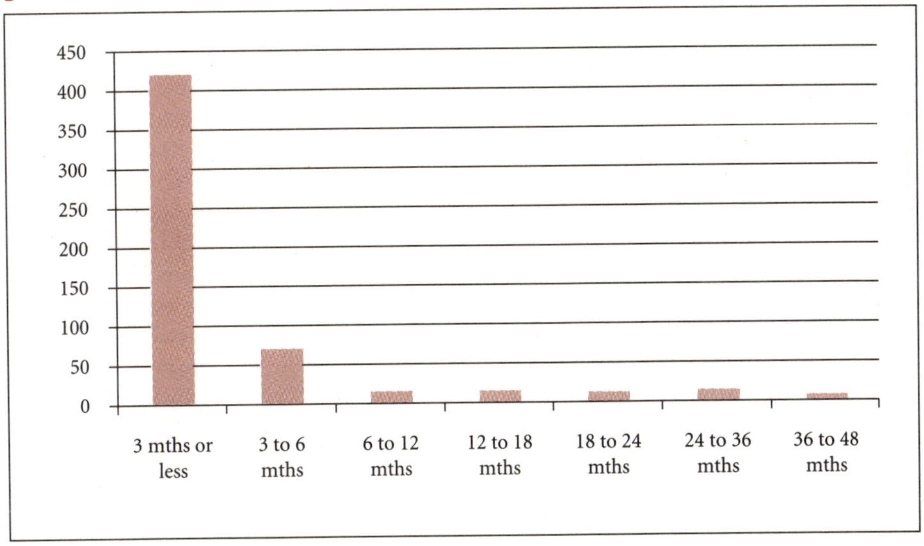

Bar chart showing course counts by duration. Y-axis 0–450. "3 mths or less" ~420, "3 to 6 mths" ~70, "6 to 12 mths" ~15, "12 to 18 mths" ~15, "18 to 24 mths" ~15, "24 to 36 mths" ~20, "36 to 48 mths" ~12.

Source: NSDC, MIS Department, as in July 2013.

shows the duration of the full list of 537 courses offered by NSDC partners, as on June 2013.

The vast majority of courses—77 per cent—are for three months or less, and only 9 per cent of courses are more than six months. When we combine this with the MoRD figures, the proportion of courses of three months or less is far higher still, since MoRD-sponsored courses are universally less than three months, typically two or even one and a half. And if we go by students, rather than courses, the proportion will be higher still, since numbers trained in short programmes are turned out much quicker than in longer programmes. The proportion of the 1.5 million students who have received more than three months training, then, would perhaps be a mere 1 lakh or so.

Short-term courses suit funders and their training providers because they give velocity: fast turnaround which meets one's targets quicker. The incentives could be quite different if trainers were required to count a different input, for example, 'person months of training provided'. But there are other reasons why short courses have swept the floor. First, it is true, as NSDC has argued, that poor people may struggle to 'take time out from work and pay for the course'.[40] Second, training providers need to manage cash flows. Payment terms for long courses often mean trainers don't get paid until the training is complete, an impossible situation when the students are in the course for a year. These institutional concerns are discussed in more detail in the next section.

The arguments demonstrate just how much concerns other than the needs of learners have taken centre stage in the new policy. For the less schooled, the norm of two months will neither repair school failure nor build core or generic employability skills. Further, it will provide scant opportunity for work-based training as part of the course. At best it can induct them well so they're less surprised or disconsolate at what they find, give them an exposure to work rules and discipline, and teach them a handful of technical skills which are most likely to be put to immediate use.

The cases below (Boxes 6.1 to 6.4) show the limitations of the trajectory of poorly schooled youth migrating into low-wage jobs, but they also highlight the opportunity which can be reaped by the tougher ones.

---

[40] Personal communication with Prateek Agarwal (analyst at NSDC, MIS Department) on 19 August 2013.

Box 6.1: *Learner Case I*

Rabi Narayan Sahoo from Odisha has been in Pune since November 2011 when he came for a placement in an auto-parts manufacturing plant following two months of training. Rabi was put in the press shop, loading and unloading cut metal sheets into a hydraulic press to create body parts, for which he earned a take-home (after deductions for food and lodging and including overtime) of around ₹5,800 per month. Following an appraisal at seven months, he was told—with the majority of his batch mates—that there was no chance for a departmental transfer and that he'd remain in the press shop for another two years at the same salary. When a year was up, he felt there was little more to

learn and decided to quit. Within a month he'd found work in a water pump parts factory, at a salary ₹4,000 higher than that offered in the first firm. Rabi was discovering his value on the open market of Pune's industrial belt. But confidence in the city can only be acquired if one can endure the harsh living conditions. Rabi and his room-mates have no ceiling fan (the landlord refuses to install one, claiming it will be stolen) and must make-do with a single bucket of water per day per head, for bathing, latrine, clothes washing, and cooking.

Source: Author's survey of workers, April 2013.

Box 6.2: *Learner Case II*

Runi is 9th pass and was hoping to earn her livelihood better than is possible in her village in rural east India. She got to know about a sewing machine operator (SMO) training course from the block office. She joined the two-month course in November 2012 and after completion, was placed in an apparel firm based in Bangalore. She was very nervous and excited about the job. But after arriving, she hardly survived a month there before returning to her village. While she was told her pay would be ₹5,000 (with some deductions for

hostel and food), at the end of the month she received only ₹1,700, far less than she was expecting. Long working hours, poor accommodation, no health check-up facilities… all in a new metro city. It was too much for her to deal with. Far away from family and friends it wasn't easy to survive so she resolved to come back, where at least she can share her joy and sorrows with her family.

Source: Author's survey of workers, April 2013.

For the better schooled, short courses can be of much greater use. India's growing challenge of educated unemployment can be usefully addressed by courses which help school leavers and graduates to connect with and gear themselves for employment opportunities which are too distant and little known for them to manage on their own. Such youth also have the financial security and network to manage more easily stays away from home. Case III (see Box 6.3) illustrates.

What sectors are the young people being filtered into? The graph (Figure 6.2) shows the distribution of trained youth across the major sectors in which NSDC partners are working. It shows that

services dominate heavily, but that there are some key exceptions, for example, in telecoms and hardware, construction, agriculture, and garments. Notable is that manufacturing doesn't appear at all, since numbers are too small (way under 5,000 trained each for 'manufacturing' and 'light engineering').

Also notable is the absence of traditional, informally organized sectors such as food processing (only 439 trained), gems and jewellery (773), and leather goods (9). With the exception of agriculture (14,585) and perhaps some of the large numbers trained inside schools and colleges (65,000), trainees are being filtered into urban-based employments, and with only 11 per cent of

Box 6.3: *Learner Case III*

Harish Arya is from Lucknow. From a middle-class family, he completed his BA and then went into journalism, following up crime stories for the racy ETV Uttar Pradesh. Then he got in trouble with the police, and with First Information Reports (FIRs) filed against him, thought it would be better to flee the city and make a new start in Delhi. He joined Shoppers' Stop and was immediately provided three months of training, outsourced to one of the leading skills providers. Now he earns ₹12,000,

organizing, manning, and assisting customers on the shop floor. He thinks it's not a bad company: they provide opportunities for more educated kids to go into management. But really he's passing time, learning enough to be able to quit and go back to Lucknow when the dust has settled, start his own retail and make money. You can't grow on these salaries, he says.

Source: Author's survey of workers, August 2013.

Figure 6.2: NSDC partners—Distribution of trainees by major sectors

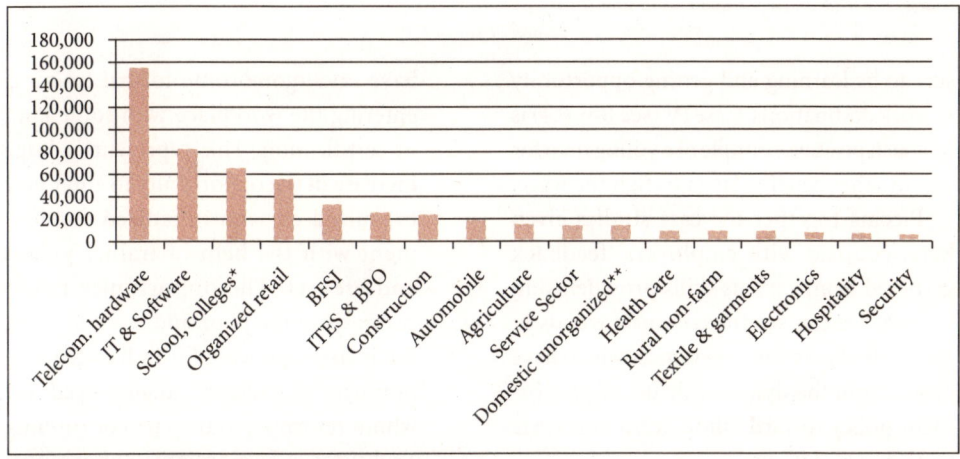

Source: NSDC, MIS Department, as in July 2013.
Note:* This refers to learners covered in the context of full-time school or college.
**This refers to housemaids, drivers, carpenters, etc., for home-based markets.

total placements in self-employment, these jobs are overwhelmingly wage jobs.

Migrating for work in India has a long and deep history, and the combined number of those who have migrated permanently, semi-permanently, and are repeatedly migrating seasonally, is estimated to be as many as 200 million.[41] But as we have seen, facilities for migrant workers are poor in most industries and regions,

and the costs of living cut into wages which are already low.

A review of the average wages offered per sector gives a key idea of job quality (see Figure 6.3). Again, this is from NSDC's partner base. Taking into account the predominance of each sector in the overall portfolio of placements, we can develop a weighted average wage of ₹7,277. Given the short period of most trainings and the poor origins of most students, this is not bad. However, if we exclude the IT and Software sector, where prerequisite qualifications are high, this weighted average drops sharply to ₹5,888.

For many trainees, this is a good wage if one can limit the costs of living, and if one is

---

[41] This excludes all the women who migrate primarily for the purpose of marriage. See Deshingkar, P. and S. Akter. 2009. 'Migration and Human Development in India'. Human Development Research Papers. UNDP. New York.

Figure 6.3: Average wages earned by placed trainees of NSDC partners, sector-wise (₹)

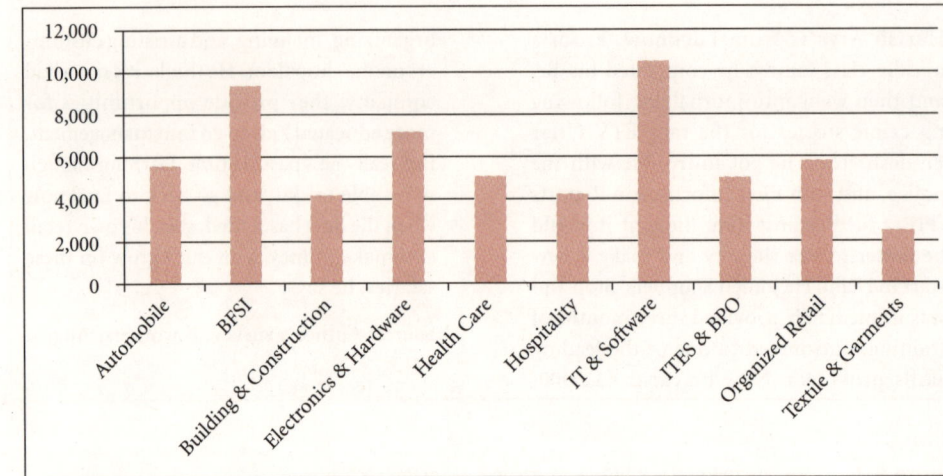

Source: NSDC, MIS Department, as in July 2013.

sure to be learning and getting opportunity in work destinations. Case IV (see Box 6.4) is one such positive example of a young man for whom other benefits far outweigh the wage.

Piecing together the case studies given here, coupled with employers' feedback garnered from various skills providers and surveys, we can see the common trends in the kinds of jobs and experiences which have arisen from the dynamic thrust of government policy towards short term and wage work-based skilling:

- More and more young people flocking to India's metros and industrial centres

have undergone some formal training, entering the workplace with some kind of certification. This represents a huge increase in the opportunity to enter new organized or semi-organized employment with the help of trainer guides and escorts. The opportunity is not confined to the poor and less educated, but is also significant for India's growing numbers of educated unemployed, for whom returning to the farm or running a subsistence-level enterprise after school have no appeal.

- Entry-level jobs which trainees fill are often poorly paid and satisfaction

Box 6.4: *Learner Case IV*

Guru Prasad, also from Odisha, is a maintenance electrician at an industrial facility in Greater Noida. He was placed in the job following completion of a two-year ITI diploma. He's only been in the job for four months but is delighted by it. The supervisors are kind and guide him well; he's learning a lot and is well accommodated in a hostel operating out of up-market family accommodation left unsold after the real estate crash in 2009–10. For each shift, he's picked up and driven the 45 minutes' distance to the company and fed in the canteen which serves fresh, oil-free vegetarian food (two sabzis, dal, raita, salad, pickle, rice, roti [offered at the table fresh off the tawa],

papad, and sweet). At ₹5,000 take-home per month, his wages are not particularly high for NCR. But Guru Prasad is reassured of opportunities for progression ahead: the company has a well publicized and transparent appraisal process which assesses all employees against criteria ranging from productivity to punctuality, adaptability to eagerness, quality to communications. Further, he is pleased to hear that the company may be entering an arrangement to offer a workplace diploma for ITI graduates like him.

Source: Author's survey of workers, April 2013.

depends on the overtime and non-monetary benefits offered. On the other hand, progression and the chance to learn, goes a long way to compensate for low wages: perhaps in the form of a supervisor who acts as mentor; a firm which observes a structured and transparent career path, or a company committed to support workers to reach the qualifications they aspire to. These are rare things and even 'skilled' workers find that progression may be better achieved by hopping between firms than by showing loyalty to the one in which they were placed.

- While learning is achieved in diverse ways, many companies have policies which ensure new entrants are kept at arm's length from the prospect of regularization, so that in-firm progression is precluded from the outset. This is achieved in a variety of ways, when ex-trainees are taken on through contractors, or as trainees (under the Apprenticeship Act or the Standing Orders of the company), or through distributors and suppliers, rather than through the lead firm.

- None but the robust and resourceful can get through the tough experience of neo-migration and the poor conditions frequently meted to such workers, a situation exacerbated by the existence of contractor intermediaries. The pull to return to the village is multifold: the farm, domestic duties, marriage… and above all, the elusive hope of a local job.

- On the other hand, for those who can tolerate it, there are various gains which go beyond the job offer. First, the exposure and freedom of being in an urban industrial centre (throb, new habits, new people, technology, anonymity) and away from the constraints of caste, family, and village. Second, new personal relationships (friendships, girl/boyfriends, new pass times). Third, the feeling of empowerment for those who acquire the confidence to make their own pathways, search and switch for the jobs which suit.

- The training offered by the new government-supported private providers tends to be short term and invariably tacked on to a weak educational base (this is discussed more below). While even a low-waged job in urban industry or services can have a huge impact on a poor rural family, the continued expansion of channels to bring entry-level workers from remote regions to employment centres may eventually help to keep wages and productivity low by facilitating labour supply.

- Indian employers demand several 'soft skills' which are widely regarded as positive attributes, such as communication skills, ability to follow-up and take initiative when problems arise, ability to learn, and team work.[42] But other attributes in demand, relate to conformity and restraint, and are, therefore, more ambivalent and may even appear to contradict the requirements above. These include: not showing behaviour which is out of line, being docile and non-emotional (not making trouble), being punctual, moving around the shop floor in an orderly and controlled way, high ability to imbibe rules and follow them.[43] This wish list of workforce norms reflects employers' concerns about security of their capital, hedging against industrial action, and a regime of maximizing output in a capital-intense environment.

4.3 Institutions

The NSDC's 74 partners collectively run an impressive 1,572 centres, many of which did not exist before 2009. Members of the new generation of skills providers are routinely

---

[42]ACCESS. 2011. *State of India's Livelihoods (SOIL) Report 2011*. New Delhi: SAGE Publications.

[43] Author interviews with HR managers of automotive components firms in Chennai, February 2013.

training and placing five, 10, even 20,000 trainees a year, numbers on a scale which was unknown before the policy change. Few training providers—even those such as Don Bosco and NIIT who have functioned without government resources for decades—have been able to stay way. But many partners concur that government scheme business is not the best and proudest part of what they do: they work on tight margins, struggle to get payments from the respective ministries, push people into substandard placements to meet their targets, and above all, cope with high levels of attrition following placement, which margins can barely cover for.

Perhaps the most important legacy of the government's frenetic and torrential thrust towards the sector, will be the private institutions it leaves behind. Many training partners who have won government contracts and even received pumb-priming support from the NSDC may not survive. But some will. And as the years go by, they will make roots, focus on their strengths, deal more with industry and less with government, and become more learner-centred. In the spirit of social entrepreneurship, they will find their feet without target-linked government money and grow more slowly but more organically towards excellence.

Boxes 6.5 to 6.7 show the relatively high impact training providers are achieving when they take time out from the gravy train to work with their best instincts of sustainable employment, career progression, and partnerships with employers.

Box 6.5:   *Gram Tarang's partnership with Café Coffee Day*

Café Coffee Day (CCD) is a division of India's largest coffee conglomerate, Amalgamated Bean Coffee Trading Company Ltd (ABCTCL) and has a penetration of 1,500 + cafés spread across the country, growing at the rate of one new café per day. The company has a huge need of skilled manpower to staff their cafes. The skills-sets required include: (i) Making and serving coffee, other food and beverage items on their menu, (ii) customer service, (iii) billing, cash handling, and management, and (iv) store and store-related procedures. Gram Tarang and CCD entered into a long-term strategic partnership to set up a joint skill development programme at the Bhubaneswar campus of Centurion University which now has the capacity to train 120 'brewmasters' at a time. This programme has been operational since November 2012 with the first batch of 120 trainees successfully placed in cafés across Chennai and Bangalore.

The programme is fully funded by CCD and free of cost to the trainee. It incorporates a three-month fully residential programme in Bhubaneswar, during which five courses are covered. Following the residential course, the trainees begin a nine-month on-the-job internship in a CCD café usually in an urban industrial centre far from their homes. They are paid a stipend and offered highly subsidized accommodation. In their seventh month as interns, they are offered the chance to sit for a test and begin training as 'operational trainees' which line them up for management roles. Once the internship is complete, they are tested and if successful awarded a Certificate in Retail Management by Centurion University. Successful graduates are hired as junior managers and permanent employees of CCD, eligible for promotion and incentives as per company's growth path.

The strong growth path offered is a key reason for the success and low attrition in the programme: the trainees are willing to stay in a new city far from home and work for a low stipend because they see the potential once the year of training is complete. Uniquely, the growth of the company's café network allows it to offer new graduates a work location of their choice, closer to their home again. The eligibility for the programme is at least 17 years of age, a qualification of 10th pass, and readiness to relocate across India.

Source: Gram Tarang's internal documents, August 2013.

Box 6.6: *B-Able's support to Common Service Centres (CSCs)*

Since 2010, Government of India's Department of Information & Technology has promoted a National e-Governance Plan with the vision of providing all government services at an affordable cost and integrated manner at the doorstep of the citizen. The pillar of the scheme is the CSCs envisioned as the delivery point for government services, including utility payments, information on products, prices and schemes, banking and financial services, to all populations, however remote.

CSCs are set up by 'village-level entrepreneurs' (VLEs), self-employed youth who run a kiosk with a couple of desktops and an Internet line, who guide local people to use the e-based system. Basix, the parent of B-Able, has been managing CSCs since 2008 and manages 3,500 across the five states of Punjab, Meghalaya, Tripura, Odisha, and Maharashtra. In January 2011, B-Able began a collaboration with Basix to develop the CSCs as mini-training centres in the core skills of English and IT literacy. The VLE receives training to become a facilitator, mobilizing local youth to sign up to the programme. Rural youth attend classes which are broadly based on interactive digital material, paying ₹500–750 per month for a three-month course. The digital learning is supplemented by face support from the facilitator who receives training to play this role. To date, nearly 4,500 young people have been trained across the five states. The income of a typical VLE increases between ₹2,000 and ₹4,000 per month when he or she becomes a facilitator, while the top-performing ones have been able to earn as much as ₹15,000 from the supplementary role. Thus the programme succeeds in buttressing the business model of the VLE, while rolling out generic employability skills to rural youth.

Source: Personal communication with B-Able representatives, August 2013.

Box 6.7: *Nettur Technical Training Foundation (NTTF)*

The NTTF is one of India's oldest technical training institutes, which has also achieved a stellar transition from the age of heavy industry and planned economy to that of globalized and high-tech automation. From its foundation in Kerala in 1963— with the help of Swiss Aid—NTTF now has 20 campuses across nine states, delivering a mix of diplomas, postgraduate diplomas, and certificate courses (requiring 10th or 12th) in mechanical, electronics, mechatronics, computer engineering, and IT. It is one of the few training institutions which has resisted entry into the government scheme business.

The fees for the certificate courses, of duration six months to 24 months— average out at about ₹5,000 per month and all have substantial on-the-job-training/internship components. Jobs at exit are guaranteed, with a starting salary billed upwards of ₹8,000 per month. This makes them comparable to the new government rates, for example, those offered in Roshni. But training periods are always much greater than the two to three month government standard (averaging nine months in the classroom and five months on the job). The equipment, training expertise, and placement cudos which this money buys is probably much greater.

Source: http://www.nttftrg.com/, accessed in October 2013.

5. Deepening the dive into root causes and solutions

5.1 The Poor base of schooling: Repair it but don't depend on it!

India's TVET sector is living a contradiction: you can't get trained without schooling, yet schooling is part of the problem.

There are huge numbers of unemployed graduates and school pass outs. Those who get through the tough 10th and 12th, then onto degrees, are frequently not favoured in the job markets they aspire to, while they shy from manual and lower status work. Yet school certificates remain a prerequisite for VET courses. On the one hand, this greatly narrows the student base to work with (since the vast majority fail at 10th or before), on the other hand, it biases the base towards the same employability problems encountered with pass outs and graduates.

Here we try to answer two questions. First, why is schooling helping so little with employability? Second, if schooling predisposes people away from manual jobs, why do TVET courses continue to insist on it?

India's 10th exam is famously difficult. While more and more children are enrolling in primary and secondary school, a high proportion—perhaps 4 million students a year—drop out before reaching 10th, and another 2 million or so fail to clear it.[44] It is above all the demanding standard in math and two languages—Hindi and English—foreign (or at least not mother tongue) to the vast majority who take it, which makes the exam so challenging. The box below compares a math problem offered in the CBSE 10th exam, with an equivalent problem offered in the UK's General Certificate of Secondary Education (GCSE).

The high standard set by the education boards is one explanation for the culture of teaching in Indian schools. Since the standard is too high for the majority, the best bet to clear it is to narrow questions tightly to syllabus and inculcate students in a way which ensures information is absorbed and understood—just enough—while not being widely applied or tested. While learners must learn to absorb information efficiently and accurately, they must be content with knowledge which often remains abstract and sometimes esoteric. They learn not to ask questions, since questions derail the schedule and, while questioning might help some students, others might stumble into confusion such that recovery to a level of certainty would not be possible in time for tests. The narrow base of learning in Indian schools is amply illustrated in the results of syllabus-neutral tests (ASER and PISA) in which India performs terribly.[46]

This classroom regime is not without its skills building: endurance, accommodation of confusion, and docility are all developed and may even have their uses in the workplace. But it is clear that these attributes and the poor versatility and critical thinking which underpins them contribute directly

---

Box 6.8: *Comparing math exam papers for 15-year-olds in the UK and India*

A small sample of five teenagers and young adults in India were asked to compare the exam paper for 10th grade maths, set for summer 2012 in UK[45] and India respectively. The response of the five volunteers was unanimous: the UK paper was much easier in almost every way, equivalent to between one and two grades (school years) lower than the Indian. While the overall technical standard of the Indian paper was significantly higher, the UK paper asked students to apply their math knowledge more creatively but at a far lower technical standard.

A small sample of the difference in standard follows in this algebra question, with each question carrying broadly equivalent marks in the set time.

Indian question:	UK question:
Solve the following quadratic equation for x: $$X^2 - 4ax - b^2 + 4a^2 = 0$$	Solve the simultaneous equations: $$2x + 4y = 1$$ $$3x - 5y = 7$$

Source: Central Board of Secondary Education, India (http://www.cbse.nic.in) and Assessment and Qualifications Alliance, UK (http://www.aqa.org.uk/).

---

[44]While CBSE pass rates have been fast rising, state boards lag behind, while they cover a growing proportion of school children.

[45] The UK has two General Certificate of Secondary Education (GCSE) levels for maths and here we took the higher level.

[46] Chavan, M. 2012. *Uphill Battle Ahead as Outcomes Go Downhill.* ASER 2012, New Delhi, Pratham; Pritchett, L. 2012. 'The First PISA Results for India: The End of the Beginning'. Available at: http://ajay-shahblog.blogspot.in/2012/01/first-pisa-results-for-india-end-of.html, accessed in October 2013.

to poor employability in India. It is because of education, as much as in spite of it, that our young people are considered unfit for work.

To date, the current skills policy has reinforced the convention that schooling should be a prerequisite for vocational training: those who didn't pass their 10th, can only get two months of training; those who did, can get two years, at least in ITI (should it not be the reverse?) But there are alternatives to relying on school prerequisites, if we can reorder our values to take these on board. Even among the new skills providers, there are those who are testing out new ways of training for work. Organizations such as Empower and IndiaCan are making huge improvements to the standard of training and learning, and codifying practice in such detailed facilitators' guides that even provincial and mediocre trainers will teach to a decent standard.

What can we learn from the way skills are acquired outside the classroom?

In the new skills policy there has been very limited discussion on the informal sector. While it is rightly assumed that the government's resources are helping to bring those who would otherwise be in the informal sector into the formal or organized sector, there is still scant attention to how skilling and job-readiness actually occurs in the milieus of smaller units, SMEs and home-based industries which fall below the regulatory radar. In fact, as Kenneth King has pointed out, the government seems quite determined not to learn from or refer back to the commendable base of reports produced by the NCEUS.[47]

Much skilling in the unorganized sector is hard to mimic because it is from parent to child. India's occupational structure continues to be somewhat caste-aligned, while the tradition of the family firm means that even those who have the financial backing and wherewithal to move freely between businesses and occupations will nonetheless expect their sons to take on the family firm. But there are many sectors where apprenticeships have grown up outside kinship relations. Here, the learner (*shaagird*) arrives to study and learn with the master (*ustaad*) as a young teenager. Such apprenticeships are far more structured than is often assumed regardless of being free from paper and pen.

Edward Simpson highlights how learning among apprentices in the ship-building cluster of Gujarat is organized according to a clear hierarchy of tasks of increasing complexity.[48] Since all learning takes place 'on the job', the context in which one is expected to undertake tasks is as important as the task itself, and learners are not allowed for a minute to forget the requirement of conformity to norms of respect, consideration for team mates and hierarchy, competencies not unlike the generic skills which formal sector employers demand of entry-level workers. The amount of guidance given to the apprentice is carefully regulated according to his/her level, and teaching input is tied to the hierarchy of task complexity.

It is important to recognize that the structure and supervision of learning in some informal sectors may well be much more organized than in the formal sector. As we showed in Section 3, government-regulated apprenticeships (or trainee contracts) are often a means through which to hire cheap and casual labour and learners complain that they're not learning enough. In informal sector firms, this problem is less likely to occur because of the much stronger imperative to train entry-level workers in a wide range of tasks and functions required in a small and labour-intensive workplace.

---

[47] King, K. 2012. 'The Geopolitics and Meanings of India's Massive Skills Development Ambitions', *International Journal of Educational Development*, 32: 665–73.

[48] Simpson, E. 2006. 'Apprenticeship in Western India', *Journal of the Royal Anthropological Institute*, 12 (1): 151–71.

Recognition of prior learning

One reason why we remain stuck with input-based, classroom and academically biased vocational training is because it is difficult to assess learning *outcomes* and relatively easy to assess if someone has received *inputs*. But there are significant efforts, globally, to assess those who are less educated and who have learned their skills at work as well as informally. The objectives of what is known as recognition of prior learning (RPL) are threefold. First, RPL assessments help diagnose training needs and better target training. Second, they identify, benchmark, and provide recognition for skills informally acquired, facilitating workers' access to job levels and bands and to trade licences. Third, the recognitions can count towards qualifications which enable re-entry into formal education.

Countries such as Australia, Netherlands, and Denmark have led the process of testing and establishing systems to measure competencies learned on the job. The experiences have not been without their problems. These partly relate to the difficulties in building credibility for, financing and then administering, assessments: these must go beyond the standardized and input-geared tests which follow a TVET course, and ideally, use a variety of ways which allow candidates to demonstrate knowledge and skill, such as observations in the workplace, detailed interviews, references from employers, and portfolios with sample works. 'The focus must be on what an individual knows, understands or is able to do at the end of a learning process, not on the inputs to a teaching process'.[49] Other challenges have included, stimulating learner demand and establishing 'parity of esteem' with other forms of assessment.[50]

The following case study outlines the work of LabourNet, Bangalore, in instituting an RPL assessment among construction workers on sites (see Box 6.5).

Box 6.9: *LabourNet's RPL programme for construction workers*

LabourNet aims to be a one-stop platform for unorganized sector workers to obtain services currently unavailable and hard to access. It provides identity, financial inclusion, and social protection services, builds worker skills (often through industry partnerships) and places them in jobs with formal sector employers mostly in the construction industry. The RPL programme started as part of LabourNet's end-to-end approach to improving livelihoods: migrant workers are poorly schooled, lack identity and evidence of skill levels. In order for LabourNet to better target its training and help its employer partners benchmark skill levels and wages, it needed an assessment system. As a representative explained, 'Based on your RPL, we should put you in the right training programme; once you are trained and skilled…, you should have a wage increase based on your skill set; once that is proven in the industry, we can enable job engagement.'

One of the challenges has been developing an assessment system with no occupational standards. Thus LabourNet evolved a team of industry and vocational and instructional design exporter to write and trial the test. The team elaborated competencies relevant to the trade and then built question banks (adapted from outcome-focused curricular) which are arranged in order of increasing difficulty on the test sheet. Then it hired a professional survey agency to administer the tests, which are conducted by verbal questionnaires at the worker's workplace. Completed tests are then evaluated centrally by industry experts. Evaluation takes about four days after which a report card is printed and sent over to workers. Results are communicated to LabourNet's labour coordinators who then advise workers accordingly with respect to training and job opportunity.

Source: Manipal City & Guilds, 2013.

---

[49] CEDEFOP. 2012. 'Curriculum Reform in Europe: The Impact of Learning Outcomes'. Research Paper. European Centre for the Development of Vocational Training, CEDEFOP.

[50] Manipal City & Guilds. 2013. 'Credit Where Credit's Due'. City & Guilds Centre for Skills Development. London.

As discussed in Section 4, the lack of occupational standards referred to here is rapidly being addressed by the NSDC-promoted SSCs, though the SSC for construction is yet to get going. While the STAR scheme is probably too shortlived and election geared to install a culture of learning outcomes, the central place given to occupational standards and assessments against these is a first and major commitment to judging the worth of a worker by job-ready skills and no longer by their schooling base and rote-learning craft.

Repairing failure at school

For a system which continues to hold 'classroom qualifications' in such esteem, India's TVET system offers little second chance for those whom school has failed. Doubtless this is because repairing school failure takes a long time. Valuing so highly as we do a person's schooling levels, few of us have thought seriously about how to really take them back to school skills. The NIOS—rejuvenated in the new skills agenda—nonetheless remains poorly equipped to take on the adult literacy agenda and ironically shares the same bias towards schooling as a prerequisite, with only 12 of 85 courses offered to those who have not passed 8th grade.[51]

In this respect, as discussed above, the community colleges of North America are an exciting model. With decades of experience teaching the 'Three Rs' to marginalized adults, their experience will be invaluable to India. Only by taking those in their early 20s through 8th, 10th, and 12th can it demonstrate its commitment to give a 'second chance' and have the potential to change trajectories.

5.2 Learning a living[52]

The World Bank's 2006 survey of TVET in India told us the shocking news that Indian firms offer less formal training to their workforce than firms almost anywhere in the world, including in India's neighbouring countries. While there is a fair bit of training in the southern, high-investment states—related to gearing to meet export standards—there is very little elsewhere. Reasons expressed for lack of in-service training were (i) technology in use is already mature, known to workforce, (ii) can't afford to train, and (iii) can get skilled workers relatively easily.[53] In-service training tends not to be rewarded in India, neither does it show up in productivity gains.

The World Bank report recommends strengthening in-house capability of firms to train, and providing incentives to companies in addressing market failures (finance, poor information, and the risk that newly trained workers might leave).

In its Labour Report (2012), TeamLease argues that India experiences limitations in on-the-job training for the following reasons:[54]

- Poor commitment from top of the firm
- Poor mutual trust and respect between institution and industry
- Poor integration of workplace learning process and curriculum
- No appropriate mechanism for assessments (which goes back to the RPL challenge)
- Monitoring and corrective action of learner not in place
- Gap in expectations between industry and learner's actual level
- Weak communication between learner and mentor

The effectiveness of on-the-job training depends on the level of intersection and overlapping in the goals and efforts of the

[51] World Bank. 2006. *Skill Development in India: The Vocational Education and Training System*. New Delhi: World Bank, p. 47.

[52] This heading is taken from the title of a new book: Hannon, V., S. Gillinson, et al. 2013. *Learning a Living: Radical Innovation in Education for Work*. UK: Bloomsbury.

[53] World Bank. 2006. *Skill Development in India: The Vocational Education and Training System*. New Delhi: World Bank, p. 66.

[54] TeamLease. 2012. India Labour Report 2012: Massifying Indian Higher Education. Bangalore, TeamLease, p. 93.

three participants to the scheme, the institution, the employer and the learner (ELI). TeamLease has summarized the effects, and resulting success or failure, in cases where these overlaps are weak, and where these are strong, shown in the following two figures (Figures 6.4 and 6.5).

As King has shown, the government's new skills policy—until mid-2013 at least—made little reference to the on-the-job training, in spite of it constituting the country's mainstay of firm workforce renewal. While on-the-job training has received recognition lately in both the MoRD's Roshni scheme and the NSDC's STAR scheme, little is documented about how this process takes place for workers. What are the skills and capabilities of workers who have learned on the job? What makes some of them more skilled and valued than others? What is it that makes one workplace offer a better learning experience than another?

Mike Rose has studied in detail the nature of skill and knowledge among manual and/or less educated workers in the US, and he tells us:

Studies of the factory floor demonstrate that frontline-workers develop skill at performing their routines. They learn to work

Figure 6.4: Poor learner-enterprise-institution overlap and on-the-job training failure

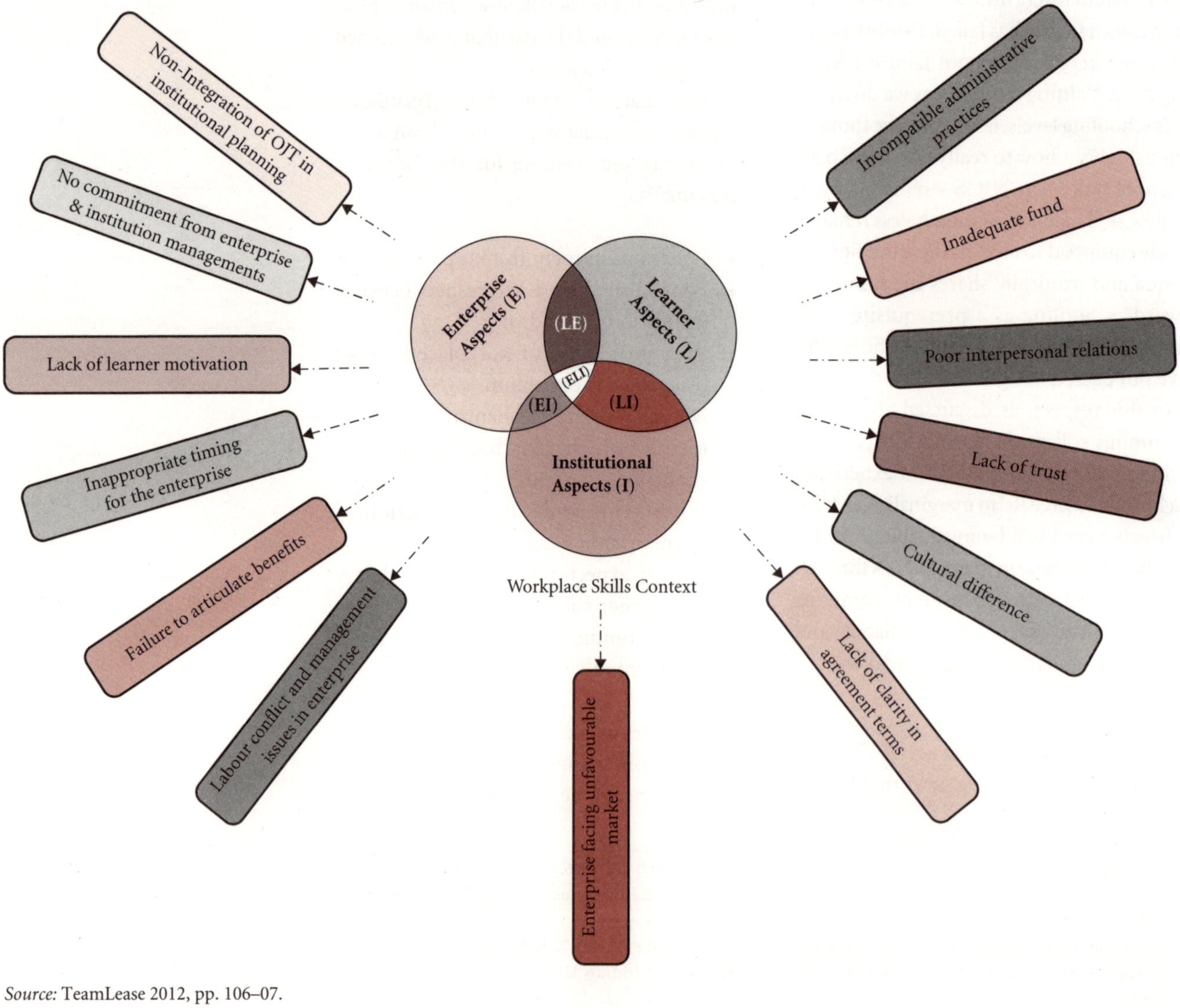

Non-Integration of OJT in institutional planning

No commitment from enterprise & institution managements

Lack of learner motivation

Inappropriate timing for the enterprise

Failure to articulate benefits

Labour conflict and management issues in enterprise

Enterprise Aspects (E)

Learner Aspects (L)

(LE)

(ELI)

(EI)   (LI)

Institutional Aspects (I)

Workplace Skills Context

Enterprise facing unfavourable market

Incompatible administrative practices

Inadequate fund

Poor interpersonal relations

Lack of trust

Cultural difference

Lack of clarity in agreement terms

Source: TeamLease 2012, pp. 106–07.

Figure 6.5: Strong learner-enterprise-institutional overlap and on-the-job training success

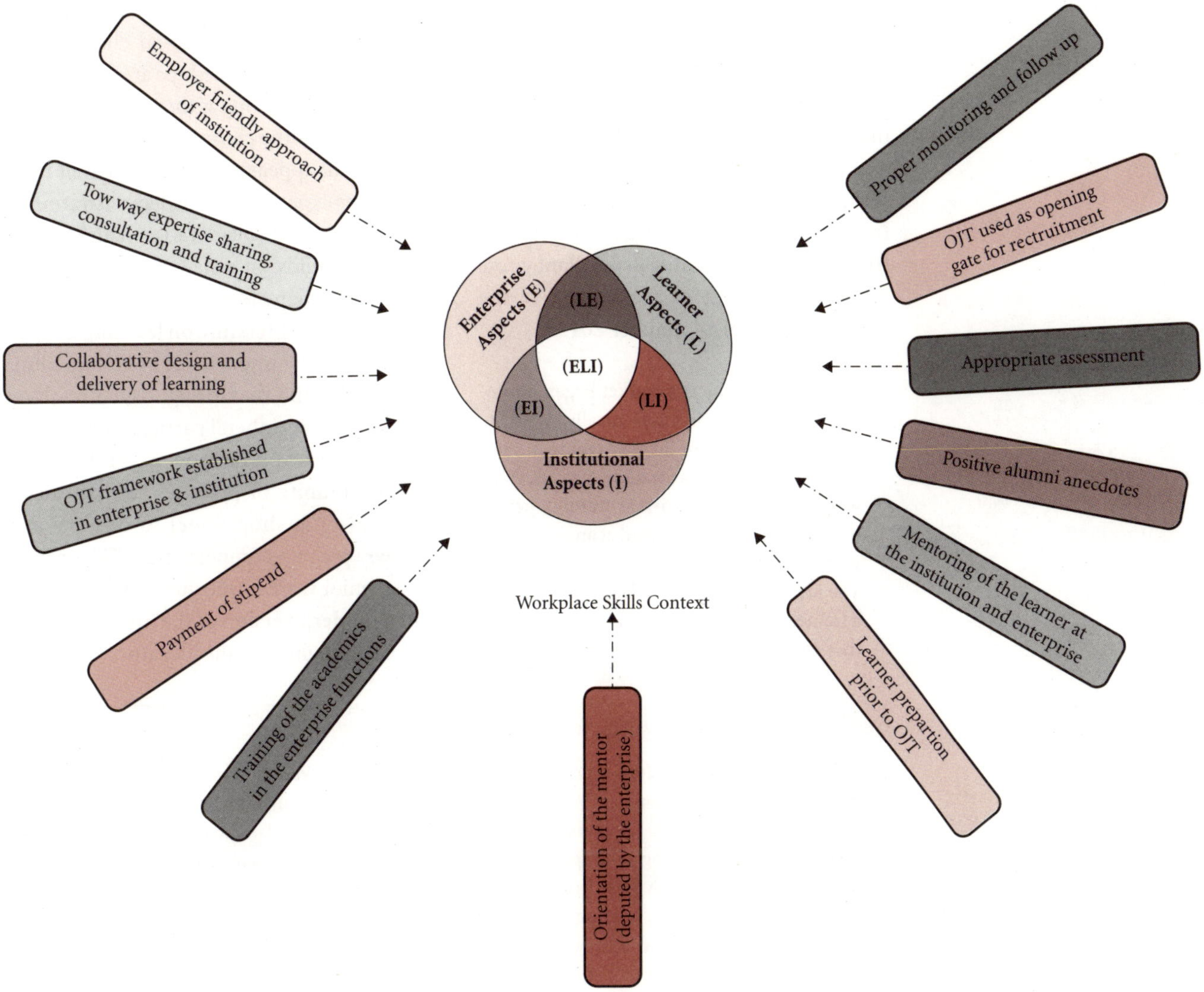

Employer friendly approach of institution

Tow way expertise sharing, consultation and training

Collaborative design and delivery of learning

OJT framework established in enterprise & institution

Payment of stipend

Training of the academics in the enterprise functions

Proper monitoring and follow up

OJT used as opening gate for recruitment

Appropriate assessment

Positive alumni anecdotes

Mentoring of the learner at the institution and enterprise

Learner prepartion prior to OJT

Enterprise Aspects (E)

Learner Aspects (L)

(LE)

(ELI)

(EI)

(LI)

Institutional Aspects (I)

Workplace Skills Context

Orientation of the mentor (deputed by the enterprise)

Source: TeamLease 2012, pp. 106–07.

smart, to maximize energy and efficiency. They come to know the properties of the materials they work with and the quirks of the machinery they operate… Mechanics, machinists, and all the construction tradespersons continually blend hand and brain. They develop rich knowledge of materials, tools and processes. They regularly troubleshoot and solve problems.[55]

Rose calls for a breakdown of the vocational-academic divide and an openness to rethink the way we have defined intelligence. Part of the problem lies in exposure and attitude. 'If we believe common work to be mindless, that belief will affect the work we create in the future.'[56]

Other than the pedagogical and managerial constraints listed by TeamLease, there are two fundamental problems for on-the-job training in the Indian context. The first is the tendency to use on-the-job training schemes to use relatively well-qualified workers as cheap labour. As a recent ILO

---

[55]Rose, M. 2009. *Why School? Reclaiming Education for All of Us.* New York: New School, p. 78.

[56]Ibid., p. 86.

study showed, in India, apprentices are routinely left un-mentored in unskilled roles and benefit from no greater learning nor progression than other unskilled workers.[57] The use of labour regulations like these to reduce the costs of entry-level workers, as well as to downgrade more mature workers, has given on-the-job training a bad name. A long-serving worker from Manesar's Maruti-Suzuki plant wrote a moving account of the run-up to the tragic violence of September 2012:

> When in 1993 the car market began booming, the Maruti workers ironically started to suffer at the hands of the management. They introduced a two-year training period. What was the need for a two-year training period for a worker who has trained at an ITI for two years and then as an apprentice for a year? The idea was to get cheap labour, to call you a trainee and pay you less than half the salary they would otherwise pay you.[58]

By contrast, the German apprenticeship system has held its standard commendably well. Governed by regional chambers of commerce, apprenticeships are coveted and competitive, leading as they do to a promising career in the chosen industry.

Maruti appears to be learning well from its bitter experience. One demonstration of this is its recent collaboration with Manipal City & Guilds on a new workplace-based training scheme (see Box 6.6).

The wider literature on learning at work highlights the importance of certain kinds of activity and mentoring. Lave's work on 'legitimate peripheral participation' stands out, wherein permission is granted from 'a community of practice' (which can be a team on a shop floor) to observe and slowly pick up competencies.[59] The power of a senior worker who guides and oversees, in a modern version of the 'master' role, is also highlighted in the literature. The term

---

Box 6.10: *Manipal City & Guilds on-the-job training with Maruti*

Known best for certifying short-term courses, Manipal City & Guilds has recently launched a two-year 'Earn & Learn' programme with Maruti Suzuki in its Udyog Vihar plant. The programme targets 10th pass and above without ITI qualifications, arguing that ITIs already have a clear path into the company, leading to apprenticeships or regular workforce. Therefore, the Maruti–Manipal City & Guilds collaboration is testing an alternative to the traditional route of ITI, to explore the possibility that there may be a quicker and more efficient route to becoming 'workplace ready' enough to get hired as regular staff. The programme is affiliated to Uttarakhand Open University and offers an Advanced Certificate in Automobile Assembly.

The programme leads trainees through an internship which combines learning across the shop floor with off-the-job classes, each closely dovetailed with the other. At the centre of the curriculum is the manufacturing process at the plant, and the mix of technical and generic skills required for its successful functioning. Much of the classroom time focuses on business perspectives and values-building: the kids must learn to view things from the viewpoint of management, running the business. Those successfully completing an exam at course-end are hired as regular workers. The programme is funded by a mix of trainees, who pay fees to the affiliating university, and the company, who pay a stipend to the trainees. The key to the programme's success is the efforts to bring supervisors on board, which depends in turn on full support at the highest level.

Source: Personal communication with Manipal City & Guilds' representative, August 2013.

---

[57] Smith, E. and R. Kemmis. 2012. 'Possible Future for the Indian Apprenticeship System'. New Delhi, ILO, World Bank, Ministry of Labour.

[58] Vij, S. 2012. 'The Maruti Way'. *Fountain Ink* (web-based journal, at http://fountainink.in/; citation from a posting on 5 September 2012), New Delhi.

[59] Lave, J. 1988. 'The Culture of Acquisition and the Practice of Understanding'. In J. Stigler, R. Shweder, and G. Herdt (eds), *Cultural Psychology: Essays on Comparative Human Development*. Cambridge: Cambridge University Press.

'situated cognition' is associated with the understanding that learning is most effective when it is situated in a meaningful context. Learning is conceived as a process of 'guided discovery' where the learner is able to set goals and prepare action plans and where mentors actively intervene, in on-the-job training as in class. It is time that India understood and implemented these things better.

The second of the fundamental problems for on-the-job training in the Indian context is the deskilling effect of technology. More and more jobs relate to feeding and supervising machines in narrow, automated, and highly regimented contexts. The implications of this are the topic of the next section.

5.3 The Skills—Productivity relationship

Increased capital intensity and automation are well known for their impact of displacing labour and—partly as a result of this—increasing productivity (defined as output per unit of labour input). What is less discussed is what impact capital intensive automation has on the skill content of jobs and on wages.

One of the Millennium Development Goal (MDG) targets added in 2007, is 'full and productive employment and decent work for all'.[60] Decent work was belatedly recognized as the best way to get out of poverty. The measurements are fourfold:

- Productivity growth (rate of GDP growth per person employed)
- Ratio of employment to population (i.e. proportion of whole population in work)
- Share of 'vulnerable employment' in the total, defined as own-account workers and contributing family members
- Proportion of the working poor, i.e. those employed living on less than US$1/day PPP.

As we showed in the 2011 SOIL report, in the years of growth through the 1990s until the mid-2000s, the Indian economy absorbed its workforce reasonably well (workforce participation grew steadily and unemployment barely increased). But it did so without delivering any improvement in the quality of jobs. In fact, 'the share of organized sector as an employer declined... Surplus labour was being absorbed into the unorganized sector, which was able to sustain jobs due to a healthy growth, but this was at the cost of job quality and security'.[61] To improve incomes (reduce poverty), growth must be accompanied by productivity. This is achieved both by improving the rate of growth of formal employment and increasing the productivity of jobs in the informal economy.[62]

India's manufacturing productivity rose steadily throughout the 1980s and faster in the 1990s to the early 2000s.[63] Productivity gains continue, though there is a great deal of progress still remaining: In 2012, India's productivity was still only 10.2 per cent of the US levels.[64]

There is clear evidence to show that skill building improves productivity (as one of several factors). High-performance workplace are regularly associated with enhanced worker responsibility, multi-skilling, and a greater responsibility of operators for quality control.[65] But, as we have shown, most Indian firms have not chosen the skilling path to reach productivity gains.

In lieu of this virtuous image of the high-performance workplace, many workers' reports highlight the lack of learning

---

[60] ILO. 2013. *Global Wage Report 2012/13*. ILO. Geneva.

[61] ACCESS. 2011. *State of India's Livelihoods (SOIL) Report 2011*. New Delhi: SAGE Publications, p. 19.

[62] ILO. 2008. 'Skills for Improved Productivity, Employment Growth and Development'. ILO. Geneva, p. 6.

[63] Goldar, B. 2004. 'Productivity Trends in Indian Manufacturing in the Pre and Post Reform Periods'. Working Paper 137, ICRIER.

[64] The Conference Board. 2013. 'Productivity Brief: Key Findings: Global Productivity Slowed in 2012 with Little Scope for Improvement in 2013', TED Talks.

[65] ILO. 2008. 'Skills for Improved Productivity, Employment Growth and Development'. ILO. Geneva, p. 69.

opportunity in such workplaces. On these shop floors, security and discipline are issue of paramount importance, due to the need to protect the value, and maximize the output, of machines. While relatively educated workers are in demand for their literacy and behavioural advantage, they complain that they are stuck in narrow and unskilled roles, manning automated machines.

There are a number of reasons why Indian firms are not bothering with skilling as they reap productivity gains:

- Work on high-tech machines can be managed with a mix of less skilled labour and highly qualified staff (degree and diploma holders). The need for blue collar skill is not always evident.
- Productivity can be realized without skilling (through such changes as the organization of work, technology adjustments, and methods improvement). If productivity is achieved without skilling workers, workers have less claim on the gains and are less likely to make new demands or to quit (see below for issue of productivity and wages).
- Skilling is done but not in the form of on or off-the-job training programmes. Instead, it is realized through commercial relationships: inter-firm learning in value chains and clusters. MNCs and large Indian corporations, even in higher tech industries, work through chains of suppliers. Lead firms have programmes for supplier education, setting standards, and even assisting suppliers to reach these. International standards especially, have forced lead firms to 'transform the supply chain into a learning chain based on a collaborative and reciprocal relationship'.[66]
- Firms face information uncertainty and moral hazard. They are not sure that training will end up with strong workers, or that the benefit of training will accrue to the firm.

Of equal concern is the fact that productivity, when achieved, is increasingly not shared with workers. Globally, the share of income to labour relative to capital in the economy has shrunk.[67]

Counter-intuitively, the periods when wage share declines most sharply are the periods of high growth and expansion: far from permitting the bargaining of their share of the gains, such periods have seen the relative power of capital increase. By contrast, in downturns and recessions, wages remain stable when compared to profits which are more volatile, and in such periods, the relative share of labour improves.[68] In spite of its shrinking growth, for example, India's organized manufacturing sector has achieved a continued rise in its profitability which is now at 48 per cent (up from 18.5 per cent in 1991). This profitability is explained by wages consistently shrinking as a proportion of output.[69]

The reasons for this declining share, on a global level, relate to the pressure to pay dividends to shareholders, the greater capital intensity of technology (so that labour's relative share declines), and the decline in labour's bargaining power, in the context of globalization and the power of financial markets.[70]

What is the solution, in India, to securing better jobs from higher productivity? To begin with, the government must ensure that their policies do not create a 'race to the bottom' among skills providers who compete to place youth in the same firms. Labour organization must be allowed to take its course: if placed workers use collective action to push for better terms and conditions, let not their efforts be thwarted by the arrival of fresh workers to replace

---

[66] Ibid., p. 138.

[67] The wage share shrinks when per capita GDP grows faster than average wages.

[68] ILO. 2013. *Global Wage Report 2012/13*. ILO. Geneva, p. 43.

[69] Economic Survey. 2013. 'Industrial Performance'. Ministry of Finance. New Delhi.

[70] ILO. 2013. *Global Wage Report 2012/13*. ILO. Geneva.

them. Second, training providers, employers, and possibly even the global customers of employers can work together to address the problems which hold back productivity and output: poor generic skills, attrition, long and unplanned leave-taking.

5.4 From competencies to capabilities

With the STAR scheme and the SSCs, India's skill policy has taken its first leap into competency-based training and assessment. There is a chance that workers will be recognized, waged, and appointed according to how they work and what they can do, not what they learnt in class and wrote in an exam. National Occupational Standards (NOS)-based and competency-geared training is a sensible response to the over-theorized and general curriculum of ITI and diplomas. But can a learner be too short of theory?

'Theory helps us to transfer the experience gained in one context to new experiences in other contexts', writes TeamLease.[71] It is our understanding of the underlying logic, principles, and rules which positions us to be versatile, to apply that logic and those rules in one context just as to another. Theoretical understanding is what enables us to see how our job fits with the wider whole.

Not only are such abilities aligned to some of the requirements voiced by employers; they are also a key to an employability which outlives a specific job role. Lifelong employability is a much flouted goal of India's policymakers and practitioners, and yet, are we getting any closer to it in gearing training to job roles than we did in teaching theory in the classroom without context or application?

The ILO defines employability as 'the portable competencies and qualifications that enhance an individual's capacity to make use of the…opportunities available in order to secure and retain decent work, to progress within an enterprise and between jobs, and to cope with changing technology and labour market conditions'.[72] The skills essential to lifelong employability are developed over a lifetime, as much at home and in communities, as they are in institutions or jobs. They are mostly 'core' or generic skills (see Table 6.1).

Of course, there is an axis between lifelong employability and short-term job-readiness. In a century where 'the illiterate…will be only those who cannot learn, relearn and unlearn',[73] where should we be on this axis?

There is a parallel here with the early years of sustainable livelihoods. As we traced in SOIL 2012, the sustainable livelihoods approach emerged in the late 1980s from a recognition that human development had to be conceptualized, beyond basic needs, as the provision of opportunity to fulfil aspirations. By the early 2000s, the 'capabilities' approach associated with Amartya Sen had become mainstream, as poverty and well-being became increasingly conceived

Table 6.1: Some important 'core' or generic skills for lifelong employability

Skill	Detailed description
Communication skills	Listening, crafting response, presenting
Teamwork	Cooperation, playing to strengths, support and guidance
Problem-solving	Application of knowledge to diverse contexts
Planning and organizing	Managing time, multitasking, flexibility
Openness, ability to learn	Accepting criticism, adaptability, capacity to assimilate and filter new learning
Grooming	Comportment, habits, and discipline
Positive attitude	Willing to try, take opportunity, find a solution
Sense of responsibility	Accountability for tasks, guidance to others, delivery against what's agreed

Source: TeamLease 2012, author's interpretation.

[71] TeamLease. 2012. India Labour Report 2012: Massifying Indian Higher Education. T. S. I. I. o. J. Training. Bangalore, TeamLease, p. 94.

[72] ILO. 2008. 'Skills for Improved Productivity, Employment Growth and Development'. ILO. Geneva, p. 23.

[73] Vamsi Madhav, Country Head, HR, CMC Ltd, quoted in TeamLease. 2012. India Labour Report 2012: Massifying Indian Higher Education. T. S. I. I. o. J. Training. Bangalore, TeamLease, p. 25.

as a matter, not simply, of access to material resources and utility, but of the capabilities one has to make use of the whole gamut of aspects (material and non-material) in one's environment. Capabilities are both the functionings of a person and the capacity (or freedom) that person has to pursue these functionings, in different combinations and circumstances.[74] In sum, 'capabilities denote a person's opportunity and ability to generate valuable outcomes'.[75] The meaning of capability, and the personal agency which realizes capabilities, resonate closely with the concept of lifelong employability discussed above.

India's civil society, policymakers, and development researchers today have a nuanced understanding of rural livelihoods. They have absorbed and responded to the elaborations and analyses of Sen, Chambers, and others. By contrast, the skills sector, just starting out, is still stuck in the equivalent of the crude age of economism and top-down modernization theory which characterized rural development until the 1980s. It is time to take the capabilities approach to the skills sector. Within the practical constraints of delivering employment to youth and jobs to industry, let us nonetheless explore how to build capability, through education, training, and working life, so that lifelong employability can remain a genuine goal.

6. Conclusions and a research agenda

The government's energetic, target-led, and pervasive skills policy is no doubt having effects, but many of these may not be intended, while other intended effects remain far from being achieved (see Table 6.2).

The skills policy prior to the Eleventh Plan was geared to serve an industrializing nation, on the one hand, and the mass of informal workers, on the other. It was lofty in its theoretical ambitions but weak in its match to market and capacity to create job-ready workers. The government characteristically played multiple and overlapping roles, leaving little scope for meaningful engagement with industry.

The new skills policy which emerged after 2007 has reacted against the old. Liberating itself from government provision and heavily regulated and theoretical curriculum, it has harnessed enormous energy from private sector providers offering short-term courses across a range of mostly service sector occupations. Turning away from both heavy industry and the informal self-employed sector, the new policy is geared to feeding new workers into casual roles in the formal sector. The new policy thus fits comfortably on the wave of labour market flexibility in which jobs are increasingly based on 'just-in-time' principles; indeed the new policy is becoming a key engine to fuel this wave.

Table 6.2: The matrix of intent and achievement in government of India's skills policy

Intended and achieved	Not intended and achieved
Assist in supply of cheap labour to low productivity industry	Superficial exposure to urban industrial centres to large swathes of young people
Getting youth out of the village into urban and formal firms	Decrease the value of skills such as ITI, therefore assuring them less purchase on the market
	Facilitation of informalization labour in formal firms
Intended and not achieved	**Not intended and not achieved**
Creation of long-term employability and more robust careers	Reintegration of school drop outs into formal education system ('second chance')
Accreditation of informal skills towards formal qualifications	Increased productivity (therefore job quality and wages) through skilled labour
Overcoming stigma of manual skill	

Source: Author's analysis.

---

[74] Sen, A. 1992. *Inequality Reexamined*. Cambridge, MA: Harvard University Press.

[75] En.wikipedia.org/wiki/Capability_approach, accessed in October 2013.

Industry, for the most part, is not a stake-holder in the new policy. It plays very little role in training, setting training standards, building curriculum or assessments. On the other hand, industry is a beneficiary, not so much of increased skill and the productivity that leads from it, but of the continually refreshed pool of escorted and accredited labour which the new policy facilitates. Industry gets this labour cheap; if NREGA moves ahead with the plan to list industries as permissible works under the scheme (see Chapter 5), industry will get this labour for free.

As growth slows, we have more time to reflect: industry demand is tapering and learner interest is also. Those who have already been through skilling and placements will be more clearly heard, and the recyclers—those who have been through the system several times in a rota of training-placement-dropout—will become more visible. And we will be forced to face the fact that neither learner nor employer has been our key stakeholders until now.

One agenda, at that point, will be to explore and test the relationship between skills and productivity: how and by what approach should skilling be done to push forward the productivity frontier of a firm? A second agenda, how to counsel, assess, and mentor well enough to create the best bet fit with a job and career path? A third, how best to build capability from competence, to build employability for life not for six months? A fourth, how to build core skills from school upwards so that our employable base is stronger? And finally, how to learn from and embed skilling within the informal sector which offers such excellence at on-the-job training and which will need ultimately to absorb the bulk of our youth?

About the Contributors

Savitha Suresh Babu currently teaches Sociology at Alliance College of Law and St. Joseph's Evening College in Bangalore, India. Previously, she has worked as a Research Associate with Azim Premji University and as a Staff Correspondent with *The Hindu*. At Azim Premji University, she was part of a landscape study on Teacher Education in North-East Karnataka and Sirohi and Tonk Districts of Rajasthan, India. Her areas of interest include education and gender. Babu holds a master's in Sociology and a postgraduate diploma in Journalism.

Resmi P. Bhaskaran has more than 16 years of professional experience in Social Policy Research and Advocacy and Project Management and Evaluation. She was heading the Policy Advocacy activities at Save the Children. Prior to Save the Children, Bhaskaran has worked with Institute for Human Development, Sa-Dhan, and Malayala Manorama Company Pvt. Ltd. She has worked closely with policymaking bodies, UN agencies, and CSOs at national and state levels. She has received the SANEI Research Award at South Asia level in 2008 and is a member in the Research Committee of National Commission for Protection of Child Rights (NCPCR) since 2012. She has published books, including *Surviving the Street—Census of Street Children* and *Literature Review on Indian Microfinance*, and articles in Indian and international journals.

Adarsh Kumar is the Founder and CEO of Livelihoods Equity Connect (LEC), an advisory group that seeks to promote investments in the Indian agricultural sector. Prior to LEC, Adarsh helped found All India Artisans and Craftworkers Welfare Association (AIACA), a non-profit organization that works to promote crafts producer-enterprises. Kumar's prior work experience includes stints at the Ford Foundation, where he worked on strengthening microcredit institutions in South Asia, and at the World Bank in Washington, DC, where he worked on evaluating client satisfaction with welfare services in the Philippines. He holds a bachelor's degree in Business Management from Georgetown University and a master's degree in Public Policy from the Kennedy School of Government at Harvard University. Kumar has been nominated as a Young Global Leader by the World Economic Forum and has been awarded both the Echoing Green and the Ashoka fellowships for social entrepreneurship.

Tara Nair is an Associate Professor in Gujarat Institute of Development Research. She has published in journals and edited books on topics such as financial intermediation and commercial banks, trends and patterns in the Indian microfinance sector, financial inclusion, micro enterprise development, and media economics and policy. She has also been part of large-scale field studies on the impact of microfinance in India, Myanmar, and Bangladesh.

Suryamani Roul is the Senior Vice President at ACCESS Development Services. He has expertise in enterprise and entrepreneurship position with intensive exposure in remote areas and tribal communities. He has earlier been Project Director, Sustainable Tribal Empowerment Project, CARE-India, Andhra Pradesh and Project Manager, CREDIT Project under CARE India's Small Economic Activities Development (SEAD) Programme supported by DFID's JFS support with World Food Programme and Rotary Foundation in undivided Bihar (Ranchi). He holds a bachelor's degree in Economics from Utkal University, a masters in Analytical and Applied Economics from Utkal University and MBA from University of Calcutta.

Orlanda Ruthven specializes, in labour standards, job quality, and skills in global supply chains, as a researcher, advisor, and trainer. Coming to India from Department for International Development (DFID) in 1998, she has since undertaken two research projects: the first, published in the co-authored book, *Portfolios of the Poor: How the World's Poor Live on $2 a Day* (2009, Princeton); the second her PhD thesis research (2008, Oxford) on work relationships and labour regulation in Moradabad, India. She has consulted extensively for UK and India-based organizations including Impactt, ODI, GIZ, and ACCESS Development Services. She is currently teaching, and helping build the vocational training and placement programme at the Centurion University in Odisha.

Ashok Kumar Sircar heads the programme portfolio of Landesa India, a unit of Landesa, a global land rights organization that works in 40 countries. Previously he worked as Professor in Development Studies and Action in Azim Premji University, Bangalore, India. He has also worked in various capacities in Indian non-profit sector. Dr Sircar's interests are on land rights, local governance, and civil society on which he has written extensively.

Kirti Vardhana, in his role as Head-Certification at LabourNet, leads the skills consulting and assessment portfolio for a wide range of vocational skills programmes. His work areas span the development of National Occupational Standards (NOS), skill-gap studies, vocational skill–related course design, training effectiveness measurement and assessment design. Kirti has over 10 years of HR experience and is keenly interested in the concept of livelihood enhancement through 'industry role' relevant training and access to jobs. Kirti holds a Bachelors' degree in Commerce and a Post Graduate Diploma in Human Resource Management.

Gayathri Vasudevan is a co-founder and the CEO of LabourNet, a Social Enterprise that enables livelihoods by focusing on 'Real Income Increase' for informal sector workers through vocational training, work linkages, financial inclusion and social security measures. Gayathri has earlier managed projects for various UN and bilateral organisations; she has also worked with the International Labour Organization (ILO) for eight years on issues related to child labour and vocational education. She holds a PhD in Development Economics from Institute of Social and Economic Change (ISEC), Bangalore.

Technical Partner

Centurion
UNIVERSITY

Centurion University of Technology & Management (CUTM), enacted by the Odisha state assembly in 2010, comprises a network of educational institutions delivering primary, secondary, tertiary, and vocational education in Odisha and Andhra Pradesh. The University has two main campuses at Paralakhemundi (Gajapati District) and Bhubaneswar, offering undergraduate and postgraduate programmes in Engineering, Management and Agriculture, as well as vocational courses. It also has three smaller campuses at Bolangir, Rayagada, and Chatrapur where vocational training is offered. In addition, it runs a +2 college and three CBSE secondary schools. CUTM seeks to bring quality, flexible, and field-grounded education to remote and poor regions of eastern India.

CUTM's promoters are management professionals and development workers committed to a vision of social entrepreneurship: building sustainable institutions which are privately funded and market-linked, free from dependence on donors and government aid. To this end, the University has incubated three social enterprises, all of which draw it deep into the poor and rural areas surrounding its campuses. The largest is Gram Tarang Employability Training Services, offering vocational training and placements to school drop outs. Second, Gram Tarang Inclusive Development Services tests and fields a range of services for rural people while providing local self-employment. Third, Gram Tarang Foods processes primary agricultural products using the latest extraction technology, thus developing and boosting local supply chains and farm-based income earning opportunities. The University's teaching and research activities are closely involved in these social enterprises, ensuring field exposure and ground-level experience for students.